MAKE THE
DEVIL
HOMELESS

MAKE THE
DEVIL
HOMELESS

VLADIMIR SAVCHUK

CHARISMA HOUSE

Further, the publisher and author do not have any control over and do not assume any responsibility for third-party websites or their content.

For more resources like this, visit MyCharismaShop.com and the author's website at pastorvlad.org.

Cataloging-in-Publication Data is on file with the Library of Congress.
International Standard Book Number: 978-1-63641-502-4
E-book ISBN: 978-1-63641-503-1

1 2025
Printed in the United States of America

Most Charisma Media products are available at special quantity discounts for bulk purchase for sales promotions, premiums, fundraising, and educational needs. For details, call us at (407) 333-0600 or visit our website at charismamedia.com.

CONTENTS

....

I THINK I HAVE DEMONS

MY INTRODUCTION TO the ministry of deliverance came through my pastor, who is my uncle. When he started our church, he was determined that we would not drift into a seeker-sensitive ministry model that mocks or minimizes supernatural manifestations. He wanted us to experience God's power firsthand. So he took us to places where we could witness it.

One of those places was a Bob Larson seminar. I was only fourteen or fifteen years old at the time, and I won't lie: It was pretty spooky. I had never seen a deliverance in real life; I had only heard stories about exorcisms. I vividly remember one session in which Reverend Bob walked through the room holding a cross. As he moved, demons manifested, and even teenagers freaked out.

Bob wasn't afraid of demons manifesting or creating disorder. It seemed like he *invited* those manifestations. This reminded me of when Jesus was in the synagogue and a demon manifested. (See Luke 4:33–36.) Jesus didn't throw the man out of the synagogue, as many of today's churches would do. No! He cast the demon out of the man.

As Bob slowly made his way through the seminar room and reached the second row, someone started screaming. I gripped my chair, silently praying that nothing would manifest in me. It was an intense but defining moment in my understanding of deliverance ministry.

But why did I grip my chair in fear? At first I didn't know why. I assumed that all the "demon stuff" scared me. The truth was that I needed deliverance. As a young teenager, I got hooked on pornography without the help of smartphones, the internet, or social media. My neighbor had asked me to mind his cats while he was on vacation.

Being new to the United States, I was curious to see how other people lived. So I watched some VHS tapes I found in his closet.

Something changed in me that day. Immediately I felt guilty and repented. But the pull was too strong. I kept returning to watch more videos. My only hope for stopping was for my neighbor to return and take back his keys.

At the time, I thought the issue was simply the lust of the flesh—a sin I needed to repent of and forsake. That's true for some people, but I kept falling back into pornography no matter how many times I repented. It was as though porn would find me. I would stumble upon it in the most unlikely places, including Christian bookstores. I felt targeted, and I wondered whether something deeper than the lust of the flesh was involved.

Eventually I realized that when you're addicted, you've got company. I'm not saying that every addicted person has a demon, but I soon realized that I did. A book opened my eyes to my struggle (and I sincerely hope reading this book will pull back the curtain on whatever spiritual realities are behind your challenges). I understood that I'd been dealing with the symptoms of my issue but missing the root cause. I was trying to eliminate spiderwebs without taking care of the spider.

My self-deliverance began with fasting and prayer, and lust lost its grip on my life. But complete deliverance happened later. Although I believe in self-deliverance and will soon guide you through the steps, most of us need someone to lead us through deliverance.

My own deliverance was very productive: The spirits of Leviathan, Jezebel, death, and lust were all cast out. You might wonder how I knew which spirits came out. Well, they spoke. I thought my problems had started with my exposure to pornography, but there was a deeper issue. Lust was a small demon running errands for the bigger spirit of death. And death itself did the bidding of higher-level spirits like Leviathan and Jezebel. To get to the root of my addiction, I also had to confront and renounce generational curses, especially curses of death.

FAMILY HISTORY MEETS ABUNDANT LIFE

Let me give you some background so you understand where I'm coming from. There were complications when I was in my mother's womb, and doctors said I wouldn't survive. Thank God I was born, but I spent much of my childhood in the hospital. During my first two years of development, the optic nerve didn't properly connect to one of my eyes, causing it not to follow the other. And before I even turned two, I died. Obviously I was revived, but it was as though something didn't want me to live.

When I was nine years old, my best friend died right before my eyes. Then, at thirteen, soon after moving to the United States, I was weary of life and wanted to die. When I started feeling better, pornography entered my life—I believe to kill the beginning of my ministry and destroy my future marriage and calling. Looking back, I can see how this "death" thing worked overtime to take me out at every stage of my life.

At one point my uncle the pastor traveled overseas to see a certain prophet of God. Our church was spiritually stuck, and my uncle was dealing with difficult family issues. Desperately seeking a breakthrough and a word from God, he fasted for forty days and visited the prophet's church. During one service, the prophet told my uncle that a curse from his own father's lineage was attacking the family.

My uncle and I went to see my grandmother, who confirmed a shocking piece of our family history. She told us that Grandpa, who had already passed away, came from a large family where death was "normal." She and Grandpa had sixteen kids. His parents and eleven of his siblings all died before he got married. One sister survived into her early twenties but developed a mental illness and died in an institution two weeks later. The story was almost unbelievable.

Then my grandfather himself experienced tragedy, accidentally running over his four-year-old child with his tractor. This terrible death seemed to make sense of everything else. There was nothing normal about the patterns of freak accidents, premature deaths, and mental illness that plagued my grandfather's side of the family.

Later, during my own deliverance, a demon revealed that many generations before my grandfather's time, his family had offered human sacrifices. In exchange for the promise of protection and health, the curse required someone in each generation to die. Of course, anything a demon proclaims needs to be tested, but it was clear that something spiritual had been at work in my family for generations.

Here's the thing: Although I grew up in a Christian family, crazy, destructive things happened. Some might think, "Well, that's just life." But I refuse to accept that kind of "normalcy." Freak accidents, mental institutions, premature deaths, addictions like pornography—these things are not my portion.

John 10:10 says that Jesus came to give us abundant life, but Satan came to kill, steal, and destroy. Don't normalize what is demonic—*neutralize it.* You empower whatever you tolerate. Accepting patterns of chaos and destruction gives the enemy room to operate. Jesus didn't come to help you cope with the devil's works; Jesus came to destroy them. (See 1 John 3:8.) Bondage isn't your portion. Freedom is.

Finding freedom brought more to me than a release from pornography and the shadow of death. Finally I was able to live without my hands being tied behind my back. Not only did breakthrough come to my personal life and ministry, but the Holy Spirit also began using me to share the power of Jesus and set other people free.

Jesus is real. Demons are real. And freedom is real. That is true in my life and the lives of those whose release from demonic oppression I have been privileged to witness. I have observed that demons are bent on destroying people, but Jesus sets people free. In fact, anyone who is demonized can be free.

FAITHFUL SHEPHERD

The reality of freedom reminds me of a powerful verse in Amos 3:12: "This is what the LORD says: 'As a shepherd rescues from the lion's mouth only two leg bones or a piece of an ear, so will the Israelites living in Samaria be rescued, with only the head of a bed and a piece of fabric from a couch'" (NIV).

What a vivid picture of the ruthless lion that seeks to capture and devour its prey—but also of the shepherd who interrupts the lion's meal and rescues from its jaws whatever remains of the sheep! The shepherd is not afraid to fight the lion. And the ultimate Shepherd, Jesus, is far better at delivering us than we are at getting ourselves into bondage. Jesus is stronger than any demon, and His power to rescue is unmatched.

Jesus will rescue even two leg bones and a piece of an ear. No one is too far gone. Even if you feel as though the lion has you in its mouth—even if you believe it's over—Jesus wants to deliver you. Yes, demons are ruthless, but Jesus is relentless. He doesn't give up, even when you do. He is better at delivering than demons are at destroying. No one is hopeless whose hope is in Jesus.

I'm reminded of the man in Matthew 8, Mark 5, and Luke 8 who was possessed by a legion of demons. The "lion" had that man firmly in its jaws, and the man barely kept himself from being swallowed. He lived among the tombs, isolated and cut off from society. He cried out day and night and cut himself with stones. He endured extreme internal anguish, and he physically harmed himself. Unclothed, he wandered without shame or awareness of his condition. He roamed the tombs and hills, unable to find peace. His torment consumed him, and his actions were dictated by demonic spirits.

People and family wrote off this Gadarene demoniac as being too crazy and too far gone. But Jesus came through a storm just to reach him. Very little was left of the man and his sanity, but it was enough for Jesus to work with. That's the power of God: Even if Satan controls 99 percent of your life, the 1 percent he doesn't have is more powerful than all the rest.

Mark 5:6 says, "When [the demoniac] saw Jesus from afar, he ran and worshiped Him." Demons don't make people run to Jesus and worship Him. That desperate man saw a small window of opportunity to get free. This was his chance. No matter how far gone or demonized he was, he had the desperation all of us need to press into Jesus for freedom. Demons might harass your mind, control your emotions, or manipulate your circumstances, but they cannot stop you from willfully seeking freedom. You can run to Jesus and be free.

Jesus delivered the demoniac and healed his broken mind. Yet because of it, the entire city rejected Jesus. Jesus willingly endured their rejection for the man's sake. He is the relentless Shepherd who goes to war with the lion for what's left of His sheep.

Jesus delivered the man in the tombs, and He will deliver you.

CHAPTER 1

WELCOME TO THE BATTLEFIELD

DURING THE COVID-19 pandemic, we held a deliverance conference in Seattle where an extraordinary number of people experienced deliverance. Afterward, my wife and I met one of the top cosmetic influencers on YouTube. She shared her incredible journey of coming to faith and undergoing deliverance, which included removing from her home roughly $300,000 worth of crystals.

She spoke about her deeply spiritual past. As a successful businesswoman, she had Hollywood elites and major YouTubers on speed dial. She also communicated regularly with a spirit guide (a demon) who helped her make decisions, and she consulted with psychics regarding her business deals.

This woman wasn't some evil-looking "crazy witch"; she was a deeply spiritual and influential person. However, when Jesus became her Lord and Savior, the spirit guides that once seemed helpful began physically tormenting her, both at home and in public places. Desperately searching for help, she met experienced deliverance ministers.

When she told my wife and me some of what occurred behind the scenes in her life, I wasn't shocked. Her story was a fresh reminder of a simple truth: "The whole world lies under the sway of the wicked one" (1 John 5:19). Her experiences provided greater insight into the surging interest in deliverance and the surprising number of people who seem to struggle with personal demonization.

The accounts this woman shared reminded me of a moment when the curtain was pulled back and the spiritual world was exposed to me. I had seen deliverances at a young age (during Rev. Bob Larson's seminars), but the full depth of the spiritual realm hit me when I read Rebecca Brown's book *He Came to Set the Captives Free*.[1] It was a captivating and terrifying volume. I couldn't sleep for several nights after reading it.

The book follows the lives of two women: Rebecca, a Christian doctor, and Elaine, a former satanist. Elaine's journey was harrowing. Dedicated to Satan within days of her birth, she was inhabited by demons and grew up with special powers. At seventeen she was recruited into a satanic cult where she witnessed raw demonstrations of demonic power. She was trained in incantations, martial arts, and other dark practices, all while she was also active in a large Christian church where she sang and taught.[2]

Elaine eventually rose to the rank of high priestess in the cult and even met Satan personally. She refused to participate in human or animal sacrifices that led to brutal torture by demons, yet she gained national influence within satanism and was given the title "Bride of Satan."[3] The cult she belonged to practiced human sacrifice, sexual rituals with demons, and frequent orgies. Elaine's life was steeped in unimaginable darkness.

However, Elaine noticed that her powers were stopped by Christians who prayed. This realization marked the beginning of her journey to freedom. Eventually she visited a genuine church and surrendered her life to Jesus. Shortly afterward, she became gravely ill and was admitted to a hospital, where she met Dr. Rebecca Brown, a devout Christian knowledgeable in spiritual warfare. Rebecca took Elaine into her home and helped her undergo deliverance from the demons that had inhabited her since birth. Rebecca, together with a strong Christian pastor experienced in casting out demons, guided Elaine toward freedom.[4]

Although *He Came to Set the Captives Free* opened my eyes to the reality of evil authorities in the spirit realm, it seemed from the book that demonic activity only involves spooky, bizarre activity happening in some hidden California basement.[5] But I now have a front-row seat to something much more domesticated. Not all of what I see comes in the extreme forms that Rebecca Brown's book chronicles, but it's undeniably from the same dark kingdom.

SPIRITUAL SHIFT

The American culture has experienced a significant shift in recent years. As traditional religious affiliations decline, many alternative spiritualities fill the void. The world isn't becoming less spiritual; it is becoming profoundly spiritual. We are made in the image and likeness of our Creator God as spiritual beings with an innate longing for our spiritual source. Denying the existence of the Creator does not stifle that longing. Instead, the enemy exploits it by offering counterfeit spirituality, his "Trojan horse" for demonization.

New Age spirituality, the twin sister of occult practices, has taken center stage. Its customization and nondogmatic approach make it highly attractive to a generation that seeks a spiritual reality that is outside of Scripture and shaped to individual preferences. Rather than calling people to submit to the Creator God whose image they bear, the New Age offers a god made in the customizable image of each human being.

In rejecting a "religion of rules," many seekers desire all-inclusive, self-empowering spiritualities that validate and legitimize every spiritual endeavor, regardless of what Scripture teaches. Unfortunately, the New Age emphasis on healing, miracles, curse breaking, and positive thinking that seems so appealing is polluted, contaminated, and impure. This counterfeit is seducing a generation thirsty for an encounter with the divine but giving seekers a demonic deception that poisons rather than satisfies the soul.

Americans are increasingly pursuing the occult and witchcraft as their presence becomes more pervasive in pop culture, social media, and entertainment platforms. Popular franchises have glamorized magic, witchcraft, and supernatural powers, presenting them as fun, empowering, and accessible rather than dangerous or taboo. TV shows and movies normalize witches and occult practices, even portraying practitioners in heroic roles. Disney has increasingly normalized witchcraft and occult themes in its kids' shows and movies, featuring magical characters, spell casting, and mystical storylines.

Mainstream artists incorporate occult imagery and symbolism into music videos, lyrics, and performances. Pentagrams, tarot cards, and allusions to spells or rituals often appear in visual presentations, making occult practices seem edgy and artistic. Some artists openly embrace New Age philosophies (including manifestation, energy healing, and spirit communication) and encourage their fans to explore them. TikTok has become a hub for "WitchTok" and "SpiritualTok" communities, where creators share content involving spells, tarot readings, astrology, and crystal healing.

Taboos once forbidden and associated with shamans have become trendy, comedic, and widely regarded as harmless. But poison is still poison, no matter how attractive the label seems. Witchcraft and demons are evil even when the culture celebrates them. The book you are reading is not about exposing the darkness as much as bringing the light to those who sit in darkness. It is in the light that they can find freedom.

The rise in occult and witchcraft practices is not limited to the American youth culture. A significant resurgence is happening across age groups and across the globe and drawing a response. In his *Harper's* article titled "The Demon Slayers: The New Age of American Exorcisms,"[6] Sam Kestenbaum highlights the growing prominence of deliverance ministry in the US over recent years.

I've sat up front in crowded stadiums as demons are cast out. I've seen massive tents packed to overflowing where deliverance breaks out even before services begin. In movie theaters, popcorn buckets have been used as vomit trays as deliverance sweeps through screenings. Thousands have shared testimonies of watching YouTube videos and experiencing demons departing as they watched.

Some people ride the deliverance wave because it's trendy or makes good clickbait. Others see it as an opportunity to attack the ministry of deliverance. I often say that some are focused on delivering the demonized, while others are busy demonizing those who deliver. Nevertheless, some real generals and soldiers are courageously fighting to set the captives free.

TWO DOMINANT WORLDVIEWS

Before diving into the topic of deliverance, it's crucial to address the worldview issue. I believe this is the root cause of why so many people struggle with the concept of deliverance.

Everyone has a worldview—a lens through which they perceive and interpret reality. Every worldview seeks to understand the world and answer the following major questions:

- Where did we come from?

- Why are we here?

- What is wrong with the world?

- What is the solution to the world's problems?

The Christian worldview answers these questions while providing moral absolutes, affirming human dignity, and offering hope for humanity's most significant problem: sin. Yet many Christians struggle with multiple-worldview disorders. Because their beliefs are unclear, they allow conflicting ideas to coexist in their minds. This approach is dangerous because the enemy thrives where understanding is lacking.

Jesus affirms this danger in the parable of the sower, saying, "When anyone hears the word of the kingdom, and does not understand it, then the wicked one comes and snatches away what was sown in his heart. This is he who received seed by the wayside" (Matt. 13:19). Despite our free access to Bibles and sermons, the enemy has sown seeds of confusion among believers. Barna's research confirms this alarming trend among practicing Christians:

- 61 percent "agree with ideas rooted in New Age spirituality."

- 54 percent "resonate with postmodernist views."

- 36 percent accept Marxist ideas.

- 29 percent align with secularist principles.[7]

This confusion confirms the urgent need for a clear, biblical worldview that equips believers to resist the enemy's lies. Without it, Christians are vulnerable to deception, and the devil exploits their confusion.

What you believe determines how you live. Christianity is not only about living differently—it's about thinking differently, which transforms how we live. A biblical worldview simplifies life by grounding us in eternal truths. As A. W. Tozer said, "The man who comes to a right belief about God is relieved of ten thousand temporal problems, for he sees at once that these have to do with matters which at the most cannot concern him for very long."[8]

Worldviews are key to how we understand life. In relation to deliverance, we must examine the two dominant worldviews within Christianity: the *blueprint worldview* and the *warfare worldview*. These perspectives profoundly shape how believers interpret suffering, evil, and God's role in the world. In his book *God at War*, Pastor Greg Boyd contrasts these views.

The blueprint worldview

The term "blueprint worldview" seems to have been coined by Boyd.[9] However, the concept predates him. Broadly conceived, it is a "Calvinist" worldview.[10] The idea is that everything that happens—whether it's a tornado, a war, or something as small as tripping over a fallen tree branch—is predetermined by God. Therefore, if you were born with a deformity or a genetic illness, you would accept it as God's choice for you. If you were born beautiful and brilliant in every way, God predetermined that too. According to this perspective, everything God does is ultimately for His glory, so even a deformity is meant to bring Him glory and serve His purposes.

The blueprint worldview holds that nothing happens by accident or human choice, and free will is an illusion. People might think they are making independent decisions, but they are doing what God previously decided they would do. Human and angelic agencies are nonexistent; God's fixed plan has mapped out everything.

The blueprint affects issues of eternity. If God decreed that you would sin and end up in eternal fire, then that is your fate. Interestingly, it is God who determined that you would sin. Even so, God is incapable of wrongdoing. Because He is God, He can do what He wants— even decree sin and punish you for it. If you suffer, God caused your suffering for His own (often unknowable) reasons. And if your life is free of suffering, He chose that too.

As a Christian, you don't really "do" anything within this framework. God does everything for you. He can reward you, but even your good actions are ultimately what He prearranged. There's no credit to be given for human effort.

The blueprint perspective often leads to prayers of resignation, in which people thank God for the bad things that happen to them. These happenings are seen as gifts God gives for reasons that cannot be understood. An unavoidable paradox arises, however: Believers who thank God for His "gift" of illness also seek the best doctors in hopes of a cure. So is the sickness a gift to embrace or an enemy to resist?

The warfare worldview

The warfare or freewill worldview sees life as a battleground between God and Satan. God has a plan to defeat Satan and uses free agents—faithful angels and redeemed humans—to carry it out. However, Satan also has a plan and works to oppose God's agents. While the final victory belongs to God, the war is ongoing.

Humans genuinely have free will and can make real choices, within limits. For example, not everyone can choose to be a professional athlete. Our options can be shaped by random events, the choices of others, or even natural disasters. A family history of alcoholism and poverty might limit a family member's opportunities. A drunk driver might cripple someone. A tornado might destroy someone's home. Or a health crisis might change someone's outlook.

In the warfare worldview, God does not cause these events; they are results of the curse that Adam's sin brought into the world. At times and for various reasons, God intervenes in our circumstances. He might be answering a prayer, honoring the faithfulness of someone long ago, or using us for His purposes in ways we can't fully understand. His sovereignty is complex and interactive. Like a master chess player, God sees every move in advance and works through a world of free agents to accomplish His aims.

The brokenness in the world—suffering, deformities, and natural disasters—does not come from God but is the result of sin. God created Adam and Eve perfectly and gave them a good and beautiful world. When they disobeyed Him, sin entered the world and corrupted everything, including human DNA, weather systems, and ecosystems. For example, God designed the reproductive system to be perfect, but the sin that corrupted genes led to deformities and disease. God has allowed these outcomes, but He did not decree them.

MILITANT MINDSET

Now that we've seen the dominant worldviews that relate to deliverance, let's talk about a mindset that proactively partners with God: It's a militant mindset that leads believers to pray prayers of resistance where evil and suffering are concerned. We don't just pray; we also use every tool and modern advancement available to alleviate pain and suffering, knowing that when God creates a new heaven and a new earth, He will obliterate all suffering.

Take sickness, for example. Some people may accept cancer as a gift from God. God can use evil circumstances to bring about growth in us, but our own bodies tell a different story about God's intent. Without any theological training, the immune system God gave us automatically fights sickness. Perhaps the human immune system understands God's will better than some of our minds do!

Whether healing comes immediately through a miracle, gradually through doctors, or ultimately in heaven, one thing is clear: Sickness is neither God's will nor a gift to be embraced. We are called to resist sickness, trusting that God is always working for our good.

Jesus' own life and character reinforce this view. He fed the hungry, calmed storms, healed the sick, and cast out demons. He didn't promote suffering or destruction. God's nature, revealed in Jesus, shows that He is not the author of evil; He is at war with evil.

For the first four centuries after the ascension, the early church fathers embraced this militant mindset. They viewed all sickness as demonic and all natural disasters as the devil's work. Their response was simply to wage war against these forces in Jesus' name.

DRAGON SLAYER

From its beginning the Bible reveals a cosmic conflict. In Genesis 3:15, after humanity fell, God spoke a prophetic word to the serpent, promising a Savior who would crush its head. This Savior would not escape suffering. The prophecy explained that His heel would be bruised. This first hint of the gospel pointed straight to Jesus.

Before there were any "demon slayers" there was the true "Dragon Slayer." Jesus' mission was to destroy the works of the devil. (See 1 John 3:8.) At every turn Jesus confronted the sickness, sin, and suffering that sprang from the serpent's influence. His miracles, healings, and deliverances revealed His authority over Satan. (See Acts 10:38.)

The greatest battle took place at the cross. What seemed like a defeat was the serpent's undoing. Jesus' heel was bruised, but Satan's head was crushed. As Colossians 2:15 attests, Christ disarmed and shamed the powers of darkness, turning death into victory for all who believe. This spiritual warfare reminds us that sin, sickness, and suffering were never God's plan. They arose from rebellion and the enemy's dark work. But through Jesus—the Dragon Slayer—the serpent's power is broken, and its final defeat is assured.

LIFE IS A BATTLEFIELD, NOT A VACATION

Having a warfare worldview doesn't mean seeing demons behind every bush. It simply means recognizing that life means warfare. The chaos on the beaches of Normandy in 1944 resembles our reality more than a breezy Hawaiian vacation does. Consider the following account of the D-Day landing on Omaha beach, as described by the National Museum of the United States Navy:

> At the beaches, [after] wading through tide-water, the men were met with extreme gun fire, rough terrain, runnels, mined-obstacles, French galets (pebbles), concertina barbed wire, and seawalls. This journey continued with being exposed in a grassy area with no cover, whilst still under extreme fire, which was then met with a climb riddled with numerous bluffs and eroded ravines.[11]

Treating your life like a vacation instead of a war is not only naive—it's immoral. Vacation mode is about approaching life with ease in mind, expecting only good things to happen. When you're on vacation, challenges are unwelcome interruptions. But a warfare mentality expects suffering and is pleasantly surprised when good things occur. This mindset cultivates gratitude for even the most minor victories.

As Christians, a warfare worldview helps us make sense of suffering and evil without blaming God or ourselves. Jesus said, "From the days of John the Baptist until now the kingdom of heaven suffers violence, and the violent take it by force" (Matt. 11:12). Jesus wasn't advocating physical violence; He was urging spiritual awareness. We are in a war, so let's wake up and realize that we're on the battlefield.

Here's how C. S. Lewis describes spiritual warfare and our role in it: "Enemy-occupied territory—that is what this world is. Christianity is the story of how the rightful king has landed, you might say landed in disguise, and is calling us all to take part in a great campaign of sabotage."[12]

THE CHURCH IS A WARSHIP, NOT A CRUISE SHIP

Jesus' vision of the church was inherently militant, not in a physical sense but in its mission to oppose the forces of hell. His choice of location was strategic when He posed a famous question to His disciples during a field trip to Caesarea Philippi. There Jesus asked, "Who do men say that I, the Son of Man, am?" (Matt. 16:13).

Caesarea Philippi was built on a massive rock at the base of Mount Hermon, a mountain with a dark spiritual history. The ancient city of Dan was located nearby. King Jeroboam established a place there to worship a golden calf, a horrible sin against the true God, YHWH. (See 1 Kings 12:28–30.)

In the Book of Enoch (a popular non-biblical book written 150 or more years before Jesus' birth) this region was believed to be a stronghold of the Nephilim, the "giants" mentioned in Genesis 6. The late biblical scholar Michael Heiser notes Enoch 6:6, the story of two hundred angels who met on Mount Hermon to agree to disobey God and marry human women. Heiser points to this mountain as "ground zero" for that rebellion.[13]

Caesarea Philippi had a lot of history. The Phoenicians considered Mount Hermon sacred to Baal and named nearby towns such as Baal Gad (Josh. 11:17) and Baal Hermon (Judg. 3:3) after him. Later, Herod the Great built a temple to honor his patron, Caesar Augustus, and established both the cult and worship of Augustus.[14] An inscription from another Roman province calls Augustus "savior" (Greek, *soter*) and "god," and says that his birthday was "good news" (Greek, *evangelion*) for the world.[15] Herod's great temple included many priests and probably administrative buildings, so a city was formed. After Herod's death, his son Philip expanded the city, naming it Caesarea

Philippi to honor both Caesar and himself. The worship of the pagan Roman emperor was strong on Israel's northern border.

The people of Caesarea Philippi also worshipped the Greek god Pan, a half-man, half-goat creature so ugly that his parents supposedly rejected him and numerous nymphs rebuffed his amorous advances. As a result, Pan became completely without moral boundaries, raping both women and boys.[16] From a biblical perspective, Pan is a demon. Full of rejection and sexually debased, he was the major god worshipped at Caesarea Philippi.[17]

It is no wonder that Jesus brought His disciples to this literal gateway to the demonic world to ask them who people claimed He was. When Peter responded that Jesus was the Messiah, the Son of the living God, Jesus declared: "I will build My church, and the gates of Hades shall not prevail against it" (Matt. 16:18). This was more than a statement; it was a battle cry. Caesar was neither a "god" nor a "savior." Pan was not a "god" either. Only Jesus is the Messiah/Savior and Son of the *living* God. He alone will liberate His people from their demonic oppressors and turn the tide of battle against the spiritual enemy!

Jesus notified His disciples that "the kingdom of heaven suffers violence, and the violent take it by force" (Matt. 11:12). The church He continues building is no passive institution. It is strategically positioned to launch an assault on the gates of the underworld, tearing down strongholds and overcoming the darkness being unleashed on the world.

It's essential to understand that Jesus' call to action was not aimed at social work, though the church *is* called to help the poor and serve others. Jesus was pointing to the church's ultimate mission: to storm the gates of hell. The church of Jesus Christ is not a cruise ship designed for pleasure but a warship piloted by the captain of our salvation, the King of kings and Lord of lords.

So at Caesarea Philippi, Jesus stood in enemy territory and declared that the gates of hell, the strongholds of darkness, could not prevail.

The church is not afraid of hell's gates. The church is built to overcome them and win.

You might be wondering, "Didn't Jesus already defeat the devil? Shouldn't we simply live in that victory?"

The answer is yes! Jesus defeated the enemy through the cross, but the battle isn't over. Acknowledging spiritual warfare does not give credit to the devil; it magnifies the power and victory of what Jesus accomplished. The church's mission is to enforce that victory, pushing back the darkness and reclaiming what the enemy has stolen.

THE WAR IS WON, BUT THE BATTLE RAGES ON

Hebrews 2:8 captures the seeming paradox of a war that continues after the battle is won, saying: "You have put all things in subjection under his feet....But now we do not yet see all things put under him." This concept, known in the theological world as "already, but not yet," reflects our current reality.[18] Jesus has already defeated Satan, but His victory will fully manifest when He returns. Until then, we are soldiers in a spiritual war, spreading the gospel and resisting the enemy.

An earthly example provides a powerful analogy for what Christ accomplished on the cross and what He will complete when He returns. D-Day (already mentioned), when Allied forces landed on the beaches of Normandy and delivered a decisive blow to the Axis powers, was the turning point of World War II. Although the enemy was defeated in principle and the ultimate victory had become inevitable, battles raged on for eleven more months. Then on V-Day (or VE Day) the war in Europe officially ended.

Christ's death and resurrection were the spiritual equivalent of D-Day. At the cross Jesus decisively defeated sin, death, and Satan, ensuring ultimate victory. The war is effectively won, but battles still rage because the enemy resists. We live in this "already, but not yet" reality—the kingdom of God has been inaugurated but not yet fully realized.

Like the Allies who fought the enemy with hope and determination after D-Day, we fight against sin and dark spiritual forces knowing that Christ's second coming will be our spiritual V-Day. Then He will fully eradicate evil, judge the wicked, and establish His eternal kingdom. The victory He secured on the cross will be fully manifested.

Until that day, every Christian is called to live as a soldier, remembering that for every Pharaoh, God raised a Moses. For every Goliath, God raised a David. And for every Jezebel, God raised an Elijah and a Jehu. I believe that amid the current chaos, God is raising an army of men and women who are breaking free from demonic bondage and are boldly entering the enemy's camp to free others.

As Isaiah 59:19 declares, "When the enemy comes in like a flood, the Spirit of the LORD will lift up a standard against him." No matter how relentless the storm or how many spiritual enemies flood in, the Holy Spirit raises a banner of victory against them. Will you be a courageous soldier on this battlefield? Or will you be a casualty of war? The choice is yours. Welcome to the battlefield!

CHAPTER 2

....

DEMONS UNMASKED

STEVE GREW UP in South Korea surrounded by Buddhism. His grandparents were devout Buddhists, and he was immersed in Buddhist temple life from infancy. By the age of six, two questions stirred in his heart: "Why was I born?" and "Why is there suffering?"

At nine years old, Steve moved to Boston but continued practicing Buddhism, praying up to eight hours a day during his teen years. Yet his questions remained unanswered. He experienced fleeting moments of peace, but the fear of evil spirits tormented him continually.

As an immigrant, Steve wrestled with his identity. He felt different and believed he needed to prove himself. This inner struggle led him into rebellion. By 1998 he was getting high and spending time with friends who did the same. One day he smoked a concoction he called a "death bowl," a mix of weed, heroin, cocaine, and PCP. The Korean word for *drugs*, which translates to "demon's medicine," suddenly became hauntingly real for Steve. For ten straight days after smoking the death bowl, Steve couldn't sleep. On the eighth day, he saw a vision of an Asian grandpa. By the ninth and tenth days, the figure appeared regularly, offering him a sinister bargain: fifty thousand fewer years in hell if he would commit suicide.

Desperate and deceived, Steve wrote a suicide note to his mom. He grabbed the largest knife he could find from the kitchen and went to the living room. Kneeling on the floor with the knife to his stomach, he hesitated, thinking, "This is going to hurt!"

At that moment Steve's mom walked in, saw what was happening, and called the police. Ignoring the chaos, Steve began cutting into his stomach, causing unbearable pain. When the police arrived, they tried to wrestle away the knife. They maced Steve and hit him with a baton, but the Asian grandpa's voice urged him: "Go for the neck!" Steve obeyed. As his artery exploded, blood covered the living room.

Immediately Steve began sinking and found himself in hell, chained through his stomach, with demons tormenting him. "I knew I was a sinner, and I knew I would never get out of that place," he recalled. The spiritual, emotional, and physical pain was beyond words. Steve said, "I realized I had been tricked."

Meanwhile, Steve's mom, a devout Buddhist who despised Christianity, reached out to her only Christian friend, Mrs. Kim. Unbeknownst to Steve, Mrs. Kim had been praying for his salvation. She quickly gathered seven intercessors from her church, and they went to the hospital where Steve was, praying for eight hours—the exact length of Steve's two surgeries.

When Steve began waking up, he didn't see Jesus, but he heard a voice say, "I love you, Steve. No more drugs and no more Buddhism."

The intercessors were still there when Steve opened his eyes. They shared the gospel with him and asked whether he wanted to accept Jesus. Overwhelmed, Steve prayed the sinner's prayer—not once but ten times, just to be sure!

Steve's life was radically transformed. He knew Jesus had saved him, and soon he was baptized in the Holy Spirit. After some time, Steve felt called to visit the underground church in China, where he spent one hundred days. There, he witnessed the faith of radical believers who had little more than a Bible and faced real persecution from the police. Their church services lasted all day, and their hunger for God inspired Steve. Before they sent him home, the underground church leaders urged him, saying, "We need you to get a degree."

Steve returned to the US, earned his Master of Divinity degree, and became a military chaplain. Today he is a passionate, on-fire evangelist sharing the power of Jesus to save, deliver, and transform lives.

Demons don't discriminate—they operate across all cultures, seeking to deceive, torment, and lead people to destruction. In Buddhist circles they can disguise themselves as spirits offering peace or enlightenment. In other cultures they might present themselves through witchcraft, ancestral worship, or even modern forms of idolatry such as addiction, power, or fame. The goal is always the same: to keep people in bondage and blind them to the truth of Jesus Christ.

Demons exploit the spiritual hunger that God placed in every human heart, twisting it to lead people down paths of deception that lead to separation from God. The good news is that no matter how deep the deception or how strong the chains are, the power of Jesus to deliver is greater. His light expels all darkness, and His truth sets people free.

DEMONS IN DIFFERENT CULTURES

Demons have been around for a long, long time. Throughout history people across the world have believed in spirits that cause harm, suffering, or chaos. These demons might be called by different names, but all of them disrupt life and bring trouble.

- In ancient Mesopotamia, people feared spirits like the *utukku* and *lilītu*.[1] These beings were blamed for diseases, bad luck, and torment. The remedy? Rituals, sacrifices, and protective charms to keep the spirits away. After the time of Jesus, Jewish people in Mesopotamia used magic bowls with inscribed incantations to protect themselves against demons.[2]

- The Egyptians believed that their four-thousand-plus demons were closely tied to their gods.[3] They believed certain spirits brought plagues or controlled specific areas of life. They relied on magic spells and amulets to ward off evil and protect themselves.

- Greek and Roman cultures introduced the idea of *daimons*. At first these spirits were not always seen as evil, but over time they became associated with madness, illness, and misfortune. People turned to priests or healers who performed ceremonies, offered sacrifices, or chanted special prayers to drive out the spirits.[4]

- In African tribal cultures demons or evil spirits were often linked to ancestral curses or angered ancestors. Witch doctors or shamans were called upon to fight these spirits through dances, chanting, and sacrifices.

- In Southeast Asia the Wa tribespeople feared the spirits they called *nats* and even killed other tribespeople and took their heads to satisfy the nats' bloodlust.[5]

- In Eastern cultures (especially Hinduism and Buddhism) people believed in beings called *asuras*, spirits that cause disorder and chaos. People meditated, chanted prayers, or used rituals to restore peace and harmony.

No matter the culture, the belief was clear: Evil spirits existed, and the people had to deal with them. Yet no matter how creative or traditional human methods were, they were (and are) no match for God's authority.

JINN IN ISLAM

Muslim belief in the unseen world is deeply ingrained and tied to the culture's understanding of demonology. Spirits known as *jinn* are seen as beings that can influence people, cause harm, and even possess individuals.[6] Islamic tradition often attributes unexplained illnesses, misfortunes, or mental struggles to the influence of jinn. To combat such oppression, many Muslims turn to exorcists known as *raqi*, who perform rituals, recite verses from the Quran, and use prescribed prayers to drive out these spirits.[7]

At one of our conferences, I had the opportunity to minister deliverance to a Muslim woman who had suffered years of spiritual torment, constantly battling sleepless nights, fear, and an overwhelming sense of darkness. Raised in Islam, she was deeply devoted to her faith. She was convinced her problem was demonic, so she sought help from the raqi. Unfortunately, they left her even more oppressed.

A Christian friend invited the woman to his church. She initially hoped to convert him to Islam, but as she continued visiting, something shifted. She noticed the joy and freedom among the people and began questioning everything she had long believed. She still struggled to sleep, and someone suggested she call on the name of Jesus. She hesitated but finally whispered His name one night, and for the first time in years, she experienced peace and sound sleep.

She wondered, "How could this be?" When her friends told her to pray to Jesus, she prayed, "Jesus, if You are real, show Yourself to me."

At a party the next day, a young woman witnessed to the Muslim woman about Jesus. So she said, "Jesus, I believe in You as my Lord and Savior." She has testified that in that moment the Holy Spirit came like a wind and filled her up. She compares the transformation to seeing the world in black and white one minute and full color the next.

Although she saw Jesus standing there in the fullness of His light and glory, when she got home, she still questioned how it could be. In her Islamic life she believed Jesus was a prophet. Now she wondered, "How can I know that the man I saw was Jesus?"

Jesus appeared to her again and said, "You belong with Me. You belong in My Father's house. I'm coming for you."

Her struggle continued, however. She knew that following Jesus would cost her everything, even her husband and daughter. It could even cost her own life. As the spiritual battles and torment intensified, she knew she needed deliverance.

This realization is what brought this woman to our conference. During the prayer time, the demons that were tormenting her began to manifest and declared their intent to destroy her. But in the name of Jesus Christ these spirits were cast out, and the chains that kept her bound for so long were broken. At the conference, this very shy, formerly Muslim woman took a huge step, publicly declaring her faith in Jesus for the first time. She said that God told her that if she didn't give Him her life, then she was not worthy to follow Him.

Today this woman stands freely and boldly, proclaiming that it was not religion or rituals that delivered her—it was the power of Jesus.

NOT-SO-HARMLESS ENTERTAINMENT

In Western culture we often see demons through the lens of movies, art, and entertainment. Movies have thrilled audiences by portraying demons as terrifying forces that possess people, haunt houses, and wreak havoc. Movies like *The Exorcist*, *The Conjuring*, and *Paranormal Activity* depict demons as powerful and almost unbeatable beings.[8] As these films provide glimpses of demonic activity, they often become open doors through which the demons on the screen inhabit movie-goers who sought only to be entertained.

Other films and shows normalize demons, turning them into antiheroes or misunderstood creatures. Movies like *Hellboy* and shows such as *Lucifer* glamorize demons,[9] presenting them as relatable and even sympathetic characters. This approach deceives people into seeing demons as harmless beings who do good. This deception dulls spiritual discernment and causes people to ignore the dangers of demonic influence.

Video games and fantasy stories often use demons as plot devices, including enemies to defeat, bosses to fight, or powers to harness. In games like *Doom*, *Diablo*, or *Dark Souls*, demons are presented as dark, destructive enemies. Harmless as games might seem, they create a fascination with the demonic. Players can become desensitized to the reality of spiritual warfare or drawn to explore occult ideas out of curiosity. Some games go further, allowing characters to use demonic powers or work alongside demons. This is another open door to the demonic.

Today's culture swings between two extremes where demons are concerned. On one hand, demons are presented as terrifying and all-powerful. This approach opens the door to fear. On the other hand, demons are glamorized, normalized, and even mocked as harmless characters who do nothing more than entertain us. This deludes people and makes them more spiritually vulnerable.

DEMONS OPERATE BEHIND THE SCENES

The Bible paints a clear picture of who demons are and what they do. In contrast to the confusion and mystery found in many cultures, Matthew 12:43–45 identifies demons as unclean spirits who oppose God and harm people.

Although demons are not mentioned as often in the Old Testament, they are still present. Sometimes evil spirits were allowed to torment those who disobeyed God, as was the case with King Saul. After turning away from God, "an evil spirit from the LORD tormented him" (1 Sam. 16:14, NIV). Deuteronomy 32:17 reveals that demons were tied to idol worship, saying, "They [God's people] sacrificed to demons, not to God." When Israel turned to other gods, they didn't simply bow to lifeless idols; they opened doors to demonic spirits. This is why the Old Testament strongly forbids consulting with spirits, practicing witchcraft, and turning to mediums. (See Leviticus 19:31.)

Some prophetic and poetic passages of Scripture specifically mention demons. Isaiah 34:14 (LEB) hauntingly describes Edom's devastation, where goat-demons (satyrs, or in Hebrew, *śā'îr*) and the well-known demon figure Lilith (in Hebrew, *lîlît*) were said to inhabit the barren, apocalyptic wasteland. Similar imagery appears in Isaiah 13:21. These are more than scary scenes; they reveal a spiritual reality of desolation and demonic presence in a land or people abandoned to destruction.

A possible reference to a demon named Azazel appears in Leviticus 16. On the Day of Atonement, one goat was sent away into the wilderness "for Azazel" (Lev. 16:10, ASV). Scholars debate its exact meaning, and some suggest Azazel represents a demonic figure connected to the wilderness, a place often symbolizing chaos, darkness, and the demonic.[10]

Demons often operated behind Old Testament scenes of idol worship, rebellion, and judgment. Although they weren't mentioned as often or as clearly as in the New Testament, their influence was very real.

WHEN JEWISH DEMONOLOGY DEVELOPED

Between the time of Malachi and the coming of Jesus, Jewish understanding of demons increased. People began to see demons as real, active forces—unclean spirits that caused harm, brought sickness, and troubled people's lives.

These ideas came in part from the Hebrew Scriptures, which provided glimpses of evil spirits at work. Outside influences such as the Persian and Greek cultures also shaped beliefs about the spiritual realm. Remember the Greek daimons; the Greeks believed these spirits could be good, bad, or somewhere in between. But in Jewish thought, a daimon was a purely evil enemy of God that worked clandestinely to torment people.

A growing belief also taught that demons came from fallen angels. Remember that the Book of Enoch connected demons to angels that rebelled against God by having intercourse with human women. Some Jews believed demons to be the spirits of the Nephilim—the offspring that resulted from the unholy unions mentioned in Genesis 6.[11] While the Book of Enoch is not Scripture, it shows how readers of that time viewed the spiritual world. They believed demons were responsible for all kinds of trouble. When inexplicable evil happened, many people believed demons were to blame.

To address the demon problem, Jewish exorcists developed ways to cast them out. They relied on prayers, rituals, and sometimes complicated incantations, often calling on the name of God or even angels like Michael to help. The Jewish historian Josephus documented the practice of exorcism in ancient Israel. In his *Antiquities of the Jews*, Josephus wrote about Solomon's God-given authority over demons, noting that Solomon composed incantations and developed rituals to expel evil spirits.[12] Tradition and historical texts such as the *Testament of Solomon* describe the use of specific prayers and commands to drive out demonic spirits.[13] The Dead Sea scrolls reference some of David's songs that were believed to have power over demons.[14] These references emphasize the role of worship and sacred writings in spiritual warfare.

Although it's often said that the four-hundred-year period between Malachi and John the Baptist was silent, it also hosted the meaningful development of Jewish demonology. This was the backdrop when Christ came with authority and power to confront and cast out demons.

FALSE GODS AREN'T MERELY IDOLS

For the Jewish people of Jesus' day, demons were no vague superstition. They were real unclean spirits that caused harm, confusion, and distance from God. They invaded people's bodies, tormented their minds, and disrupted their lives. They were feared, avoided, and difficult to confront.

Jesus' ministry began with His wilderness triumph over the devil. (See Matthew 4:1–11; Luke 4:1–13.) Soon afterward, in an early public demonstration of His authority, Jesus cast out a demon in the synagogue. While deliverance wasn't new to Jesus' audience, His approach was. He didn't use or need rituals, formulas, or sacred objects. His authority was enough. He simply spoke, often with a simple command such as, "Come out of him!" (Mark 1:25), and demons obeyed.

The New Testament uses two key Greek words to describe demons: The one we've already seen is *daimon* (δαίμων), which makes only one New Testament appearance, in Matthew 8:31.[15] The second word is *daimonion* (δαιμόνιον), which is used more than sixty times in the New Testament. Prior to Jesus' arrival, Jewish thought rejected any positive connotations of *daimon*. As for *daimonion*, it was a general word for something divine or connected to fate. But when the Hebrew Scriptures were translated into Greek in the Septuagint, *daimonion* took on a darker meaning. Psalm 96:5 declared, "All the gods of the nations are demons" or "devils," and Psalm 91:6 warned of "the noonday demon" or the "evil spirit at noonday." These verses revealed what many had missed: False gods were more than empty idols. Behind them were demonic forces that spiritually opposed God and deceived nations.[16]

EVERYDAY ISSUES, SPIRITUAL ROOTS

The demons behind idols were also responsible for issues that many would call purely physical or psychological. During His earthly ministry, however, Jesus made the spiritual issues clear. In Luke 13:11–13, for example, a woman who had been bent over for eighteen years was set free when Jesus revealed that a spirit of infirmity had caused her physical state.

I've seen medical doctors confirm many healings in people who received deliverance from unclean spirits. This does not mean that every sick person has a demon, but some illnesses have demonic roots. Acts 10:38 says that Jesus healed "all who were oppressed by the devil," showing that, in some way, the enemy often causes physical suffering.

I recently met Lorraine, who shared an amazing testimony about how severe pain in her leg became a significant barrier in her life. It impacted everything from daily tasks to her role as a church elder and worship team member. Unable to climb stairs or stand without pain, she felt hindered from fully pursuing God's calling. Despite medical help and physical therapy, her condition persisted.

One day, Lorraine watched a sermon I preached. At the end of the message, I led a prayer for healing and first prayed deliverance prayers that targeted the spirit of infirmity. During the prayer, Lorraine realized that this might be the root of her pain. She felt warmth and tingling as she prayed and laid her hand on her leg. Instantly, the pain was gone. She could walk, climb stairs, and move freely. Her physical therapist was stunned, unable to explain the sudden change.

You might be wondering whether something as simple as leg pain can have spiritual roots. But if it's hindering your life, why would a spiritual cause surprise you? Lorraine's testimony shows that God cares about every part of our lives and wants to remove even the seemingly small barriers that oppose us.

DELIVERANCE MIGHT BE WILD, BUT IT'S NOT WEIRD

I find it interesting that Jesus' deliverances were personal and public and even occurred in synagogues. Jesus had no reservations about allowing people to witness God's power firsthand. He didn't worry that it might make people afraid, and He didn't believe it would distract them from God. In fact, in every place where I've witnessed people being delivered, I've also seen the fear of God fall on those watching.

As for people becoming gripped by the fear of demons, what really happens is quite the opposite. Horror films instill fear because that is their purpose. But people who witness deliverance are not only seeing demons cast out; they're seeing the power of God on display. Deliverance doesn't exalt the devil any more than healing exalts sickness. I can't tell you how many times people have told me, "We believe in deliverance, but we don't want to draw attention to demons or freak out new visitors during our services."

That's interesting! Nobody worries about the worship team distracting people from worship, or the preacher distracting people from God's Word. Yet a manifestation that occurs as someone is being set free is a problem? How can that be? God's glory is revealed when chains are broken, demons are cast out, and the sick are healed. Yes, some individuals manifest to get attention, just as some people take the platform for the wrong reasons. But we don't throw the baby out with the bathwater. We discern, address issues wisely, and focus on the life-transforming power of Jesus.

Regarding new visitors, I believe there is something far stranger than seeing biblical realities unfold; what is really weird is *never* seeing what you read about in the Bible. Exorcism might seem strange to some, but most unbelievers experience far stranger things in their lives. I have found they are more open to deliverance and the reality of demons than many believers are. In fact, some visitors who don't believe in God still believe in demons.

One touch of God's power can do more for a person than hundreds of sermons can. We need sermons, but we also need the demonstration of God's power. A few years ago, our team and I ministered deliverance in another city. There was a woman there who had suffered severe grand mal seizures for seven years. The condition was debilitating. Doctors couldn't find its cause, and the medication they prescribed cost approximately $2,000 per month.

The woman's life was completely disrupted by seizures so severe that her driver's license was suspended. Often she would forget her name or what she was doing. When she attended the service where we prayed for deliverance, God set her free as we prayed. From that moment, she has not had a single seizure. She no longer takes medication, has had no further ER visits, and her medically incurable condition was totally healed by God's power.

INVASION OF THE KINGDOM

Deliverance from demons is not only about setting the demonized free; it's also a proclamation of God's kingdom. Jesus said, "If I cast out demons by the Spirit of God, surely the kingdom of God has come upon you" (Matt. 12:28). Deliverance is a sign that the reign of God is breaking into the world. Because there is no sickness in God's kingdom, Jesus healed the sick. Because there are no demons in God's kingdom, Jesus cast them out. And because there is no death in God's kingdom, Jesus raised the dead.

Nothing Jesus did was done only to improve our lives (although it does that); it was also to give us a glimpse into the eternal reality of His kingdom. Miracles, including deliverance, are appetizers of His coming kingdom. Jesus inaugurated this kingdom at His first coming and gave us a foretaste of restoration. Upon His return, however, Jesus will consummate His kingdom. The devil will be bound and cast into the lake of fire. There will be no more curse and no more torment.

During the early stages of our ministry, deliverance became part of our church culture. Because many churches don't engage in deliverance, people flooded into our church, seeking help. While deliverance freed many of them, it also stirred up criticism from other leaders. Some pastors and bishops called me names, warned me to stop, and even made deliverance a topic of contention. I later learned that my name had been placed on a blacklist, barring me from speaking at youth conferences and camps.

That was more than a decade ago. One Friday night, during prayer, I found myself broken and crying out to God. I was hurt and confused, wondering why people couldn't celebrate the freedom others were experiencing. We had fasted and prayed for this breakthrough, believing God would move, and now we felt surrounded by rejection.

Lying on the floor, I wrestled with thoughts of toning things down to regain favor with certain circles or appease well-meaning pastors. But as I prayed, the Holy Spirit reminded me of King Saul's failure to destroy God's enemy, Amalek. (See 1 Samuel 15:2–3, 9.) Saul flinched because he feared people more than he feared God, and his compromise cost him the anointing. As I remembered his choice, conviction gripped my heart.

In that moment, I repented of my complaints and renewed my commitment to obey Jesus, even if it meant being misunderstood or rejected. I decided that God's anointing mattered more than human opinions. Demons are God's enemies, and they hurt His people. Deliverance is a war against them. It isn't about being popular or cool; it's about setting captives free and pleasing the One who called me.

DELIVERANCE IS A MIRACLE

Deliverance from demons is also called a miracle. Jesus said, "Do not forbid him, for no one who works a miracle in My name can soon afterward speak evil of Me" (Mark 9:39). Here Jesus was addressing

His disciples who told another deliverance minister to stop because he wasn't part of their group.

Jesus referred to deliverance as a miracle, and it often is, not only because of the visible changes people experience but also because of the profound release that happens when the bound are finally set free. Sometimes deliverance is the immediate healing of what was broken. At other times it's the untangling of everything that was trapped and suppressed by demonic influence.

A woman named Christy shared a powerful testimony of deliverance. Born into a broken home, she experienced abandonment and trauma early in life. By the age of ten, she battled severe depression and demonic oppression from being raised in a drug-filled environment. In her teenage years, self-harm plagued her, and terrifying voices commanded that she kill herself. Fearing death, she felt unable to tell anyone about her struggles. At nineteen, she found herself living with a boyfriend who was involved in witchcraft. Seeking safety, she ran to the church she grew up in and surrendered her life to Jesus, realizing that only He could protect her.

Years later, Christy's life spiraled into cycles of deep depression, drinking, and partying. Her now-husband, once a drug dealer but saved by Jesus, brought her to HungryGen. Despite her fear (which she now recognizes as demonic resistance) she attended a service where deliverance prayers were being offered. As prayer began, the many voices in her head manifested audibly, and she was delivered from those unclean spirits. Since then, Christy's life has been transformed. She is full of joy, peace, and kindness, and she is no longer bound by anger or torment. When she senses darkness, she boldly rebukes it and lives a life of freedom and victory in Christ.

During His earthly ministry, Jesus performed thirty-seven recorded miracles: sixteen healings, seven exorcisms (including the man in the synagogue, the Gadarene demoniac, and the Syro-Phoenician woman's daughter), and other acts such as raising the dead.[17] Yet in many

Charismatic circles, those eager to see the miraculous often overlook exorcism as a miracle, even though Jesus said it was.

Miracles don't only involve blind eyes seeing, deaf ears hearing, or the dead being raised. Transformation in the life of someone who is freed from demons is nothing short of miraculous.

DELIVERANCE IS DOING WHAT JESUS DID

Deliverance didn't end with Christ. He gave His disciples authority to cast out demons, and this became a regular part of their ministry. Today, people attend seminary to prepare for ministry. Jesus prepared His disciples differently: He commissioned the Twelve to drive out evil spirits and later sent out the seventy, who returned rejoicing because demons submitted to them in His name. (See Mark 3:14–15; Luke 10:1–19.) The disciples experienced moments of struggle, however, like when they couldn't cast out a demon due to their lack of faith and prayer. (See Matthew 17:19–21.) All of it was part of their training.

Deliverance from demons wasn't limited to Jesus' earthly lifetime. In the Book of Acts, His followers continued the work boldly. In Acts 8:6–7, Philip cast out demons in Samaria. Paul drove out spirits on multiple occasions, and even ordinary believers operated in this authority. (See Acts 16:16–18, 19:11–12.) Romans 15:19 shows that Paul performed "mighty signs and wonders" through the Holy Spirit.

Although Paul didn't focus on exorcism in his letters, he addressed something unique in 1 Corinthians 5:1–5: a kind of "reverse exorcism." When an unrepentant man persisted in sin, Paul instructed the believers to "deliver [him]...to Satan" (v. 5). They weren't only removing him from fellowship but acknowledging that his sin gave the enemy legal ground to attack him. The hope was that through this process and the suffering of his flesh, his spirit might be saved.

The early church did not see casting out demons as something weird. It was a natural extension of the apostles' calling as they followed what they saw Jesus do. Those closest to Him understood that delivering people from demonic oppression was a key part of advancing God's kingdom on earth. It was their mission and should be ours too.

DELIVERANCE: MINISTRY OF MERCY

Deliverance is not about fame or spectacle. It is a ministry of God's mercy. It is not a show to gain attention but an act of compassion that reveals the heart of Christ. Some argue that miracles, including exorcism, were meant only to confirm Jesus' divinity and validate the writing of the New Testament. According to this cessationist view, miracles ceased after Jesus ascended to heaven and the New Testament was completed. But if this were true, demons should have ceased to exist as well, which they didn't.

The four Gospels make it clear that Jesus cast out demons not merely to demonstrate His power but because He was moved by compassion for those suffering torment. Deliverance was always an expression of Jesus' mercy and love. Hebrews 13:8 reminds us that He "is the same yesterday, today, and forever." Jesus still loves people today, and demons haven't changed. Deliverance is as necessary now as it was two thousand years ago. It's not an outdated practice but a living expression of Christ's authority and compassion for a hurting world.

A recent interview I had with Rev. Bob Larson highlighted the reality of deliverance ministry.[18] He shared a defining moment from the early days of his calling: After a service, a teenage girl approached him, desperate for help. She was tormented by compulsive behaviors stemming from her father's hidden addiction to pornography. He was a deacon in the church and had unknowingly opened a door for the enemy to attack his family.

Because the girl was underage, Bob invited her father and pastor to be present during her deliverance. As Bob prayed, the demon manifested but was cast out through the power of Jesus Christ. The girl was completely delivered. Her compulsive behaviors stopped, and her father repented. This led to the healing of their family.

Rather than celebrating the miracle, the church leadership rejected Bob's actions. The very next Sunday morning, the pastor publicly condemned Bob from the pulpit and said he was of the devil. The pastor claimed the church leadership didn't believe in deliverance or in Christians having demons.

Someone gave Bob a cassette tape of the pastor's sermon and all his hurtful words against Bob. This left Bob devastated, questioning his future in ministry. Days later, he received a letter from the girl. She shared how she was now free, her father had turned back to God, and their family had been restored. In that moment, God spoke to Bob's heart: "What matters more—the approval of men or the deliverance of one soul?" That question solidified Bob's calling: to set captives free, regardless of the rejection or criticism he might face.

This reminded me that deliverance is all about God's mercy reaching people in bondage, even when it's misunderstood or opposed. Deliverance is a ministry born out of love for people and obedience to God. It is an integral part of fulfilling the Great Commission and should be embraced by the church. Jesus didn't hesitate to confront the works of darkness, and neither should we. His mercy is still at work, setting captives free, one soul at a time.

THE UNBROKEN CHAIN OF DELIVERANCE MINISTRY

The ministry of deliverance did not end with the apostles but was carried forward by subsequent leaders and church fathers. Their writings and testimonies confirm that exorcisms were widely practiced and recognized as evidence of Christ's power working through His people by the Holy Spirit. Let's now explore some of these leaders and their perspectives.

Justin Martyr (AD 100–165) explicitly wrote about Christians casting out demons in the name of Jesus Christ: "For numberless demoniacs throughout the whole world, and in your city, many of our Christian men, exorcising them in the name of Jesus Christ... have healed and do heal, rendering helpless and driving the possessing devils out of men."[19] This shows that exorcisms were not isolated events but a widespread practice in the Christian community.[20]

Tertullian (AD 160–225) boldly challenged non-Christians to bring demon-possessed persons into their courts, asserting that any Christian could cast out the demon in the name of Jesus Christ. He declared that because of their authority in Christ, the mere presence of a Christian would terrify any demons. Tertullian's words indicate that exorcism was viewed as a natural, ongoing part of Christian life and ministry.[21]

Origen (AD 185–253) wrote the following in *Against Celsus*, which is about the continuation of Christ's power over demons: "The name of Jesus can still remove distractions from the minds of men, and expel demons, and also take away diseases."[22] Obviously the early church saw deliverance as a key demonstration of God's kingdom.

WHEN DELIVERANCE WAS DIMINISHED

As Christianity became popular and was made the official religion of the Roman Empire, reliance on the supernatural diminished. When the church gained political power under Emperor Constantine and beyond, the perceived need for dependence on God's miraculous power decreased, along with the emphasis on spiritual warfare. The focus then shifted to institutional structures, political influence, and theological debates. As a result, supernatural ministry declined.

Are we in the West finding ourselves in a similar position today? We've built systems, structures, and marketing strategies that cause us to depend less on the power of God and more on human effort. It's been said, "It's shocking how much Christians in the West can accomplish without the Holy Spirit."

While some modern methods draw people to our churches, they cannot drive out demons. Without the power of the Holy Spirit, captives remain bound, and the supernatural ministry of Jesus is neglected. The church is at its strongest when it depends fully on God's Spirit rather than worldly methods or influence. Christians are most free when the church does what Jesus did.

THE ORIGINS OF DEMONS

In concluding this chapter, let's address the centuries-old question of where demons come from. Although the Bible is not explicit about demons' exact origins, there are some theories.

Some believe that demons are the spirits of evil people who have died. This idea is more aligned with pagan beliefs than biblical truth. Hebrews 9:27 makes it clear that after death, the spirits of people do not roam the earth but await judgment. After death, every human being faces judgment. There is no biblical support for the idea that human spirits become demons.

Another theory is that demons are the disembodied spirits of a pre-Adamic race that existed before Adam and Eve. This belief stems from what is called the "gap theory," which suggests an interval of time between Genesis 1:1 and 1:2. This theory proposes that a previous creation was destroyed and reconstructed. However, this is not taught anywhere in Scripture. Therefore, the gap theory is intriguing but speculative.

A common assumption among Christians is that demons are fallen angels who were cast out of heaven along with Satan. This view is often tied to Revelation 12:4–6, which describes Satan as a dragon whose tail drew "a third of the stars of heaven" and cast them to earth. The context of Revelation 12 does describe heavenly conflict, specifically referencing events surrounding the birth of the Messiah. However, the idea of a "primeval fall" of angels originates more from church tradition and literature (notably John Milton's *Paradise Lost*) than from clear biblical evidence.

A more compelling theory gaining much interest is one already mentioned. It is rooted in Genesis 6:4 and suggests that demons are the disembodied spirits of the Nephilim, the offspring of the "sons of God" and the "daughters of men" who perished in the great flood. The ancient Jewish text 1 Enoch expands on this concept. Although it is not in the canon of Scripture, 1 Enoch describes how the Nephilim's spirits became earthbound and corrupt: "Now, the giants, who are produced from the spirits [angels] and flesh, shall be called evil spirits upon the earth, and on the earth shall be their dwelling....The spirits of the giants afflict, oppress, destroy, attack, do battle, and work destruction on the earth" (1 Enoch 15:8, 11).[23]

This theory seems to explain the differences between angels and demons. Angels seem to have their own bodies and typically inhabit the "heavenlies," according to Ephesians 6:12 and Jude 6. But demons are earthbound and seek to inhabit physical bodies, as Matthew 12:43–45 and Mark 5:11–13 indicate. Unlike angels, demons seem to rely on occupying bodies to fulfill their mission. This distinction gives weight to the theory that they are disembodied spirits seeking bodies to inhabit.

When people ask me where I think demons come from, my answer is simple: The Bible doesn't give us a clear answer. However, the Bible is crystal clear about where demons are going—to the lake of fire. Speculating about theories involving disembodied Nephilim spirits and other ideas is interesting, but obeying Jesus and casting out demons through the power of the Holy Spirit is what truly matters.

Next, let's dive into one of the most controversial topics about demons: the demonization of believers.

CHAPTER 3

SPIRIT SQUATTING

Don Dickerman was raised in a home with parents who were believers but not churchgoers. During a certain service in a Baptist church in Texas, the Holy Spirit convicted eleven-year-old Don deeply. Overwhelmed with emotion and encouraged by a friend, he walked down the aisle and received Christ. That day changed his life forever, and his passion for serving the Lord began.

Don's ministry journey started with serving as a pastor in Southern Baptist churches. Driven by a heart for evangelism, he transitioned to full-time prison ministry in 1974. Over the years, Don preached in more than 850 prisons across North America, the Caribbean, and Europe. He saw tens of thousands of inmates come to Christ—perhaps more than one hundred thousand. His Baptist background equipped him as an evangelist focused on salvation, but his theological training had not prepared him for what would come next.

In 1995 Don's ministry shifted dramatically. While he was preaching in a federal prison, a corrections officer shared a vision with him. The officer described Don standing in a pot of bubbling oil that overflowed onto a crowd of people and healed them, replacing the stench of sickness with the fragrance of freedom. This vision stirred something in Don's spirit, but he didn't know how to respond. He recalls crying to God, saying, "I don't know how to get people healed."

The Holy Spirit impressed upon him, "Healing them is not your job. Just keep preaching."

Shortly after the officer shared his vision, Don began receiving letters from inmates describing spontaneous healings that happened during his services. This marked the beginning of a new ministry in healing and deliverance.

One of Don's early encounters with deliverance involved a prisoner suffering from a severe colon issue. During a service, Don had a vision of a swollen colon with a rat gnawing inside. Unsure of how to proceed, he called it out. A man came forward, but he wasn't the one Don saw in the vision. Later another inmate slipped Don a note saying, "I'm the one."

Don prayed for him, rebuking the spirit behind the illness, and the man experienced instantaneous healing. When Don returned to the prison a month later, the man greeted him, declaring that he had been pain free since that prayer. Experiences like this gave Don the boldness to step into deliverance ministry.

Don's first dramatic deliverance happened in Canada, where a woman in prison approached him, saying he was "the one" God had sent to help her. She'd been raised in a satanic cult and had endured horrific abuse. Don called another minister experienced in deliverance to get involved, but when the minister didn't show up, Don had to handle it himself. The woman manifested demonic resistance and taunted him, saying, "You don't know what you're doing. We'll kill you."

Despite his doubts, Don stood on Luke 10:19, commanding the demons to leave in Jesus' name. One by one the demons obeyed, and the woman declared her freedom.

Through these ministry experiences, Don came to understand that Christians can face demonic oppression. He explains that while the Holy Spirit resides in a believer's spirit, demons can inhabit the soul or body if they have legal grounds, such as unrepented sin, generational curses, or trauma. Just like Jesus cleansed the temple, believers need to drive out whatever doesn't belong in their lives. Don teaches that deliverance involves recognizing the legal rights demons claim, canceling them through repentance and confession, and commanding the demons to leave in the name of Jesus.

Don Dickerman, a seasoned minister with more than twenty-five thousand personal deliverances, has become a friend of mine. When

I jokingly asked if he had stopped being a Baptist, he replied with a smile, "No, I'm a Baptist who casts out demons."

Don's ministry has grown far beyond the prison walls where it began. He now reaches pastors, doctors, lawyers, engineers, house-wives, and even children. Don often emphasizes that deliverance isn't reserved for the "crazy" or visibly broken. "It's for anyone who wants to be free," he explains. He likens deliverance to spiritual house-keeping: "If you leave the door open, pests will come in. But if you close the door and command them to leave, they have to go."

CASTING DEMONS OUT OF UNBELIEVERS

There are many opinions where deliverance and miracles are con-cerned. There is a small group of Christians, primarily in cessationist circles, who don't believe in either one. Most conservative Christians acknowledge that deliverance is relevant today, but many believe it mainly happens on foreign mission fields where unbelievers steeped in witchcraft or idolatry encounter the gospel.

I've also heard numerous pastors and influencers say that only unbelievers can have demons and that our role is simply to cast the demons out. Sometimes I wonder whether they themselves have ever cast demons out of unbelievers. It is one thing to believe in deliver-ance; it is another to practice it and witness the results.

I remember praying for a girl at church who began manifesting during prayer. As I tried, with little success, to cast out the demon, I stopped and asked her, "Are you a Christian?"

She said, "No, I don't believe in this stuff," and went on to explain that her parents were practicing satanists who dedicated her to the devil at the age of five.

No wonder the demons didn't want to leave! They had every right to be there. I asked her if she wanted to give her life to Jesus. She said she did. After she surrendered to Christ, the demons were cast out, and she was filled with joy and the Holy Spirit.

From a spiritually legal perspective, casting demons out of

unbelievers isn't as effective as some might think. It's like trying to evict someone from a house they legally own—it doesn't work. For those who say we should just cast demons out of unbelievers, my advice is to go ahead and try it. You'll hear demons screaming, "This person is mine!"—and in many cases, they're right. Through consent, sin, or generational rights, those demons have a legal claim to stay.

I'm not prepared to say that demons cannot be cast out of unbelievers. After all, Jesus cast a demon out of a Gentile woman's daughter. (See Matthew 15:21–28.) However, He also made it clear that deliverance is "the children's bread" (v. 26), meaning that deliverance is for God's children.

"I DON'T BELIEVE CHRISTIANS CAN BE DEMONIZED"

Someone once sat in my office and told me he was leaving our church because we believed that Christians could have demons. I asked him for a Bible verse that proved it wasn't possible, but he couldn't name one. So I asked him a simple question: "Do you believe Christians can give place to the devil?"

Before I even finished the question, he said, "Of course they can."

Then I followed up: "If Christians can give place to the devil, how can you say that they cannot have demons?"

He had no answer.

It's very common to hear people say, "I used to believe Christians couldn't be demonized. I didn't even have a Bible degree! But then something happened: I manifested and was delivered, and now my perspective has completely changed."

Others might say, "I prayed for a fellow Christian, saw them set free through deliverance, and that experience transformed my understanding."

As Leonard Ravenhill so wisely put it, "A man with an experience is never at the mercy of a man with an argument." Personal encounters have a way of cutting through debates, leaving no room for doubt.

In the twentieth century, an influential voice shaped the belief that demons cannot inhabit Christians. That voice belonged to the respected biblical scholar Merrill Unger, a man once very critical of Pentecostals. Unger was also known for *Unger's Bible Dictionary* and many other reference works. He initially believed that Christians could not be demonized. However, after encountering genuine believers who experienced deliverance, he reexamined the Scriptures and church history. This led him to change his position, and he published two books about his revised understanding: *Demons in the World Today* and *What Demons Can Do to Saints*.[1]

TESTIMONY OVERCOMES THE DEVIL

While we should never base our theology solely on experiences, we can't ignore the filters many seminaries and Bible teachers have imposed on us—filters often disconnected from history, Scripture, and reality. Testimonies really do matter!

In Mark 5:1–13, Jesus delivered a demon-possessed man. The man had no theological training, yet Jesus sent him to preach in his region. (See Mark 5:18–20.) And what was the man's sermon? "I had demons, and Jesus delivered me." Testimonies glorify God and build faith in the hearers. (See Psalm 22:22; John 4:39.) Scripture also explains that testimonies defeat the devil, declaring, "They overcame him by the blood of the Lamb and by the word of their testimony" (Rev. 12:11).

Testimonies are seeds that produce more testimonies. When someone hears a deliverance story, it plants faith in their heart that God can do the same for them. Scripture does say that "faith comes by hearing, and hearing by the word of God" (Rom. 10:17). I often tell pastors that if they want to build a culture of seeing more of God's answers in their church, they must prioritize sharing testimonies in their church services, even from the platform.

Too many leaders focus on preaching why God doesn't heal or why people can't have demons in our present day. Their doctrine revolves around explaining why things don't happen. But we don't always know why certain things do or don't happen. Instead of dwelling on the unknowns, we must focus on God's promises, His power, and what He is currently doing. Highlighting His works stirs faith and expectation in others.

For more than a decade in our church, we have shared testimonies in every service. These testimonies come from our congregation, from people online, and sometimes from other ministries. Why? I want our people to live with the expectation that God is able and willing to move in our day. They need not settle for explanations of why He might not do something He did through Jesus and the early church.

A testimony is more than a story; it declares God's power and invites Him to move again. Let's be honest: If you remove all the stories of God's dynamic power from the Old Testament, the Gospels, or the Book of Acts, there wouldn't be much left. These stories of deliverance are not only powerful but also essential to understanding and proclaiming God's work.

THE TERMINOLOGY DEBATE

The discussion over whether a Christian can be "possessed" or merely "oppressed" often boils down to semantics. The term *demon-possessed* carries dark cultural implications, especially in the West. Thanks to Hollywood dramatizations, the term conjures images of total domination or ownership by ugly, wicked demons—something that most people who have demons don't experience. That is why most deliverance ministers (myself included) prevent unnecessary offense or misunderstanding by avoiding the use of the term *possessed*.

In the New King James Version, the Greek word *daimonizomai* is translated "demon-possessed." (See Matthew 4:24, for example.) Standard Greek dictionaries variously define this word as meaning "to be possessed by a demon," "to be controlled by a hostile spirit," or "to be under the power of a demon."[2]

However, the word *possession* is misleading because it implies ownership. Derek Prince clarifies in *They Shall Expel Demons* that demons cannot own a Christian because Christians belong to Jesus ("For you were bought at a price," according to 1 Corinthians 6:20).[3] Prince rejects the term *possessed*, noting that it doesn't capture the nuances of the Greek meaning.[4] Similarly, Frank and Ida Mae Hammond, in *Pigs in the Parlor*, state that demons can indwell but not possess believers.[5] Neil T. Anderson, author of *The Bondage Breaker*, agrees, stating that ownership is never at stake. Christians are possessed only by the Holy Spirit. He highlights the idea that believers can experience oppression, but they cannot be "possessed" in the sense of ownership.[6] Rev. Bob Larson, in answer to the question of whether a Christian can have a demon, writes: "A Christian can be demonized in their soul (mind, thoughts, feelings, emotions) but not in their spirit which has been born again."[7]

Many respected scholars and pastors, such as the aforementioned Merrill F. Unger, C. Fred Dickason (author of *Angels Elect and Evil*), and Sam Storms (author of the article "Can a Christian Be Demonized?"), prefer the term *demonization*. Unger notes that *demonization* allows for varying degrees of influence, from minor demonic harassment to more profound control, without implying ownership. Storms emphasizes that "demonization" describes cases where a demon indwells, influences, or controls only certain aspects of a person's life. He also warns that the New Testament never uses the term to refer to someone who is merely tempted or harassed.

Having a demon or being demonized means having a demon indwelling, controlling, or influencing part of a person's being. The degree of demon control varies from person to person. Scripture recounts severe cases in which demons had significant control (the Gadarene demoniac), but it also shows that not all demonic influence is equally severe. The woman with a "spirit of infirmity" in Luke 13:11 suffered physical affliction, not mental control.

What all such cases had in common was that they resolved when deliverance was ministered and the demon or demons were removed. These were not matters of resisting the enemy from without but of removing the enemy from within. Therefore, although the term *possessed* might align with the word *daimonizomai* in extreme cases, it is often misunderstood in modern culture, making *demonization* a better term to use. As long as we acknowledge the seriousness of demonic influence, the exact terminology becomes secondary. The primary concern is to set captives free through the authority of Jesus Christ and the power of His blood.

WE REPLACED DELIVERANCE WITH THERAPY

When preachers claim that Christians cannot have demons, they leave many believers who are experiencing demonic torment with no place to get help. Instead of receiving pastoral support, they are often shamed from the pulpit or mocked, and sometimes the sincerity of their faith is questioned. Because some church leaders refuse to consider the possibility of demonic involvement in a Christian believer, they offer solutions that don't address the real problems some Christians are facing.

Today, professional counseling has largely replaced deliverance, and therapy has taken the place of exorcism. While I fully support the amazing advancements in medical and psychological care, I know demons cannot be removed with pills or counseling. If the issue is demonic, treating it as something else fails to resolve the problem and often makes it worse—an outcome that leaves demons very pleased.

Imagine having cancer and being treated with Advil. It might make you feel better temporarily, but it cannot cure the disease. I fear that many demonized people are misdiagnosed because the starting assumption is wrong: It's the belief that Christians cannot have demons. If your doctor doesn't believe cancer is real, a legitimate cancer diagnosis will be missed, and the results could be fatal.

Consider Angela from Oregon, whose struggles began in childhood. Little Angela suffered severe abuse, which opened doors to witchcraft and demonic torment in her life. She experienced years of spiritual attacks, doubt, pain, disease, and curses. These assaults affected her health, marriage, and finances. Despite being a lifelong churchgoer, Angela didn't realize that Christians could be demonized until she came to our special event in Vancouver, Washington.

During Angela's deliverance, the demons revealed how they had caused disease, poverty, and generational curses in her life. After being set free through prayer, Angela described feeling lighter, washed, and empowered in the Lord.

A few weeks later she came back to get water baptized, and she shared her testimony of all that had happened: She was healed of sleep apnea, which had required her to use a CPAP machine at its highest setting for eight years. Also, she was freed from allergies that plagued her every day for twenty years. For the first time, she experienced clear breathing without congestion or drainage. Even her asthma was gone, and she no longer needed inhalers.

Misdiagnosing spiritual issues causes believers to suffer needlessly. Deliverance is a much-needed ministry in every church, and one that Jesus Himself practiced. Acknowledging the possibility of demonic influences in Christians allows for the correct diagnosis and absolute freedom that only Jesus can bring.

DON'T GIVE PLACE TO THE DEVIL

Scriptures such as Ephesians 4:27 make it clear that Christians can "give place" to the devil. The Greek word for *place* in this case is *topos*, which often refers to an inhabited space. For example, Mary and Joseph couldn't find a topos (a room) in the inn for Jesus. (See Luke 2:7.) A seat at the dinner table could also be called a topos (as in Luke 14:9). And in John 14:2–3, Jesus promised to prepare a topos, or dwelling place, for believers in heaven.

The word *topos* is also used to describe someplace a demon can live. Jesus explains in Luke 11:24 that when a demon is cast out, it wanders through arid topoi (places) seeking rest before deciding to return to the "house" it had left.[8] A person is represented here as a house, and demons are depicted as seeking a place to inhabit in that house. Paul's warning to believers not to "give place" to the devil implies that doing so is possible.

Someone who stayed at our house once left a window open. So a thief came in, stole my keys, and took my car. The thief didn't own the house. He didn't even move in. But he had access and was free to take something of value. If you've ever had a mouse in your house, you know that your presence did not keep the mouse from entering. When entry points are not secured, all sorts of unwanted things can wander in. This idea applies both spiritually and physically.

Some time ago, my wife and I rented out two rooms of our house. The tenants weren't thieves or animals, but they had access to our dwelling and occupied parts of it. Although they didn't own the house, they had a key and permission to enter. Similarly, when believers open themselves to practices like witchcraft, they hand demons the keys to their minds, bodies, and emotions. Unlike invited tenants who legitimately live in the home, demons bring in torment, harassment, and bondage.

EVICT THE SQUATTERS

During the COVID-19 pandemic, when housing costs skyrocketed, unlawful land squatting became more common in the US. Squatters covertly move in to properties they don't own, rent, or have permission to use. They occupy the space illegally, not to claim ownership but to have a place to stay. Demons operate the same way. They don't care who owns the house—they just move in, make a mess, and wreak havoc. Worse yet, the longer spiritual squatters stay, the harder it is to remove them.

Once a Christian is saved, their spirit belongs to Jesus, and He is the rightful owner! However, if we Christians neglect any area of our lives or leave any unguarded, demons can still squat there. This means the human soul (which includes the mind, will, emotions, and habits) can be made vulnerable.

Of course, demons aren't content with access. Once inside, their goal is to gain as much control as possible by influencing, inhabiting, and tormenting their hosts. But even torment isn't their final goal. Their agenda is to kill, steal, and destroy. (See John 10:10.) Demons aim to bring some hell into people's lives and then drag them there for good.

JESUS STILL CLEANSES TEMPLES

Our bodies are the temples where the Spirit of God lives. (See 1 Corinthians 6:19.) Some argue that the Holy Spirit's presence leaves no room for anything else. This might sound logical, but it is not biblical. First Kings 8:10–11 states that the temple King Solomon built as God's dwelling place here on earth was initially filled with His glory. Yet history shows that even this sacred building, set apart for God's presence, could be defiled or destroyed whenever an enemy took possession.

In Nehemiah's time, Tobiah, an adversary of Israel, was allowed to use a room in the temple. To restore the temple to its proper use, Nehemiah had to confront the leaders, remove Tobiah's belongings, and cleanse the structure. (See Nehemiah 13:7–9.) Later, King Manasseh desecrated the sacred temple by setting up altars to foreign gods and placing an Asherah pole inside. This brought God's judgment on Judah, but King Josiah eventually cleansed the temple and restored true worship in it. (See 2 Kings 21:4–7; 23:4–7.)

During the intertestamental period, Antiochus IV Epiphanes defiled the temple by erecting an altar to Zeus and sacrificing pigs on it—a foul, offensive act according to Jewish law. Scripture also warns of the defilement of a future temple. Paul writes that the Antichrist will sit "as God in the temple of God" and proclaim himself to be God (2 Thess. 2:4; see also Matt. 24:15). These examples show that any physical or spiritual temple can be defiled if we give the enemy access to it.

At the time of Christ, the Jewish temple was situated on roughly thirty-six acres of Mount Zion.[9] Temple sections included a building containing the holy place and the holy of holies, where only the high priest could enter. In the surrounding outer courts, priests offered sacrifices, and certain sections were designated for Israelites, women, and Gentiles.[10] The portion allotted to the Gentiles was where non-Jews and "all nations" could pray and worship God (Mark 11:17). But it had instead become a noisy marketplace where priests rented booths to merchants selling animals for sacrifices and men exchanging money into the local currency. The sacred space served as a commercial hub.

When Jesus entered this part of the temple, He saw how His Father's house had been defiled. With righteous anger Jesus drove out the merchants, flipped their tables, and rebuked the corruption, declaring that the temple was designed as "a house of prayer," not a "den of thieves" (Matt. 21:12–13). Jesus wasn't concerned only about what happened in the temple's innermost sanctuaries; He cared about its purity throughout.

SPIRITUAL CLEANSING

Deliverance is nothing more than Jesus, the Son of God, driving greedy merchants out of the temple of our lives. While our spirits belong to God, the "outer courts" of our lives—our minds, emotions, habits, and even our physical bodies—can become cluttered and corrupted. These areas might not seem as sacred as the holy of holies within us, but when we let unrepented sin, actions, or even demonic influences linger there, we give access to demonic forces that bring noise, distraction, and defilement into a holy place of prayer and worship.

Deliverance is a cleansing of our temple. It's Jesus stepping into the neglected, chaotic areas of our lives and driving out what doesn't belong. Just as He didn't tolerate corruption in the temple, He won't ignore it in us. He flips over the tables of lies we've believed. He drives out the "merchants" of addiction, torment, and oppression. And He restores order and peace to His dwelling place. This is the process of sanctification: It is a deeper cleansing of the areas where the enemy has taken residence.

Deliverance is not a one-time event but part of the ongoing process of sanctification as Jesus continually works to purify our bodies, minds, and souls until we reflect His glory. He desires to cleanse every "court" of our lives, ensuring that every area is touched by His transforming power.

CAN LIGHT COEXIST WITH DARKNESS?

A common argument against Christians having demons comes from 2 Corinthians 6:14: "Do not be unequally yoked with unbelievers. For what partnership has righteousness with lawlessness? Or what fellowship has light with darkness?" (ESV). However, the context of this passage involves relationships not with demons but with Christians marrying unbelievers. Paul focuses not on coexisting with others but on being "yoked," or integrally linked with someone. He's not forbidding Christians to coexist with unbelievers. After all, we work with them, go to school with them, and even sit next to them in church.

Paul's point is that Christians shouldn't enter into covenant relationships such as marriage with unbelievers, not because it's impossible but because it's not God's will. The same principle applies to demons. The Holy Spirit and demons can coexist within a believer—not in fellowship but in conflict.[11]

Think about this: God is omnipresent—He exists everywhere—yet the devil also operates in this world. God and Satan coexist in the spirit realm, but they are not in agreement or partnership. God's presence doesn't automatically remove all evil. If it did, Satan wouldn't exist in this world. But in Job 1:6–7, Satan came before God to accuse Job. In the New Testament, Satan tempted Jesus in the wilderness, even though Jesus was filled with the Holy Spirit. Coexisting is not the same as being in unity or agreement.

Not one verse in the Bible suggests that Christians who have the Holy Spirit cannot also have other influences present in their lives.

Galatians 5:17 teaches that the flesh and the Spirit coexist within every believer. A Christian's relationship with demons is similar to their relationship with the flesh, which is defeated and considered dead according to Romans 6:11, where Paul wrote, "Reckon yourselves to be dead indeed to sin, but alive to God in Christ Jesus our Lord." But the flesh is still present and actively tempting us. The power of sin, the curse, and Satan has been broken, but its presence remains until our death. Fleshly "passions and desires" lead us astray and produce "nothing good" (Gal. 5:24; Rom. 7:18). They constantly wage war "against the Spirit" (Gal. 5:17). Similarly, demons can try to influence and attack, but they no longer have control or dominion over a believer unless the believer yields to them.

DOCTRINE AND THE BIBLE

When it comes to the topic of demonization, we say, "Let's get into the Bible. It has all the answers." No Christian would deny that statement, but each sees the Bible through their subjective "eyeglasses." Therefore, believers reach different conclusions about exorcism.

A common belief among Evangelicals separates New Testament accounts that occurred before the cross from those that came after. The idea is that only the epistles teach doctrine, while the Gospels and the Book of Acts illustrate it. The late scholar Gordon Fee is famous for this teaching.[12] Although scholarship and theology are shifting from this perspective, it persists in some quarters, including in the pews.

Those who disagree with Fee's view now believe that Scripture's narrative portions (the Gospels) are not only descriptive but prescriptive, containing illustrations (and moral guidance) *and* theology.[13] This is important. If only the epistles taught theology, there would be no biblical basis for casting demons out of Christians, and what Jesus did and said before the cross could not inform current doctrine and ministry. That would be like saying, "Don't get your doctrine from Jesus!"

However, this idea doesn't hold up when considering how the Bible was written and understood in its original cultural context. In ancient

Greek and Roman culture stories weren't written purely for entertainment or historical recordkeeping—they were tools for teaching moral values and showing how people should live.[14] The Roman historian Livy speaks on the importance of history for examples, both good and bad:

> There is this exceptionally beneficial and fruitful advantage to be derived from the study of the past, that you see, set in the clear light of historical truth, examples of every possible type. From these, you may select for yourself and your country what to imitate and also what, as being mischievous in its inception and disastrous in its issues, you are to avoid.[15]

The stories included in the Gospels and the Book of Acts were written to shape the lives of believers, not just to inform them of past events. Luke did not need Paul to "confirm" his teaching. Accounts of Jesus casting out demons or Paul driving out spirits in Acts are more than stories to admire; they are examples inspiring us to do the same. The same Holy Spirit who was in Jesus now lives in all His followers, empowering us to do the works that Jesus did. Deliverance stories in the Gospels are instructions for the work of setting captives free.

DELIVERANCE IS THE CHILDREN'S BREAD

Many deliverance stories from the Gospels teach valuable lessons, and I will highlight two here. The first is in Mark 7:25–30, where Jesus delivered the Syro-Phoenician woman's daughter from a demon. When this Gentile woman begged Jesus to cast the demon out of her child, He responded, "Let the children be filled first, for it is not good to take the children's bread and throw it to the little dogs" (v. 27). We have already seen that when Jesus called deliverance "the children's bread," it meant that deliverance was intended for the Jewish children of God. Although the woman's daughter was not among God's covenant people, Jesus honored the woman's faith and granted her child deliverance. As Christians under the New Covenant, that deliverance is most certainly for us, just as it was for the ancient Jews. We are God's children, and deliverance is our right. We should seek it whenever we need it!

The second story is one mentioned earlier. In Luke 13:10–16, Jesus healed the woman who was bound by a spirit of infirmity for eighteen years and could only walk doubled over. Jesus referred to her as a "daughter of Abraham" and declared that she should be "loosed from this bond" (v. 16). Jesus' words reveal that a member of God's covenant people—a daughter of Abraham—was afflicted by a demon.

Some might argue that this story is irrelevant because it occurred under the Old Covenant before the Holy Spirit indwelled believers. However, if we understand biblical narratives as teaching tools showing us how to live in a Christian community today, this story remains relevant. Luke intended for his readers to see that demons can afflict members of God's community, and deliverance is the solution.

If people in our church communities are suffering from any kind of demonic influence, whether it is physical illness, infirmity, or any other form of oppression, we are called to follow Jesus' example and set them free.

GOD DELIVERS HIS PEOPLE

We have seen enough to know that God is in the business of delivering His people, which seems to indicate that His people might need deliverance! Consider Peter, one of Jesus' closest disciples. In Matthew 16:23, Jesus rebuked Peter, saying, "Get behind Me, Satan!" (similar words to those He used to rebuke the devil in Matthew 4:10). Although Peter had received divine revelation mere moments earlier, he was now influenced by Satan. Whatever the degree of this influence, whether inside or out, this account proves that a believer can be influenced by Satan, even if it's only momentary.

Another of Jesus' disciples, Judas Iscariot, was greatly influenced by the enemy. Luke 22:3 and John 13:27 explicitly say that "Satan entered" Judas. Yet Judas was a chosen apostle who was "counted among [the

Twelve] and received his share in this ministry" (Acts 1:17, LSB). Unfortunately, Judas' heart was inclined to greed and betrayal, which allowed Satan to get a foothold and lead him to destruction. One cannot argue that Judas was merely a bystander—he was Jesus' disciple and a trusted apostle.

Satan is always in active pursuit of victims. In Acts 5:3, Peter confronted a Christ-follower named Ananias, asking, "Why has Satan filled your heart to lie to the Holy Spirit?" The same Greek word is translated "filled" in Ephesians 5:18, in reference to believers being filled with the Holy Spirit. If Ananias was demonized, why didn't Peter cast out the deceiving demon? And why did Jesus allow Judas to self-destruct instead of delivering him? These are good questions.

The answer involves the fact that Jesus doesn't force deliverance on anyone. Deliverance is for those who truly want to be set free and are willing to surrender to God. Without willingness, deliverance cannot happen. Some people say, "If God wants to set me free, He will do it," but the Bible shows that demonized people either willingly came to Jesus, or someone came on their behalf. Deliverance is available, but it requires our motivation to act.

The Bible is clear: God delivers His people and did so even before Jesus appeared in the New Testament. God sent Moses to deliver not the Egyptians but God's own people from bondage. (See Exodus 3:10.) In the Book of Judges, God repeatedly delivered Israel from the armies of opposing nations. In the Book of Esther, God delivered His people from the evil plot of Haman.

The Psalms are filled with promises and examples of God delivering His people. David frequently cried out to God for deliverance, saying in Psalm 34:17 that He hears the righteous person's cries. In Psalm 91:14, God says that because the righteous person "has set his love upon Me, therefore I will deliver him." The Lord's Prayer contains a petition: "Do not lead us into temptation, but deliver us from the evil one" (Matt. 6:13).

From beginning to end the Scriptures confirm God's heart to rescue His people from danger, sin, and spiritual enemies. God wants to deliver!

REMOVE THE GRAVECLOTHES

When people get saved, they are delivered from the kingdom of darkness and made new creations in Christ. As Colossians 1:13 states, He has "delivered us out of the power of darkness, and translated us into the kingdom of the Son" (ASV). However, the Christian's journey doesn't end at the altar. Salvation is the starting point, and the process of sanctification continues afterward. This includes renewing the mind, healing past wounds, and experiencing deliverance from demons.

But what happens to the demons people have before they come to faith? Do demons leave the moment a person gets saved? The Bible doesn't say that. When Jesus encountered demons, He cast them out. Scripture emphasizes that demons do not "go out" when Jesus enters someone's life. Matthew 8:16 and 9:33, Mark 1:34 and 3:15, and Luke 13:32 show that simply praying the sinner's prayer is not the solution for demons. The solution is deliverance.

Nowhere does the New Testament point to salvation alone as the remedy for demon possession. Even when Jesus sent His disciples to preach the gospel, He instructed them to "heal the sick, cleanse the lepers, raise the dead, cast out demons" (Matt. 10:8). If salvation alone eliminated demons, why did Jesus add these commands?

John chapter 11 provides a beautiful example of this truth in the story of Lazarus. When Jesus raised His friend from the dead, the man was alive but still bound in his graveclothes. This is a picture of many believers: They're saved but still struggling with baggage from the past. Graveclothes can include strongholds, curses, or even demonic spirits. Often trauma, rejection, abuse, mistaken identity, unforgiveness, bitterness, and soul ties also need to be addressed. Salvation breathes new life into one's spirit, but remnants of the old life in sin must be removed for unhindered spiritual growth to occur. God calls us to partner with Him, through the power of the Holy Spirit, to help others walk in freedom.

That's exactly what Philip did in Samaria, where he "preached Christ" (Acts 8:5). The people responded "with one accord" as they heeded his words and were drawn by the miracles they witnessed (Acts 8:6), and many believed and were raised into new life. But Philip didn't stop there; he also loosed these new believers from their grave-clothes. Unclean spirits cried out as they left, and the infirm were healed, so that the good news wasn't just heard but also experienced. (See Acts 8:7.) Lives were transformed as the fullness of the gospel was preached, demonstrated, and received in power.

Paul's ministry in Ephesus followed a similar pattern. The Ephesians knew that he regularly cast out demons. In Acts 19, even exorcists tried to imitate his deliverance methods. Paul ministered in Ephesus for two years, so effectively that "all who dwelt in Asia heard the word of the Lord Jesus, both Jews and Greeks" (Acts 19:10). Paul's ministry involved the preaching of the gospel followed by exorcism. Even handkerchiefs or aprons that had touched Paul were taken to the sick, "and the diseases left them and the evil spirits went out of them" (Acts 19:12). Obviously those who had heard the gospel still needed deliverance.

WHY THE EPISTLES ARE SILENT ON DELIVERANCE

Some argue that if deliverance was a significant issue, the epistles would have addressed it explicitly. However, this claim overlooks several key points.

First, the epistles are not silent on this topic. Paul warned the Corinthians against receiving "a different spirit" (2 Cor. 11:4). He rebuked the Galatians for being "bewitched" (Gal. 3:1). In 1 Timothy 4:1, Paul prophesied that in the last days some believers "will depart from the faith, giving heed to deceiving spirits and doctrines of demons." In Galatians 4:9, Paul also warned that Christians could fall back into bondage to demonic powers if they returned to old sins or idolatrous practices. This idea is echoed in 1 Corinthians 10:14–22, where Paul cautions believers about participating in pagan rituals and idol worship, explaining that such actions create "fellowship with demons" (v. 20).

In 2 Timothy 2:25–26, Paul notes the possibility of people falling into Satan's traps and being held "captive...to do his will" (v. 26). In 1 Peter 5:8, Peter compares the devil to a "roaring lion" seeking someone "whom he may devour." In 1 Corinthians 5:5, Paul writes about delivering a believer over "to Satan for the destruction of the flesh, that his spirit may be saved." While many interpret this as excommunication (removing someone from the protection of church fellowship to encourage repentance), Paul indicates something more profound. This action is a deliberate spiritual handover to Satan's authority—almost a reverse exorcism in which the person's unrepentant sin gives Satan a legal claim over them. Unable to shield them any longer, the church formally acknowledges this reality.

Clearly the epistles are not silent about demonic influence. Nor would any silence prove that deliverance wasn't happening. The exact phrase "Christians can be demonized" doesn't appear in the epistles, but neither does the word *Trinity*, and the concept of the Trinity is foundational to Christian doctrine. Similarly, the word *disciple* is not used in the epistles, yet no one would argue that (1) the apostles didn't make disciples or that (2) the Great Commission doesn't apply to us because Paul, Peter, or James didn't use that exact term in their letters. Tithing isn't taught in the New Testament either, yet pastors teach about it and use the term freely.

The absence of mention doesn't equal the absence of practice. Take the Gospel of John. John didn't record a single exorcism in Jesus' ministry, yet no one doubts that Jesus performed all the deliverances mentioned in the synoptic Gospels. Just because John didn't discuss those events doesn't mean they didn't happen. The same is true of deliverance in the epistles. The absence of a specific term does not invalidate an idea or suggest that it wasn't put into practice.

THE CHURCH FATHERS ON CHRISTIANS NEEDING DELIVERANCE

Following the apostles' deaths, the early Christian church continued to practice deliverance among believers, even connecting exorcism with water baptism. If the apostles had not practiced or taught this, why did the early church make such a connection?

Before being baptized, new Christians publicly declared their rejection of Satan, his works, and his influence. This included renouncing Satan's "pomp," which church fathers such as Tertullian and Cyril of Jerusalem saw as sinful spectacles common in their respective lifetimes. (Examples include gladiator games, theater shows, and rituals of idol worship.)[16]

Tertullian explained that candidates for baptism first renounced the devil and his pomp.[17] In approximately AD 350, Cyril of Jerusalem wrote that candidates turned westward (symbolically facing Satan) and renounced him before entering the baptistery.[18] The Apostolic Tradition of the second through the fourth centuries mentions that candidates underwent daily deliverance before being baptized. Bishops and leaders would lay hands on each person, exorcising them to confirm their spiritual purity. Those found to be under demonic influence were denied baptism until they were freed.[19] Imagine that! Then, just prior to the baptismal act, candidates were anointed with the oil of exorcism. Once purified and free of demonic influence, they were baptized into the faith.[20]

Renunciation made it clear that baptism was more than a cleansing ritual; it was a deliberate break from sin and any allegiance to Satan. Today's Evangelicals believe that people about to be baptized are already Christians. This is noteworthy: The early church performed exorcisms on believers. This is a pivotal point in the discussions about whether Christians can have demons.

The early church fathers believed that Christians could get demons through willful sin. Tertullian recounted a story about a Christian woman who attended a theater show and was demonized when she returned home. The demon cast out of her claimed the right to possess her because she had entered its "domain" by attending the show.[21] Tertullian used this example as a warning against participating in sinful activities. Referencing Matthew 6:24 and 2 Corinthians 6:14, he emphasized that Christians cannot serve both God and worldly sinful pleasures.

Cyprian of Carthage (AD 200–258) noted that demons are expelled during baptism through the believer's faith. However, he warned that if a Christian returned to sinful living after baptism, demons would take advantage of the person's weakened faith and come back.[22]

Allow me to share some final remarks to end this chapter. As a youth pastor for fourteen years and now a senior pastor for eight years, I've seen the power of deliverance firsthand. For more than ten years our church has publicly held monthly deliverance services and has made deliverance an essential part of our discipleship strategy. From my ministry experiences I can assure you that many Christians are struggling spiritually. Even after coming to salvation, some resemble Lazarus: They are alive but still bound.

This is not only my personal observation; it's the testimony of countless pastors and believers worldwide. Deliverance isn't a minor aspect of the gospel. It's at the heart of Jesus' mission to set captives free. His disciples carried on His mission, and the early church fathers embraced it in their discipleship approach. Today this powerful ministry is being rediscovered and reclaimed by the church, bringing freedom to many who desperately need it.

CHAPTER 4

....

HUNGRY FOR A HUMAN HOST

I N MARCH 2020, Robert, a dedicated police officer who loved his job, suffered a tragic, life-altering experience. While on duty in his patrol car, he was poisoned by carbon monoxide. He was rushed to the hospital, but the damage was done: A traumatic brain injury affected every aspect of Robert's life, leaving him trapped in hopelessness.

Robert's brain injury unleashed severe depression. As his mental health spiraled, he took comfort in alcohol. What started as occasional drinking soon became heavy everyday consumption. "My drinking led to my being fired," Robert recalls. "But that was just the beginning of my downfall."

Despite his efforts to regain control, Robert's addiction took over and brought him terrifying experiences. As a Christian, he found moments of comfort in worship music but also battled demonic oppression. The spiritual torment manifested as seizures, uncontrollable anger, and violent outbursts.

Robert vividly remembers a certain encounter: "While fasting and seeking God for help to quit drinking, I was attacked by a demonic entity. It looked like a stronger version of me, and it pinned me to the floor. My screams filled the room. Then I felt the presence of an angel that I could not see. The demonic entity fled, and the angel lifted me off the floor and onto my feet. My wife, who was frozen with fear, witnessed all of this and said there was no way I could have physically done what she saw."

Robert's wife saw his struggle and refused to give up. She knew her husband was not himself, and she prayed persistently for his freedom. As a follower of Christ, she sought God's intervention and stumbled upon my deliverance teachings online.

"My wife became convinced I had a demon, but I refused to believe it," Robert admits. "We weren't Charismatic believers, and I thought Christians couldn't have demons."

The faith of Robert's wife never wavered, and she encouraged him to seek deliverance. Just before Christmas in 2022, Robert reached his breaking point and agreed to join his wife in watching one of my online prayers for deliverance. What happened next was life-changing.

"As I prayed along with the video, I started sweating and feeling sick. My body ached, and I wanted to run away, but my wife insisted that I fight through it. I played the prayer again, renouncing demons and commanding them to leave in Jesus' name. Whenever the prayer mentioned 'Holy Spirit fire,' I felt shooting pains throughout my body. Finally, after the second round of prayer, I collapsed, exhausted. But for the first time in years, I felt relief and joy."

After his deliverance, Robert's life was transformed, and he received the gift of speaking in tongues. His depression and addiction disappeared, his anger subsided, and he felt like himself again. He recommitted his life to Christ, and even his physical health improved. Doctors eventually cleared him to return to the police force after a four-year hiatus.

Reflecting on his journey almost two years after his deliverance, Robert said, "I am completely healed from the brain injury and addiction. I'm now an ordained chaplain. I believe in miracles, healing, and deliverance, and I have a deep hunger for the Word of God and the power of the Holy Spirit."

HUNGRY FOR A HOST

Demons are disembodied spirits who want to do more than influence people through external temptations. Their ultimate goal is to find a comfortable base of operation—a place to inhabit. From there the demon can affect its host's thoughts, emotions, and actions by gaining more and more control over their life.

In Matthew 12:43–45, Jesus explained that unclean spirits wander through dry places seeking rest. When they find none, they return to their former "house" (providing it has been left vacant and unguarded). Demons don't enjoy dry places. They desperately crave human or animal hosts to inhabit. When Jesus cast a legion of demons out of a demoniac, the evicted spirits begged to enter a nearby herd of pigs. (See Matthew 8:28–32.)

Open doors are essential if demons are to infiltrate human beings. Sin, trauma, or spiritual negligence can provide the access demons need to establish strongholds. Like squatters, demons don't need to own you; they just need access to "property." That's why Paul warns us in Ephesians 4:27 not to "give place to the devil." Once demons gain entry, they cause chaos, destruction, and bondage, fulfilling their ultimate mission: "to steal, and to kill, and to destroy" (John 10:10).

THE DEN OF DARKNESS

What drives the relentless desire of spirit beings to infiltrate human lives and operate from within? Demonic actions are not random; they are calculated to defile and control people and oppose God. Demons are deceitful imitators who lack originality. God's Spirit dwells in believers, making their bodies His temple. So Satan and his demons seek to counterfeit this arrangement. God's indwelling transforms, empowers, and sanctifies people, but resident demons corrupt and manipulate their hosts. Satan doesn't create; he can only distort. If God lives in His people to bring life, Satan indwells them to bring death.

We humans are not ordinary creations; we bear the image of God. (See Genesis 1:26–27.) This sets us apart from animals, making us unique in God's eyes and prime targets for demonic attack. If demons can indwell us, they will work to utterly corrupt the image of God within us. They cannot touch God Himself, so they attack what He loves most—His children.

When demons enter a human, they degrade what was meant to reflect God's glory. They take something sacred and make it a vessel for their rebellion. They seek to use humans as tools of destruction—against others, against creation, and ultimately against God Himself. This is more than an attack on people; it is about vengeance against God and assaulting His image. Demons are not satisfied with control. They want desecration, so they corrupt what God loves.

Demons don't settle for whispering temptations into the human soul from the outside. They prefer inside operations. With internal control they can amplify their influence, wreaking havoc and confusion on the host and everyone around them—even entire nations.

We need to remember that demons are restless beings tormented by their own nature. Jesus said in Matthew 12:43 that demons are looking for somewhere to rest. This rest is not peaceful but a twisted satisfaction that is derived from fulfilling their dark purposes. Indwelling a human being allows demons to feed their insatiable desire for destruction. It's a parasitic relationship: The demon thrives while the host suffers.

Remember, demons are spirits without bodies. To manifest their will in the material world they need hosts to indwell, and humans are the perfect choice. This is why Satan entered Judas and led him to betray Jesus. (See Luke 22:3.) He needed a human being to carry out his plan of destruction. With access to the physical realm demons can influence actions, relationships, and even societal structures. They have more in mind than tormenting individuals. Inhabiting humans extends their reach and enacts their plans on a much larger scale.

THE DEADLY TRIO

Demons don't work alone. They have three allies: the flesh, with its sinful desires; the world, with its temptations and ungodly values; and the devil, who is the demons' boss. The flesh makes us weak and more open to demonic influence. The world creates an environment in which sin feels normal. These work together to move the devil closer to his goal, which is control.

Without God's protection, we are easy targets. Thomas Aquinas, an ancient scholar of the Catholic Church, summarized "the flesh, the world, and the devil" and cited Hebrews 4:15 to remind us that the sinless Christ "was in all points tempted as we are."[1] These three enemies often collaborate in seamless harmony. The flesh might crave something sinful, the world normalizes it, and Satan sells the lie that it's harmless. This is a dangerous and coordinated assault.

The flesh

As C. S. Lewis vividly portrays in *The Screwtape Letters,* Satan and his demons take great pride in using fleshly weakness and the world's distractions to set their plans in motion. The flesh represents our sinful nature's ungodly passions, ways, and desires—the parts of us that crave what is contrary to God's will and create vulnerabilities for demons to exploit. Humans can so easily turn from God and lean toward the devil. Even legitimate longings can become twisted and corrupted, pulling us into sin and rebellion.

The world

The world is not only the physical earth but a system of values, beliefs, and practices actively opposing God. Biblically, the world isn't neutral but is "under the sway of the wicked one" (1 John 5:19), the "god of this world" that blinds human minds (2 Cor. 4:4, KJV). In the Bible he is also known as the "ruler of this world" (John 12:31) and the dragon "who deceives the whole world" (Rev. 12:9).

The devil

Finally, there is Satan himself, "a liar and the father of [lies]," who partners with the flesh and the world to lead us into sin (John 8:44). Satan orchestrates temptations that match internal desires with external opportunities. Temptation is the flesh's blind date with the world, and the devil arranges it! The flesh provides the inner hunger for pleasure, power, and self-gratification. The world offers alluring opportunities to indulge in the sin that masks as fulfillment. A master manipulator, Satan ensures the seamless working together of these elements, drawing us away from God and deeper into disobedience and bondage. This sets the stage for demons to enter and begin their destructive work from within.

THE BARK BECOMES A BITE

The enemy never stops with luring us toward sin. Once we embrace his lies, his goal is to indwell, enslave, and torment us. An old saying says the devil is like a dog on a leash—he can only go as far as God permits. A barking dog contained within its boundaries might seem powerless to hurt us, but if we enter its territory, its bite can cause serious harm.

I learned this lesson during my childhood in Ukraine. My neighbor, a doctor who helped me with math, owned a German shepherd, a fierce dog he always kept on a leash. I quickly learned to respect the boundaries of that leash. As long as I stayed beyond its reach, I knew I was safe.

But one day I got curious and crossed the line. I didn't see the dog at first, so I approached its house to see where the chain was secured. Little did I know, the dog was hidden from sight, napping behind its shelter. In a flash it lunged at me and sank its teeth into my leg. Had it not been for my math tutor's skills as a doctor, my injury could have been far worse. She quickly stitched me up and likely saved my life.

That experience taught me a sobering truth: When curiosity draws you into dangerous territory, the progression can be swift and cause great harm. What starts as a bark suddenly turns into a terrible bite. The bark might be intimidating, but the bite leaves scars.

This mirrors what happens when we yield to sin and cross into Satan's domain. The devil's temptations and taunts might seem harmless and easy to dismiss. But when willful disobedience pushes us into his territory, the door to danger swings open, and no boundary can prevent lasting damage.

Temptation is external, like an annoying bark. But when the enemy gains access through sin, torment begins. Then he can attack your mind, emotions, dreams, and physical body. Like the German shepherd that finally got me, the devil isn't content with making noise. He's waiting to lunge at someone who will let him sink his teeth into them. His strategy is both cruel and cunning.

Staying outside Satan's reach is essential for protecting our souls.

THE CROUCHING PREDATOR

Temptation is a universal experience. Even Jesus, who was sinless, faced temptation from the devil during His time on earth. (See Matthew 4:1–11.) Being tempted does not mean you have a demon. It means you're human, and an evil enemy is seeking to exploit you. Demons operate subtly, presenting sin as harmless and appealing. They twist truth to plant doubt in your mind, much the way Satan did with Eve in the garden. (See Genesis 3:1–6.) A demon's ultimate aim is to defile God's temple by nudging you toward compromise, sin, and bondage.

James 1:14–15 reveals the progression of temptation within us. It starts with desire. When we entertain and act on that desire, sin is conceived. Left unchecked, sin grows and gives birth to spiritual death. However, the story of Cain in Genesis 4 uncovers an even more profound truth about temptation. Cain was already angry and jealous when God issued him a grave warning: "Sin is crouching at your door; it desires to have you, but you must rule over it" (Gen. 4:7, NIV).

Notice the language God uses—sin is described as "crouching." The Hebrew verb that the NIV translates as "crouching" is *rabas*. This often refers to lying down, as in resting;[2] but here *rabas* conveys the image of a predator lying in wait for its prey.[3] So sin "lurks" at the door. Even more chilling is a possible connection to *rabitsu*, an Akkadian word with a similar sound. In Mesopotamian belief, *rabitsu* refers to a demonic being that lurks around entrances—a door demon, so to speak.[4]

The sin personified in Genesis 4:7 is not idle temptation or a moral struggle. Instead it suggests a demonic force eager to lunge at Cain from the doorway. God's warning emphasizes the spiritual threat: "It desires to have you." The Hebrew word translated "desire" here is *tešûqâ*.[5] It also appears in Genesis 3:16, where it describes Eve's desire for her husband. In both cases this desire is an aggressive craving for control. Through temptation demons aim to infiltrate your will, enslave your thoughts, and dominate your actions.

Fueled by demonic influence, sin is neither passive nor content to remain external. Like a predator sin awaits moments of weakness, when resistance is low. Sin thrives on compromise, grows through neglect, and devours those who underestimate its power. Sin does not seek coexistence but total domination; Jesus said, "Whoever commits sin is a slave of sin" (John 8:34). Sin leaves destruction in its wake, making way for demons to gain access and desecrate God's dwelling place within us.

Nevertheless, God's warning to Cain carries hope: "You must rule over it." This is a call to vigilance, self-control, and reliance on God. Sin is relentless but not unbeatable. Through the discipline of righteous living, repentance, the armor of God, and the power of the Holy Spirit, sin's grip can be broken. But make no mistake—demons are sinister and relentless, always crouching and waiting to spring upon their prey in order to infiltrate and take control. This is the devil's nature; he is "like a roaring lion, seeking whom he may devour" (1 Pet. 5:8), and some people are "taken captive by him" (2 Tim. 2:26).

The warning to Cain is also for us: We must "submit to God" and "resist the devil" (Jas. 4:7), keeping our lives fully occupied by God's Spirit and leaving the enemy no room through which to enter.

THE TRAITOR WITHIN

Let's focus more deeply now on an ally of Satan that resides within us. The Bible uses the term *flesh* in various ways. It can refer to the physical body or to humanity as a whole. (See Leviticus 14:9, KJV; Genesis 6:17.) In the New Testament, however, *flesh* usually describes the sinful nature inherited from Adam. (See Romans 7:5; 8:12, 13.)

The flesh is not a demon, but if we continually yield to it, the flesh offers demons a way to enter. Twentieth-century Baptist Bible teacher W. Graham Scroggie explains, "The flesh...is the evil principle in man's nature, the traitor within who is in league with the attackers without. The flesh provides the tinder on which the devil's temptations can kindle."[6] In other words, the flesh is a traitor or spy working for Satan. By aligning with the enemy, the flesh weakens our defenses, making us vulnerable to spiritual invasion.

In the 1300s the army of Peter the Cruel approached the city of Teruel. A judge who feared he would be tortured when the city fell made a secret pact with the enemy outside. He opened an entrance in the wall through which the invading army entered and captured the city. If you visit the city of Teruel in modern Spain, you can still see the place where the traitor opened the door: It is called "Traitor's Gate."[7]

The flesh operates much as the traitorous judge did. Someone once said the flesh is the devil's gift wrapped in rebellion and weakness and delivered to everyone who is born in Adam. This inside traitor makes us vulnerable to the kingdom of darkness. The flesh is a dangerous ally to the enemy, always ready to throw open the gates of our lives and watch as the demonic influence enters.

DATING DELILAH

Judges 16:4–21 is a visceral reminder of the flesh's ways. It reveals Delilah as not only a woman but a symbol of compromise, temptation, and betrayal. Delilah was to Samson what the flesh is to the Christian. Samson was romantically entangled with Delilah and was either unaware or willfully ignorant of her alliance with the Philistines. Compromise cost Samson his sight, his freedom, his anointing, and ultimately his life.

Delilah was captivating, seductive, and relentless, much like the sinful nature. Every time Samson entertained her, he moved closer to his own destruction. What he failed or refused to see were the Philistines who waited in Delilah's house, poised to strike at the first opportunity.

At first Samson believed he was in control. Confident that he could walk away at any time, he played games with Delilah and teased her about the secret of his strength. But the flesh is never satisfied. Although it is not a demon, the flesh collaborates with demonic forces. Like Delilah, the flesh is persistent, wearing us down daily until we give in. The danger of dating Delilah is clear: The longer you entertain the flesh, the stronger its grip becomes, and the closer you move to spiritual disaster.

When Samson finally surrendered to Delilah, the Philistines were ready. They not only captured him but also gouged out his eyes, bound him in chains, and stripped him of all freedom. The man anointed by God to deliver Israel became a slave grinding grain in a Philistine prison. He forfeited much more than his strength; Samson's compromise allowed his enemy to desecrate the anointing God had placed on his life.

The flesh is the devil's willing accomplice. Feeding it strengthens its ability to betray you. The flesh isn't neutral; it continually works against your spirit. Starving it through self-discipline, fasting, prayer, and immersion in the Scriptures weakens flesh's hold and strengthens your spiritual defenses. But never make the mistake that Samson made. Don't linger in Delilah's house and deceive yourself into thinking you can handle the temptation. Follow Joseph's example in Genesis 39:12, and flee all temptation.

Dating Delilah is a game that always ends in loss. Delilah didn't start by cutting Samson's hair—she began by captivating his heart. Be vigilant about what you allow into your life. Be wise where relationships, media, or habits are concerned. What you entertain can draw you away from God, ultimately blinding you and grinding you down. Don't flirt with destruction; starve the flesh and strengthen your spirit.

CRUCIFY THE FLESH BY CUTTING THE TRIGGERS

When Samson continued to ignore the dangers of playing with Delilah, the Philistines gouged out his eyes. Jesus later used graphic language to warn us, saying, "If your right eye causes you to stumble, gouge it out....And if your right hand causes you to stumble, cut it off" (Matt. 5:29–30, NIV). Christ, the ultimate authority on exorcism and spiritual freedom, teaches that drastic action is needed to deal with the triggers of sin that invite demonic control.

Of course Jesus isn't calling for us to mutilate ourselves. He uses this vivid imagery to stress the danger and our need to resist. The hand or eye is necessary and valuable, but when it opens us to oppression, we have to remove it—not physically but symbolically. Social media, certain friends, TV shows, and other activities might be fine in moderation, but for some people they become entry points where the flesh gains ground and demons are free to exploit.

Jesus' point is clear: If you are not willing to practice some painful self-discipline, you're not ready to be free from sin's grip. Removing your sin-triggers is how you crucify your flesh. If social media leads you into lust or comparison, deactivate it. If a particular TV series tempts you into compromise, stop watching it. If unstructured free time invites temptation, replace that time with activities that build your spirit and guard your heart.

Consider how differently Joseph and David approached similar temptations. When Potiphar's wife enticed Joseph, he fled, choosing to protect his purity despite the cost. (See Genesis 39:11–13.) But when David relaxed on his balcony instead of joining his men on the battlefield, his idleness led to adultery and devastation. (See 2 Samuel 11:1–2.)

Removing ourselves from tempting situations is a critical spiritual safeguard that cuts off access to sin. If an ex with whom you had a sexual relationship tempts you in moments of weakness, block that person from your life, both physically and mentally. Find an accountability partner from your local church. Install a filter on your computer to block any explicit content. Build spiritual habits to strengthen your defenses: Fast for twenty-four hours once a week. Schedule thirty to sixty minutes of daily prayer. Meditate on Scripture and commit to reading the Bible from cover to cover in a year. Join a small group for fellowship and serve in your local church.

This isn't only about staying busy; it's about staying on the altar. Keeping your flesh crucified requires daily surrender and discipline. Removing triggers today will protect your heart and mind tomorrow.

Don't let flesh-triggers open doors in your life. Stay vigilant, disciplined, and surrendered to God.

WHEN DISCIPLINE FAILS

The way we deal with the flesh is very different from how we deal with demons. The flesh must be crucified, but demons must be cast out. Galatians 5:24 says, "Those who belong to Christ Jesus have crucified the flesh with its passions and desires" (NIV). This means denying every sinful desire daily and choosing to live in harmony with the Holy Spirit. (See Luke 9:23.) You cannot crucify a demon or cast out the flesh—each requires its specific remedy.

But what if the struggle with the flesh persists despite your efforts to crucify it? This could indicate a demonic issue rather than a fleshly one. If you've repented, denied yourself, and submitted to the Holy Spirit but still experience a relentless, overpowering struggle, you may be experiencing demonic control. For example, someone battling lust could remove all access to temptation, establish accountability, and fast regularly, yet the compulsion remains—or even intensifies—indicating that a demon might be involved. Self-discipline can restrain the flesh, but it cannot remove a demon.

When the source of temptation, such as a toxic environment, is removed, sin should lose its grip. But if oppression continues, it is likely spiritual rather than internal. Another way to identify a demon is by the presence of intrusive voices. The flesh is part of you; it does not speak but manifests internal desires or inclinations. Demons, however, attack with persistent, irrational, or violent intrusive thoughts that seem impossible to control.

When demons are involved, the issue moves beyond crucifying the flesh, and deliverance is needed. Demons must be evicted through exorcism and the authority of Jesus. When demonic oppression takes root, call on the name of Christ to break its hold and reclaim your freedom.

NOT EVERYTHING IS A DEMON

It is interesting that when people told Jesus they had demons, He didn't question their assessment. Nor did He mock them for seeing a demon behind every bush. Instead He immediately got to work, delivering them and bringing the freedom they needed. It's true that not everything is caused by demons, but 1 John 5:19 makes it clear that the world lies under Satan's control. Paul also warns us not to be "ignorant" of Satan's schemes, lest he take advantage of us (2 Cor. 2:11). Unfortunately some use the "not everything is a demon" rationale as an excuse to avoid dealing with deliverance.

Having a fleshly struggle doesn't mean you have a demon, but if you keep yielding to the flesh, you can "give place to the devil" (Eph. 4:27). Having a sickness also doesn't mean you have an unclean spirit, but if that sickness cannot be diagnosed or doesn't respond to medical treatment, it may have spiritual roots. Acts 10:38 says that Jesus healed "all who were oppressed by the devil." Sickness is a form of demonic oppression, whether caused directly by the devil or by living in a broken world. Sometimes, however, it's just a cold and not a demon. At the same time, it is wrong to assume that no sickness has demonic roots.

The same principle applies to physical disorders. Some issues are purely physical needs that require medical treatment. But demons can cause disorders. In Matthew 17:15–18, a boy suffered seizures. In Mark 5:1–15 and elsewhere, a man was possessed by demons. By today's standards this man would likely be diagnosed with a mental illness. Yet Jesus delivered both individuals from demons, and afterward, they were also healed.

Whether a demon is directly involved or not, two things are clear: The devil is not innocent, and God is not guilty. Viewing the world as being broken only by Adam's fall while ignoring the entities that are orchestrating covert agendas is ignorant at best, and potentially dangerous. Blaming God for the devil's works contradicts His character, which was revealed through Jesus' ministry. (See John 14:9–10.)

It also plays right into Satan's hands and leaves us shadowboxing an enemy whose identity we have not acknowledged.

THOSE IN BONDAGE CAN'T DO BATTLE

Recently I had an interview with a well-known pastor who raised a complaint against deliverance ministry. He said that exorcists make people overly dependent on them, and he argued that "all we need to do is point people to Jesus for deliverance." I submit that his argument overlooks the practical realities of deliverance ministry and denies the biblical model. Imagine telling the Israelites under Pharaoh's harsh rule to "try harder" to free themselves. That would never have worked. You don't get delivered from Egyptian oppression by trying harder. The Israelites needed someone to confront Pharaoh and lead them out of captivity.

Israel had long cried out to God in their bondage, and God answered by sending a deliverer. However, once they entered the Promised Land, they had to fight to take possession of their promise. Similarly, those bound by demons can't achieve deliverance by applying more pressure to their flesh. That's why Jesus sent His disciples to cast out demons in Matthew 10:1. Deliverance isn't about making people dependent on deliverance ministers—it's about providing the help they cannot give themselves.

When Lazarus exited his tomb, he was wrapped from head to toe in graveclothes and needed help to get free of them. So Jesus told the bystanders, "Loose him, and let him go" (John 11:44). Likewise, we are called to set the captives free by continuing the ministry of deliverance and bringing freedom to those bound by spiritual chains. They are seeking answers from God, and those answers often come through men and women of God who cast out demons, as Jesus did.

Many critics of deliverance don't understand how it works. Their arguments are weak because they lack firsthand knowledge. Deliverance is not a crutch; it's a biblical process for freeing those who are bound. Perhaps the critics are missing the difference between spiritual bondage and spiritual battle. Spiritual bondage is like living in Egypt: You need deliverance to break free. Spiritual battle is like possessing the Promised Land: You fight from a position of victory to claim what God has already promised. Enslaved people are not soldiers. Battle is the privilege of free people, but those in bondage are trapped in the torment of enslavement.

Asking slaves in Egypt to fight for their freedom is a poor strategy. Telling someone entering the Promised Land to wait for deliverance is equally misguided. You should exercise dominion while you're fighting to enter the Promised Land. But people can only do that after they are free. The journey to freedom is about moving from deliverance to dominion: Freedom comes first, and then you can fight for the promises of God.

THE DEVIL MADE ME DO IT

A humorous story captures the balance between temptation and personal responsibility: A mother who is disciplining her misbehaving son asks him why he kicked his brother. The boy replies, "The devil made me do it." When she asks why he pulled his brother's hair, he pauses and says, "That was my idea."

While the devil tempts and moves us toward sin, we must ultimately bear responsibility for our actions. In the Garden of Eden, Eve blamed the serpent for deceiving her. She wasn't entirely wrong—the devil did deceive her—but she ate the forbidden fruit. God judged both the serpent and Eve, as well as her husband, Adam, who also tried to shift the blame. God rightly cursed the serpent, but humanity still suffers the consequences of Adam's selfish choice.

The devil will bear responsibility for his role in humanity's suffering, but we will be judged whenever we obey the devil as Adam did. We cannot blame Adam for all of our suffering, however. "All have sinned and fall short of the glory of God" (Rom. 3:23).

The same principle is seen in King David's story. According to 1 Chronicles 21:1, "Satan...moved David to number Israel." Satan tempted David, but David willfully chose to act. When the prophet Gad confronted him, David took responsibility, repented, and accepted the consequences of his actions. (See 1 Chronicles 21:11–13.) Unlike Eve, who shifted the blame, David humbled himself and sought forgiveness. Eve and her husband lost paradise, but David retained his palace.

Although the devil might influence, tempt, or move us to do wrong, God holds us accountable for our choices. Making excuses for sin will not do; repentance is what brings restoration. The devil will face eternal judgment for his actions, but those who yield to him will bear the consequences of their sins. Blaming the devil only leaves us stuck. Battling him with the power of the Holy Spirit sets us free. James 4:7 doesn't call us to fear the devil but to submit to God and resist the devil. True freedom comes not by denying Satan's schemes but by identifying, confronting, and resisting him.

Just yesterday I interviewed a young man whose childhood was challenging. He grew up in a broken home and was exposed to pornography at the tender age of six. This opened the door to many other struggles and led to him being sexually abused by boys and older men. After moving to a new place, he was targeted with bullying and name-calling, which left him feeling lost and alone. In search of identity, he turned to a destructive lifestyle and engaged in promiscuous behavior, even distinguishing himself as a member of the LBGTQ+ community.

Though this man knew about God, he had never committed his life to Him. He began having disturbing dreams of being attacked by snakes, and he sensed an increasing darkness closing in. Desperate for help, he searched online and found a video that described his condition and experiences. As he watched a deliverance session, he felt a physical sensation, as though something evil was trying to harm him. During this intense spiritual warfare, the video abruptly ended before he could be fully delivered.

Not long after that, a friend invited him to a Christian retreat, where he surrendered his life to Jesus. During ministry time, he repented and renounced the curses, witchcraft, and spiritual attachments that had tormented him. A powerful demonic entity manifested right then, and it was cast out, setting him free.

Demons are looking for human hosts to invade and harass. But Jesus beckons, "Come to Me, all you who labor and are heavy laden, and I will give you rest" (Matt. 11:28). Jesus is standing at the door knocking, wanting to dwell richly in your heart by faith, not only to empower your resistance but also to cleanse your temple from any demonic defilement. So go ahead. Open the door to Jesus.

CHAPTER 5

YOU NEED DELIVERANCE

JOSHUA BLAHYI, WIDELY known as General Butt Naked, was a Liberian warlord notorious for his gruesome deeds during the First Liberian Civil War. He was born into the Sarpo-Krahn tribe, a warrior tribe in West Africa, and his life was steeped in spiritual darkness from an early age.[1]

Joshua's father, a wealthy and educated government accountant, unexpectedly became a tribal priest when a supernatural event bestowed the mantle of priesthood upon him.[2] Following tribal tradition, his son Joshua underwent a harrowing initiation into the service of the demon Nya-ghe-a-weh, the deity worshipped by his tribe.

When Joshua was seven, he spent three days and nights at the rock that served as Nya-ghe-a-weh's throne. The rock opened, and Joshua descended into its depths, encountering that demon in terrifying visions. For eleven days he remained underground, absorbing occult knowledge. He emerged from this period as a vessel of Nya-ghe-a-weh and was marked for a life of bloodshed and spiritual bondage.[3]

At the age of eleven Joshua was ordained as the high priest of Nya-ghe-a-weh. This role came with unthinkable requirements, including regular child sacrifices. Joshua presided over 3,929 priests, each with their own altars and followers, effectively ruling over much of Liberia's spiritual landscape. Even the president, Samuel K. Doe, a member of his tribe, was subject to this spiritual hierarchy.[4]

Joshua transitioned from priest to warrior as the Liberian Civil War ravaged his country. Under the General Butt Naked moniker he led his troops into battle wearing nothing but his shoes and a gun, believing this made him invincible. Ritual sacrifices that included human victims preceded every battle, with Joshua's child soldiers often consuming the hearts of children as a part of their demonic rituals.[5] He wielded the "spirit of fear" to terrify and overpower his enemies, successfully capturing soldiers and equipment. Yet despite his spiritual dominance, Joshua found that his power faltered when the faith of strong Christians shielded them from his dark forces.[6]

One fateful day, after sacrificing a three-year-old girl and consuming her heart, Joshua heard an audible voice call out to him. Turning toward the voice, he saw a blinding light and a ten-foot-tall figure with a cloud at His feet. The figure said, "My son, why are you enslaving yourself?"

Confused, Joshua asked, "Why are You calling me a slave when I am supposed to be a king?"

The figure replied, "You are supposed to be a king, but you are living like a slave. Repent and live, or refuse and die."[7]

This encounter triggered Joshua's inner conflict. During battles his weapons began to malfunction, and Nya-ghe-a-weh no longer provided adequate protection. The demon's demeanor toward him grew cold and distant, signaling that Joshua's spiritual bond with it was weakening.[8]

Unknown to Joshua, a prayer group called Soul Winning Evangelistic Ministry (SWEM) had been interceding for him. To protect his identity, they renamed him Joshua in their prayers, and they targeted him with intense spiritual warfare. Prophetic prayers that once asked for his death turned to pleas for his salvation.[9]

One day, a brave member of SWEM visited Joshua's home, prayed with him, and left unnoticed by his soldiers. This act of courage and continued prayer began to break the chains of demonic oppression surrounding Joshua.[10]

One night, Nya-ghe-a-weh failed to appear for their usual spirit journey. Instead, Joshua fell into a trance. A cloud enveloped him, and dew poured over his head. His body began expelling black smoke as the power of darkness was driven out. The next morning, Joshua went to church, despite Nya-ghe-a-weh's attempts to dissuade him.

At the church door, he saw an angel standing guard, and during the service Joshua surrendered his life to Jesus Christ.[11]

Joshua burned his occult tools and surrendered his weapons to his military commander. He began evangelizing and boldly proclaiming the gospel with nothing but a microphone. Despite his newfound faith, however, Joshua faced intense spiritual battles. Nightmares, visions of his past atrocities, and demonic oppression haunted him. The accusations of those he killed seemed to echo in his mind. He often struggled with condemnation, wondering whether God's forgiveness could extend to someone with a past as dark as his. These thoughts became the ground from which the enemy attacked him. Satan tried to convince Joshua that he was unworthy of God's love and destined for perpetual spiritual torment.

Joshua frequently cried out for help, repeating phrases such as "the blood of Jesus" and "Holy Ghost fire." Yet the years he'd spent as a high priest of Nya-ghe-a-weh meant that breaking free from every stronghold required intense prayer, fasting, and the spiritual intervention of deliverance.

Joshua's search for spiritual freedom brought him to Nigeria, where he attended a worship service at a Pentecostal church renowned for its deliverance ministry. There Joshua experienced one of his most intense and transformative moments in his walk with Christ. During the deliverance session, the spiritual weight of his past manifested physically. As the ministers prayed over him, Joshua began to convulse violently, a sign of the demonic forces resisting expulsion.

The deliverance was dramatic and exhaustive. At one point Joshua vomited cowrie shells that had been placed inside him during his childhood initiation into Nya-ghe-a-weh's service. These shells symbolized his covenant with the demon and served as a spiritual anchor for demonic powers. Vomiting them out was a tangible sign that those covenants were being broken and that the demonic grip on his life was being dismantled.[12]

During this session, the Holy Spirit revealed specific demonic strongholds tied to Joshua's past spiritual practices. Each revelation led to targeted prayers that uprooted the darkness. Joshua described the lifting of an immense weight from his being as numerous spiritual chains were broken.

Today, Joshua Blahyi is an extraordinary testament to God's saving and delivering power. The once-feared warlord and high priest of darkness now serves as a preacher and evangelist, leading others out of spiritual bondage. His story has been featured in various articles and documentaries, including the 2011 film *The Redemption of General Butt Naked*, which premiered at the Sundance Film Festival. In 2013 he published his autobiography, *The Redemption of an African Warlord*, which provides an in-depth account of his journey from darkness to light.[13]

I had the privilege of speaking with Joshua and hearing firsthand accounts from those who work alongside him. Their testimonies confirm the radical nature of his salvation and the profound impact he has had in leading others out of spiritual bondage.

Extreme cases of demonization, such as those of General Butt Naked and Elaine (the satanist whose story we read in chapter 1), resemble the biblical story of the man possessed by a legion of demons in Mark 5. But most cases of demonization aren't this extreme. Whatever the degree of demon control, the remedy is the same as what it was in Mark 5: deliverance.

DEMON TEST

How do you know whether you are experiencing common struggles or need to be delivered of a demon? Certain spiritual symptoms and practices can help you detect a demon's presence. One is the gift of discerning of spirits, mentioned in 1 Corinthians 12:10. This gift of the Holy Spirit is the supernatural ability to perceive spiritual activity and distinguish God's workings from human or demonic ones.

Those who are gifted this way often sense or "see" demonic influences in a person's life. A powerful example is in Acts 16:16–18. Paul encountered "a certain slave girl" with a "spirit of divination" (v. 16). She followed Paul and his team, shouting, "These men are the servants of the Most High God, who proclaim to us the way of salvation" (v. 17).

Although the woman's words were true, Paul discerned the demonic entity that wanted to disrupt his team's mission. By the power of the Holy Spirit, Paul commanded that spirit to leave her, and it departed immediately.

Another telltale sign of a demon at work is the onset of manifestation when a deliverance prayer is offered. Especially when an anointed servant of God prays such a prayer, demonic activity often manifests as though an X-ray were exposing what's hidden. Signs may include screaming, sweating, coughing, yawning, falling, shaking, sobbing, lightheadedness, heat or burning sensations, muscle spasms, stiff hands, twitching, vomiting, dizziness, violent outbursts, chest tightness, foaming at the mouth, or resistance.

In Mark 1:23–26, a demon-possessed man cried out in a synagogue while Jesus was teaching. Jesus rebuked the demon, which convulsed the man before leaving. Similarly, in Acts 8:6–7, Philip preached in Samaria, and unclean spirits came out of many people. This shows how God's Word and power affirm His authority by exposing and expelling demons.

I remember when a young woman, a transplant from another state, attended one of our services after being invited by a coworker. During the service, I led a prayer against witchcraft. As I prayed, she began to feel heat in her feet and tingling in her stomach. Suddenly she started gasping for air and screaming as she manifested a demon. The demon revealed it had entered through a soul tie and abuse in her past. As the power of the Holy Spirit moved, the demon was cast out, and the woman experienced complete freedom.

A third way to recognize demons is by their strange activities. In your own life you might notice strange or uncontrollable behaviors. Remember the Gadarene demoniac's extreme behaviors: He lived among tombs, was violent, went naked, and had supernatural strength. (See Mark 5:3–5; Luke 8:27, 29.) These abnormal actions exposed the extensive demonic activity that held him captive.

Demons can also manifest more subtly, through persistent fear, uncontrollable anger, destructive habits, or chronic feelings of oppression. When your thoughts, emotions, or actions seem beyond your control, deliverance might be needed.

ACTIVITY OF DEMONS

The kingdom of Satan is not chaotic or disorganized, as many assume. It is highly structured and operates strategically. Jesus said, "Every kingdom divided against itself is brought to desolation" (Matt. 12:25). Satan's forces work together with a chilling level of unity and purpose. His kingdom is built on military ranks, assignments, and a clear sense of mission to carry out destruction.

The Bible provides glimpses of this dark structure. Ephesians 6:12 speaks of principalities, powers, rulers of darkness, and spiritual hosts of wickedness. These entities represent a hierarchy within the demonic realm. High-ranking demons are assigned to territories, controlling regions and influencing entire communities. In Daniel 10 we read about "the prince of the Persian kingdom" (Dan. 10:13, NIV), a territorial spirit that delayed an angel sent to answer Daniel's prayer. Similarly, when Jesus exorcised the Gadarene demoniac, the demons begged to stay within their territory, even if it meant entering a herd of pigs. (See Mark 5:10–13.) This reveals their territorial nature and desire to remain in their assigned areas of influence.

Demons are often identified by names that reflect their assignments and functions. Some demons specifically target physical health, like the "spirit of infirmity" that kept a woman crippled for eighteen years (Luke 13:11). Other spirits attack the mind and emotions. The Bible mentions the "spirit of fear" and the "spirit of heaviness" (2 Tim. 1:7; Isa. 61:3), which bring despair and depression. These spirits exploit emotional vulnerabilities and intensify people's internal struggles. They don't just influence—they overwhelm, making ordinary struggles and challenges feel unbearable.

In his International School of Exorcism, Rev. Bob Larson breaks down the demonic kingdom into four levels.

- The first level includes high-ranking demons, or principalities with specific names.

- The second level consists of demons named after their actions, such as "murder, rage, or destruction."

- The third level involves demons that exploit emotional wounds such as "rejection, depression, or jealousy."

- The fourth level includes demons tied to states of being, such as confusion, "indecision, or aggression."[14]

Although these feelings are sometimes human, they become "overwhelming and destructive" when demons are involved.[15] The point is to attack every area of human life, including relationships, mental stability, physical well-being, spiritual growth, mission, and destiny, to hinder people from fulfilling God's plans for their lives.

Demons' roles and methods are targeted and deliberate, but the degree of their influence and control varies widely from person to person. This raises the question of how much control demons can exert in a person's life.

DEGREES OF DEMONIZATION

The spectrum of demonic control ranges from subtle demonization to severe domination. Oddly enough, the same word in Scripture that described severely demonized people also applied to those whose demonization was less extreme. In the Western world we like to compartmentalize demonization, labeling severe cases as "demonic possession" and milder or more "domesticated" cases as "demonic oppression."

As we have seen, mainline church circles tend to attribute demon possession (in which demons are believed to live inside a person) only to non-Christians. However, they believe that "demonic oppression" (which refers to external demonic influences) is possible for Christians. This distinction can be comforting because no one likes thinking they are as demonized as the Gadarene in Mark 5. However, the Bible doesn't seem to categorize demonization all that neatly. In fact, demonization seems to operate as more of a spectrum than a filing system.

Although Jesus makes no overt distinctions, the Gospels suggest that some people were more severely demonized than others. In Matthew 15:22, a Gentile woman cried out to Jesus, saying, "Have mercy on me, O Lord, Son of David! My daughter is severely demon-possessed." We are not given parameters pinpointing the severity of the daughter's struggle, but her mother clearly described the situation as being extreme.

In Luke 13:10–13, Jesus encountered a woman we have previously discussed. For eighteen years a spirit of infirmity had crippled her. Her situation seemed less severe than the Gadarene's demonization; nevertheless, she needed Jesus' power to restore her and set her free.

I don't have an issue with labeling severe cases as "demonic possession" and less severe ones as "demonic oppression," as long as we do what Jesus did: spend less time debating semantics and more time battling demons.

INFESTATION, VEXATION, OBSESSION, AND POSSESSION

In learning about the degrees of demonization, I found the insights of Catholic exorcists helpful. There are significant theological differences between Roman Catholics and Protestants, yet the Roman Catholic Church has a well-structured system for exorcism that is rooted in centuries of tradition. They follow the Rite of Exorcism, an official set of prayers and rituals to cast out demons. And to ensure responsible handling, only specifically appointed priests and bishops can perform major exorcisms. The Catholic Church also hosts annual conferences for exorcists where they receive training and share their experiences. Additionally, the International Association of Exorcists (founded in 1990 and recognized by the Vatican) supports exorcists globally in their ministry.

Catholics aren't alone in having a structured approach to exorcism. Much as the early church fathers did, the Orthodox Church integrates into the sacrament of baptism exorcism prayers that are recited to renounce Satan and his works. All ordained Orthodox priests are trained and authorized to perform exorcisms. Unlike the Roman church, they don't have an international association of exorcists. But they do produce documents discussing the history and modern practice of exorcism.

The Catholic Church also describes four primary types of demonic manifestation: infestation, vexation, obsession, and possession.

- **Infestation** refers to demonic disturbances affecting places, objects, or animals rather than individuals. Manifestations include unexplained noises, moving objects, foul odors, and disturbances involving animals.

- **Vexation** involves bodily attacks on individuals by demonic forces. Symptoms can include cuts, burns, scratches, bruises, and other unexplained physical injuries.

- **Obsession** is characterized by persistent, intrusive thoughts that the afflicted person cannot overcome. Unlike vexation, which affects physical bodies, obsession primarily affects the mind, making it hard to distinguish from psychiatric conditions.

- **Possession** is the most severe form of demonic influence, in which a demon temporarily takes control of a person's body but not their soul. During episodes, the individual might exhibit superhuman strength, speak unknown languages, or display an aversion to sacred objects. The possessed person often has no recollection of their actions during these episodes.[16]

Infestation can be related to so-called haunted houses or other physical places where demons have access. Although they are rare, infestations do exist. Unexplained spooky sounds, footsteps, doors opening and closing, or the sensing of an evil presence sometimes indicates demonic access. Many times infestations are tied to a history of occult activity or crimes committed on a property. You can pray deliverance prayers over places that belong to you or where you've been given permission by the owner. You'd be surprised how far dedicating your house to God can go.

Vexation, as seen in the physical marks demons inflict on a body, is even rarer than infestation. I've ministered to people who had visible marks inflicted by demonic forces. Some dismiss their stories as crazy tales, but recently, Tucker Carlson shared a startling experience in which he believes he was mauled by a demon. One night, while asleep next to his wife and dogs, he woke up in severe pain and unable to breathe. He found bleeding claw marks on his ribs, underarms, and shoulder—marks he couldn't have inflicted himself. The next morning he found blood on his sheets and realized his experience wasn't a dream.[17]

The obsession (as Catholics call it) or oppression (in Charismatic terms) is the most common level of demonic influence. Here demons attack the mind, disturb sleep, manipulate emotions, and might even control behavior, leaving a person to wonder what has happened. Luke 6:18 speaks of "those who were tormented with unclean spirits." The Greek word *tormented* is *enochleō*, which means "to interfere or bother to the point of causing discomfort, trouble, annoy,"[18] to "be afflicted, [or] suffer."[19] This torment can include mental, emotional, or physical harassment.

Demons absolutely torment people. Ironically, when Jesus encountered demons, they cried out, "Have You come here to torment us before the time?" (Matt. 8:29). Demons torment people now, but they will suffer torment in the future. Every deliverance is a preview of that judgment. That's why demons often scream, kick, and show their anger. It's as though the fire of God gives them a taste of their future agonies.

YOU MIGHT NEED DELIVERANCE IF YOU EXPERIENCE *DEMONIC DREAMS*

One of the most common signs of demon activity is the attack on someone's dreams. The devil particularly loves to target our sleep, which consumes approximately one-third of our lives. During this vulnerable time, divine dreams and demonic attacks often occur.

When Jacob went to sleep at the place he named Bethel, he met God in a dream. God is still interested in revealing Himself through dreams. However, God's appearance in dreams doesn't always indicate a dreamer who worships God. After all, God visited pharaohs and Babylonian kings who weren't believers. Similarly, being demonically attacked in your sleep doesn't necessarily mean you have a demon.

However, if you experience persistent, unsettling sexual dreams, nightmares, terrors of being chased or attacked, feelings of being restrained, or recurring visions of dead people, snakes, or your own death, demonic influence is the likely cause. Job's friend Eliphaz possibly described spiritual oppression when he said, "When deep sleep falls on men, fear came upon me, and trembling, which made all my bones shake" (Job 4:13–14). Psalm 91:5–6 also speaks of God's protection against terrors at night, hinting that spiritual attacks and fear can occur during nighttime hours. The demonized man in Mark 5:5 cried out "night and day" and was "cutting himself with stones," suggesting continuous spiritual torment.

Remember that Delilah cut off Samson's hair while he was asleep. The enemy loves to undermine our peace and power. The parable of the wheat and tares states that "while men slept, his enemy came and sowed tares among the wheat and went his way" (Matt. 13:25). The enemy loves to sow confusion, doubt, and fear into our dreams.

Isaiah 34:14 mentions a "night creature" called *Lilith* in the Hebrew.[20] (See chapter 2.) Some interpret this creature to be a female night demon, which is often linked to a demon that claims someone as its spouse, regardless of consent. Another name for such spirits is succubus (Latin for to "lie under"),[21] a demon that takes the form of a woman and has sexual relations with men. The male counterpart, incubus, is associated with nightmares and takes the form of a man who assaults women sexually.

Almost every deliverance minister has encountered demons that harass people in their sleep through nightmares and sexual dreams. Even Saint Augustine referenced these spirits in his book *The City of God*, saying, "There is, too, a very general rumor, which many have verified by their own experience, or which trustworthy persons... corroborate, that sylvans and fauns, who are commonly called 'incubi,' have often made wicked assaults upon women."[22]

One woman shared with us how she faithfully served as a pastor at her church but experienced tormenting spiritual attacks. Despite being a Spirit-filled believer, she struggled with night terrors and horrifying encounters with demonic spirits. These attacks often followed personal losses (including the deaths of loved ones and her dog) that left her feeling as though every good thing was being stripped away.

One night she saw a demon, the darkest figure she'd ever seen, physically manifesting in her room. On another occasion she experienced violent attacks as she slept, including being choked and feeling a demonic presence jump on her. Despite her fear, she managed to cry out the name of Jesus, which momentarily halted the attacks. However, the torment continued for months, making her afraid to sleep in her own bedroom.

Desperate for deliverance, she found our church and attended our deliverance service. There, during prayer, a demon claiming to be her husband manifested. This spiritual spouse admitted it had destroyed her family and marriage and had planted lies in her ex-husband's mind. Through the power of Jesus, the demon was commanded to leave her body.

After the woman's deliverance, she described feeling physically and spiritually renewed and said her relief was "better than a spa day." Since then her nights have been peaceful, and she learned to invite the Holy Spirit into her dreams. Even when the enemy tries to spring minor attacks, she boldly declares, "The blood is against you!" Each time, she stands in victory through Christ.

YOU MIGHT NEED DELIVERANCE IF YOU EXPERIENCE *MENTAL TORMENT*

Another sign of demons happens in a person's mind and involves intrusive, tormenting, blasphemous, and compelling thoughts, as well as suicidal thoughts. These thoughts can come from voices in the mind that mock, intimidate, accuse, threaten, or try to strike bargains. Sometimes a voice even refers to the person in the third person (speaking to *he* or *she* rather than *you*).

The Gadarene demoniac is a classic example of how demons mess with people's minds. Today he would be diagnosed as having a severe mental disorder. Yet after Jesus delivered him, the demoniac was "sitting and clothed and in his right mind" (Mark 5:15). Demons love to torment the mind. Everyone experiences stress, but distress caused directly by a menacing spirit brings mental torment.

For Christians, the mind is a battlefield; but for the demonized, it's a place of utter torment. Even those who wear God's armor get hit with the devil's fiery darts, as Paul mentions in Ephesians 6:16. But when you don't wear the armor and those darts penetrate your mind, the devil gains a foothold and entices you into agreement with him.

In John 13:2, Satan planted the thought of betrayal in Judas' heart. Later, Satan "entered" Judas (John 13:27). Judas opened the door to demonic control when he embraced what likely began as a passing thought. Then Judas agreed to Satan's idea and developed a plan of action. A similar situation happened when Satan prompted Ananias and his wife Sapphira to lie. (See Acts 5:1–11.) They agreed to do Satan's bidding. (See chapter 3.)

For better or worse, our hearts and minds get filled. A 2019 survey by the Pew Research Center found that 70 percent of teens aged thirteen to seventeen view anxiety and depression as significant problems among their peers.[23] Suicide remains in the top three causes of death among adolescents.[24] In 2017, for individuals aged "15 to 19 years, the rate of suicides was 11.8 per 100,000," as compared with 8 per 100,000 in the year 2000.[25]

To deal with this pandemic of mental health crises among youth, counseling and therapy have been offered. But if we don't bring spiritual deliverance into the battle, we might be bringing butter knives to a gunfight. The thief comes to "steal and kill and destroy" (John 10:10, esv). Satan "was a murderer from the beginning" (John 8:44). A person struggling with constant intrusive thoughts of suicide might need more than counseling. Yes, they might need deliverance.

YOU MIGHT NEED DELIVERANCE IF YOU EXPERIENCE *EMOTIONAL ANGUISH*

The third sign of demonic control is evident when demonic forces manipulate our emotions, making them a source of torment rather than joy. This emotional control often manifests as overwhelming, irrational, or crippling feelings that are more severe than everyday negative thoughts. Let's explore several types of emotional anguish.

Heavy depression

Heavy depression isn't a type of sadness that comes and goes. It's a deep, persistent weight that feels impossible to lift. The Bible calls it the "spirit of heaviness" (Isa. 61:3). This oppressive force steals joy and creates a sense of hopelessness, leaving an individual feeling trapped. Someone suffering under this spirit might experience continual sadness or despair, profound loneliness even when surrounded by people, or the loss of all pleasure in life. This spirit often causes people to feel overwhelmed, trapped, or tempted by self-destructive thoughts.

Fear

Fear is another emotion that demons can easily manipulate. While some fear is natural and protective, a spirit of fear is crippling, irrational, and invasive. The Bible warns about this, saying, "God has not given us a spirit of fear, but of power and of love and of a sound mind" (2 Tim. 1:7). This spirit might manifest as irrational phobias, chronic worry, or sudden, uncontrollable panic. It can cause us to fear people, failure, sickness, and even death. Nightmares, paranoia, or a sense of constant dread are also common. Unlike natural fear, which is rooted in reality, this fear seems to take over, making it difficult to function normally or with confidence.

Feelings of rejection

Rejection is another common emotional stronghold. A person influenced by a spirit of rejection often feels unwanted, unloved, or excluded, even in affirming situations. The perception of being overlooked can lead to bitterness, isolation, and a desperate fear of abandonment. Those plagued by rejection often overreact to harmless situations, misinterpret innocent comments, or even reject themselves. They sometimes accept lies such as "I'm not good enough" or "No one cares about me." This mindset fosters a performance-driven lifestyle in which one seeks approval and always feels inadequate. The spirit of rejection often partners with an orphan spirit, compounding a person's struggle and driving them further into isolation.

Hatred and uncontrolled rage

The Holy Spirit produces the fruit of self-control, but demons manipulate emotions and cause people to become uncontrolled. Hatred and uncontrolled rage are signs of emotional manipulation by demons. People influenced by a spirit of hatred or anger can find themselves unable to manage their emotions, leading to destructive behaviors and damaged relationships. These feelings can flare up suddenly and with disproportionate intensity, causing harm to others and leaving the individual trapped in cycles of guilt and shame. Affected people can lash out, harbor resentment, or justify their behavior by saying, "I couldn't help it."

It's crucial to distinguish between natural emotions and those influenced by demons. Natural emotions arise from life's challenges, personal experiences, or circumstances. They are temporary and can often be managed through prayer, Scripture reading, talking with others, or seeking counseling. In contrast, demonic emotions feel overpowering and lead to destructive behaviors and spiritual bondage. People experiencing this type of torment frequently say, "It feels like something is overtaking me." This is a key sign of possible demonic intrusion.

A young man whose life was plagued by torment came to one of our services. At the age of seventeen he lost his brother. Overwhelmed by sadness and feeling that God wasn't answering his prayers, he went to a cemetery at midnight and made a pact with the devil. Seeking happiness and power, he told the devil, "You can do whatever you want with me."

Initially the young man felt a fleeting sense of happiness, but it quickly turned to torment. He experienced terrifying supernatural occurrences. He saw dark figures moving around his house. He heard footsteps when no one was there. He felt an invisible presence walking alongside him during late-night walks.

During that night at the cemetery something entered him, causing him to lose control of his emotions and act out violently. He found himself throwing things at his family members. His fits of rage became so severe that he was kicked out of school and eventually went to jail.

When he attended the prayer line at HungryGen, an evil spirit inside him manifested, identifying itself as "Legion" and admitting it had entered through the pact the young man made at the cemetery. The demon confessed its mission was to destroy his life and take him away from God. The young man had no recollection of what happened as the demon screamed, fought back, and resisted being cast out. Ultimately, through the power of Jesus Christ, the spirit was expelled, and the young man experienced deliverance.

Not only did joy replace this young man's torment, but the strange presence left his house, and he gained control of his emotions. Rage no longer ruled him, and everyone around him noticed the change. Deliverance from demons completely transformed this young man's life.

YOU MIGHT NEED DELIVERANCE IF YOU EXPERIENCE *STRANGE ADDICTION*

Some addictions can be resolved through self-discipline, account-ability, and practical strategies, but others seem to resist all human effort, pointing to a deeper spiritual issue. Addictions involving sub-stances like drugs, alcohol, and nicotine, or destructive habits like gambling and pornography, can indicate demonic influence. But it's important to distinguish between issues that stem from personal habits and those that involve demonic spirits.

Many addictions begin as misguided choices made to cope with stress, pain, or trauma. These actions can quickly escalate into com-pulsions that feel uncontrollable. Demons are happy to leverage these vulnerable moments and use addiction as an entry point. To gain influence and control, they feed on the defilement and sin associated with addiction and create cycles of bondage that leave individuals feeling trapped and hopeless.

Certain signs can help us identify demon involvement. Some addic-tions remain unbroken regardless of all our efforts in self-discipline, counseling, or accountability. Other people experience bizarre phe-nomena such as hearing voices, seeing disturbing images, or feeling tormented by their addiction in other ways. Unnatural cravings, such as intense desires for what is ungodly, harmful, and contrary to one's values, also indicate deeper spiritual issues. During prayer or deliver-ance ministry there may even be violent reactions or manifestations of demonic spirits.

Recently I received a letter from a sixteen-year-old man in Uzbekistan. For as long as he could remember he habitually chewed paper and the collar of whatever shirt he wore. This concerned his Christian parents, who restricted him and took him to doctors, yet nothing stopped his challenging behaviors. He also had an allergy that doctors couldn't treat.

To avoid further upsetting his parents, the young man eventually developed a secret habit. One day, as he read one of my Russian-language books about the demonic spirits behind addictions and the power of deliverance, he fervently prayed the prayer at the end of the chapter. Immediately he felt something leave him. He experienced deliverance right there and then.

Soon his skin cleared up and his allergy disappeared without any medication. His shirt-chewing habit also vanished. He wrote that even though this strange behavior never seriously affected his health, he now feels disgusted just thinking about it.

This story is a powerful reminder of how combining the truth from God's Word with the prayer of faith can bring freedom—even while reading a book. The story also shows how demonic addictions marked by overwhelming compulsions are more than bad habits and are deeply rooted in the spiritual realm. The enemy uses chemically addictive substances such as drugs, alcohol, and nicotine to spiritually enslave people. Psychedelic drugs particularly invite demonic spirits to enter.

Pornography is another of the enemy's powerful tools. It creates an insatiable appetite, often leaving the individual powerless to resist regardless of how much repentance or effort is applied. This addiction also serves as a significant entry point for demonic spirits.

Alcohol affects millions of lives. A young lady came to our deliverance service seeking freedom from the alcohol addiction she had battled for much of her life—a generational curse passed down from her father and grandfather. Alcohol became her coping mechanism for emotional pain, unprocessed anger, and depression. It also opened the door to self-harm, sexual lust, and even suicidal thoughts. Over time, the addiction consumed her, and her emotional torment became unbearable.

During this woman's deliverance, the demon identified itself as a spirit of death and admitted its mission: to destroy her life by keeping her bound to addiction and overwhelming anger. The demon also confessed to causing division in her family and pushing her toward self-harm and other destructive behaviors. The demon manifested violently during the intense deliverance. The woman described feeling heat in her body, shakiness, and a gripping sensation in her throat as though something wanted to silence her.

Nevertheless, the demons were cast out, and she was freed! The bondage of alcoholism was broken. The anger, addiction, and torment she once carried were gone. She described feeling like a child again—lighthearted, joyful, and at peace. For the first time she felt like the version of herself God intended her to be.

Other strange and extreme behaviors can go beyond what is natural or psychological and indicate demonization. They include compulsions to eat inedible objects (ice, sand, or even human feces) or to hoard items. Whatever the strange addiction might be, those trapped by addiction often describe their cravings as foreign, as though they don't belong to them. This is because demons impose their own desires, using the victim's body as a vessel to gratify their twisted appetites.

While discipline and self-control can help crucify the cravings of the flesh, the urges imposed by demons cannot simply be subdued or managed. Demons relentlessly fuel these compulsions, making freedom impossible without deliverance. The demon itself *must be cast out*. When it is, cravings leave with it, and the person is finally free to walk in the peace and wholeness that only Christ can bring.

YOU MIGHT NEED DELIVERANCE IF YOU EXPERIENCE *CHRONIC ILLNESS*

Sickness often feels like an uninvited guest that interrupts our lives and leaves us searching for answers. For many the natural response is to turn to doctors, medications, or changes in lifestyle, which are good and necessary responses. However, some sickness defies explanation. The medical tests come back normal, and yet the body continues to struggle. Could there be something deeper—something spiritual—at work?

The Bible provides clues. Jesus healed people often and sometimes revealed that their physical suffering had a spiritual root. They include the woman we saw in Luke 13 who spent eighteen years of her life unable to stand upright. When Jesus rebuked the spirit of infirmity, she was immediately healed. Similarly, the boy who suffered seizures in Mark 9 was under the grip of an unclean spirit. When Jesus cast out the spirit, the boy was healed.

One of our small group leaders, Sarah, endured four miscarriages and battled depression before coming to our church. Her health took a devastating turn during her sixth pregnancy when she was diagnosed with Diamond–Blackfan anemia, a rare condition that stopped her bone marrow from producing red blood cells. Dependent on blood transfusions every two months, Sarah's energy was drained, and she struggled to care for her family.

Desperate for healing, Sarah attended our deliverance conference. During prayer she felt what she described as "the finger of God" touch her forehead. A demon manifested, confessing that it had caused her miscarriages and sickness. After her deliverance, Sarah's blood count began rising, and she no longer needed transfusions. Three years later, she is fully and miraculously healed, as doctors have medically verified.

Sickness isn't always a purely physical issue. Chronic conditions that resist medical treatment, mysterious symptoms that doctors can't explain, and sudden illnesses tied to trauma or curses can signal demonic influence. At the same time, we need to recognize that many illnesses result from living in a fallen world. When Jesus healed the man born blind in John 9, His disciples assumed the blindness was caused by sin. Jesus corrected them, explaining that the man's condition wasn't due to his personal sin or a spiritual attack. It existed so that the works of God could be displayed in his life.

So how do we distinguish between demonic influences and other causes of sickness? One of the clearest signs of spiritual sickness is when the physical condition manifests alongside unusual spiritual resistance. If someone's symptoms intensify during prayer, worship, or times of deliverance ministry, it may point to a spiritual root. I've witnessed people whose migraines vanished the moment a demonic spirit was cast out. The sickness wasn't physical but spiritual. Certain other illnesses that seem tied to generational curses or occult practices linger over families until the issue is addressed through prayer and deliverance.

We must always avoid jumping to conclusions. When sickness persists and medical answers fall short, seeking God is the best course of action. Ask Him to reveal the root cause. It may be a natural issue requiring patience and conventional medical treatment. Or it may be an opportunity to confront the enemy and claim the healing and freedom that Jesus has already secured on the cross.

YOU MIGHT NEED DELIVERANCE IF YOU EXPERIENCE *RESTLESSNESS IN SPIRITUAL ENVIRONMENTS*

A less obvious sign of demonization is hostility toward deliverance workers or restlessness in spiritual environments. Often this reflects a spiritual battle within. Demons love to remain anonymous, attacking from their hiding places, much like thieves whose success depends on being undetected. However, when the fire of the Holy Spirit is present, demons cannot remain hidden. When Paul was on the island of Malta, fire drove the snakes out of hiding. (See Acts 28:1–6.)

When pastors tell me that none of their people have demons because demons never manifest, I remind them that first-century synagogue leaders probably thought the same thing. Yet when Jesus showed up, demons manifested. As Mark 1:23–24 recounts, "Just then a man in their synagogue who was possessed by an impure spirit cried out, 'What do you want with us, Jesus of Nazareth? Have you come to destroy us? I know who you are—the Holy One of God!'" (NIV). Jesus didn't bring the demons; His anointing exposed them.

The same anointing of the Holy Spirit still causes demons to manifest today. Those who walk in the anointing of the Holy Spirit often attract demonic hostility. Demons are unfriendly toward deliverance ministers, and demonized people often exhibit extreme aggression toward those who carry God's authority to deliver them.

When confronted with God's power, demons stir hostility and restlessness in the people they inhabit. I've seen individuals scream, "I hate you!" during deliverance sessions. Yet after being set free, those same people have expressed gratitude and love, clearly showing that they hadn't lashed out; a demon had.

This hatred isn't always overt. Unusual fatigue, yawning, or an inability to focus during prayer, worship, or church services can also reveal demonic hostility. While occasional tiredness is natural—like in Matthew 26:40 when the disciples fell asleep as Jesus prayed—consistent lethargy in spiritual environments can indicate a deeper issue.

Although not everyone who resists deliverance is demonized, sudden antagonism—especially toward an anointed servant of God—should prompt consideration of spiritual roots.

YOU MIGHT NEED DELIVERANCE IF YOU EXPERIENCE *EXTREME BEHAVIOR*

Demons can influence sleep, thoughts, emotions, and desires. They can even take temporary control of a person's behavior. One of the clearest signs that a person might need deliverance is the presence of extreme, uncontrollable, or obsessive behavior. The Bible vividly describes individuals under demonic influence who exhibited such behaviors, often leading to harm for themselves and others.

After King Saul turned away from God, an evil spirit tormented him, driving him to paranoia and impulsive violence, even against those who were loyal to him. Similarly, the Gadarene man's condition was so severe that he lived in isolation among tombs and exhibited violent behavior toward himself and others.

A common thread in these stories is the loss of human instincts for self-preservation. Most people are inherently aware of danger and limits, even during moments of frustration or anger. However, when demons are working, these boundaries vanish. King Saul's irrational rage led him to target David, his key ally and son-in-law. Likewise, the Gadarene man acted with complete disregard for his own well-being, crying out in torment and cutting himself with stones.

We've seen the boy with seizures who was repeatedly thrown into fire or water by a demon who tried to destroy him. (See Matthew 17 and Mark 9.) And when Jesus cast demons into pigs in Matthew chapter 8, the animals immediately rushed off a cliff to their deaths.

Demon-provoked rage and aggression that are not turned inward can turn outward, provoking acts of homicide and even mass murder. An infamous example is David Berkowitz, the self-labeled Son of Sam. During his killing spree in the 1970s, Berkowitz claimed that a demon-possessed dog commanded him to kill. An investigative journalist, Maury Terry, theorized that Berkowitz had been involved in a satanic cult called "The Children," which "was tied to another Satanic cult...alleged to have been associated with Charles Manson."[26]

Berkowitz was already interested in witchcraft and satanism, but his new friends told him about a bookstore called Magik Child and urged him to buy a satanic bible. Friends also invited Berkowitz to occult ceremonies where dogs were sacrificed.[27] In extensive interviews with a Christian psychologist, David explained, "We worshipped the Druid god Samhain who demanded...(David's eyes well up, his voice crackling) the sacrifice of young virgins. Samhain is where the name, Son of Sam, comes from."[28] Berkowitz, who became a born-again Christian in 1988, had initially said that he "fell under some kind of spell" but then retracted his demonization story, only to finally explain that demonic powers had possessed him.[29]

Arne Cheyenne Johnson's 1981 case also brought the topic of demonic possession into public view. Johnson claimed that a demon had possessed him, causing him to kill his landlord in a fit of uncontrollable rage. His trial defense of demonic possession became famous and inspired the movie *The Conjuring: The Devil Made Me Do It*.[30]

Viewed alongside biblical examples, these contemporary cases reveal a consistent pattern regarding demons: They love death, destruction, and torment, and they aim to destroy both their hosts and the people around them. Wherever demonization causes mayhem in human lives, deliverance is the only remedy.

YOU MIGHT NEED DELIVERANCE IF YOU EXPERIENCE *PARANORMAL ACTIVITY*

One more sign that a person might need deliverance is the presence of paranormal activity. Often it involves unexplained and unnatural phenomena that disrupt normal life. People report objects moving or disappearing without explanation or shadowy figures appearing in their homes. Some have heard disembodied voices and other strange sounds. Still others experience uncontrollable, involuntary movements or noises or extraordinary physical strength (like that of the Gadarene demoniac). Some individuals display knowledge or insight beyond human capacity or exhibit unnatural, telekinetic abilities.

These occurrences are not coincidences or tricks. They point to the spiritual battle that is happening beneath the surface of our material world, and they remind us that unseen forces are real. When spiritual oppression is behind the many kinds of manifestations we have explored, deliverance confronts it and brings individuals back into the peace and wholeness only Christ can provide.

CHAPTER 6

DOORS TO DEMONS

RICARDO GREW UP in a home that was more like a war zone than a safe place. In this environment of fear and pain, Ricardo's physically abusive father crushed him emotionally, leaving deep, lasting scars.

Ricardo watched his father beat his mother and siblings. When he was eight years old, his parents separated, and Ricardo was relieved. Yet he struggled to cope with his father's absence. "Even though he was terrible, not having him there at home left this unexplainable hole in my heart," Ricardo explained. That void drove him to seek a sense of belonging and love in the streets.

As a teenager, Ricardo was sucked into a life of drugs and gangs. "The streets became my escape," he admitted, "but they also became my prison."

When the best friend with whom Ricardo shared everything was killed in a gang-related fight, grief crushed Ricardo. But it also became his wake-up call. "I knew if I didn't change, I'd end up like him—either dead or behind bars," he said.

One Sunday, Ricardo walked into our church service. He didn't know what to expect, but something about the worship touched him. The sermon also seemed to cut straight to his soul. For the first time, Ricardo had hope and thought there really was a way out of the mess his life had become.

Not long after his visit, Ricardo attended a deliverance service. He was nervous and didn't fully understand what deliverance was about, but he knew he needed help. As he received prayer, something inside Ricardo resisted. He began shaking and crying uncontrollably. Then, a voice that wasn't Ricardo's spoke through him. "I entered him when he was eight," the demon snarled. "I've kept him isolated. I've made him believe no one could ever love him."

Ricardo remembers how powerful that moment was: "I felt this thing inside of me battling to stay," he said. "It was like it didn't want to let go of my life. But the pastor kept commanding it to leave, in Jesus' name."

After what seemed like a long struggle, the demon left. Instantly Ricardo felt a huge weight being lifted off him, and a new chapter in his life began. "For the first time, I felt free—truly free," he shared.

Deliverance had shattered chains of anger, fear, and self-destruction. Ricardo began attending church regularly, surrounding himself with people who encouraged him to grow in his faith. His relationship with God became the anchor he'd never known. Now I see him every week, serving with a smile and full of joy from the Lord.

Ricardo's deliverance is a reminder that trauma, bad decisions, and unforgiveness can give the enemy access to our lives. But Jesus has the power to close any open doors and free us from Satan's grip. Ricardo's life proves that God's love and power are greater than any darkness.

SATAN STEALS

As I mentioned earlier, my wife and I had as many as four people living with us at one time during our first decade of marriage. One of the house rules everyone had to observe involved shutting and locking all doors and windows in the house.

Late one night my wife and I returned home from an event we attended. As I entered our living room, I felt a cool breeze and thought about the wind in Acts 2:2. Then I heard a sound coming from another room. When I investigated, I found drawers pulled out, shelves disturbed, and one of the windows thrown wide open.

The window screen had been removed, and glove prints marked both the walls and the window frame. Someone had broken into our home.

Oddly, our computer, iPad, and jewelry were untouched. But a car was gone. It wasn't even ours; someone loaned it to us when we gave away both our cars. The thief had apparently studied us, waited until we were gone, and entered through the single window that one of our guests left unlocked.

Later that night the guest whose room was violated spotted the stolen car in a nearby parking lot. The police recovered it and found a note inside. It said, "I'm sorry for stealing your car."

We were relieved to have the car returned to us, but the experience taught us a valuable lesson: Thieves are always looking for openings to exploit.

Satan operates the same way a thief would. In fact, John 10:10 calls him a thief. All he needs is one opening: A single compromise, unconfessed sin, or area of disobedience becomes an open door to your spiritual life. In Ricardo's case, his parents' divorce gave demons an entry point. The same can happen generationally, when grandparents or other ancestors practiced witchcraft or dedicated their family line to Satan.

Satan studies you and waits for the right moment to steal the blessings God has given you. This is not the same as losing something— that's usually a matter of carelessness, and you can often retrace your steps to find the lost item. Theft is different; it's a deliberate, malicious act. So if your peace, joy, or purity is missing, there may be an unlocked door in your life. Whether it's something you've done or someone else has allowed, the open door needs to be shut.

LEGAL RIGHTS AND OPPORTUNITIES

The devil doesn't need an opening to attack us, but he needs a legal right to enter. Think of it this way: I don't need permission to walk past your house, but if I want to enter it, I need some form of access— a key, a means to force myself in, or an open door—even if it was granted by mistake.

The Bible warns not to give the devil any opportunity to exploit us. Peter likened Satan to "a roaring lion" who's ready to "devour" (1 Pet. 5:8). This paints a vivid picture of a watchful enemy patiently waiting for even the slightest opportunity to attack. The devil doesn't need much—just one crack in our spiritual defenses is enough.

The apostle Paul warned us not to "give place to the devil" (Eph. 4:27). To "give place" is also to give opportunity, such as legal rights and situations that imply permission. The devil is swift to exploit any lapses in godly vigilance in order to gain a foothold in our lives.

We grant legal rights through actions that invite the enemy's malignant presence. A perfect example is unrepented sin. Psalm 66:18 reminds us that if we "regard iniquity in [our] heart, the Lord will not hear." Holding on to our sin gives the devil a spiritual agreement he can leverage. Unforgiveness does the same. Jesus warned in Matthew 6:15 that "if you do not forgive men their trespasses, neither will your Father forgive your trespasses." Our refusal to forgive hinders God in blessing us and leads to bitterness, which affords the enemy ample room to operate against us.

Other legal rights the devil exploits include generational curses, ungodly agreements, involvement in the occult, and sexual sin. (See Proverbs 26:2; Amos 3:3; Deuteronomy 18:10; 1 Corinthians 6:16.) Thankfully, through repentance and the power of Jesus and His blood we can revoke these legal rights (as we'll soon see).

Even when we haven't granted the devil legal rights, we must remain vigilant to avoid sins of opportunity that occur through carelessness or compromise. For example:

- Unchecked anger becomes an entry point. Paul warns in Ephesians 4:26–27, "'Be angry, and do not sin': do not let the sun go down on your wrath, nor give place to the devil."

- Fear does the same. Second Timothy 1:7 tells us that "God has not given us a spirit of fear." When we allow fear to rule, we're agreeing with the enemy's lies instead of trusting in God's promises.

- Envy also opens doors. James 3:16 says that "where envy and self-seeking exist, confusion and every evil thing are there."

- Careless words can create openings: Proverbs 18:21 reminds us that "death and life are in the power of the tongue." When we speak words of doubt, negativity, or cursing over ourselves or others, we align with the enemy's plans and not God's truth.

- A lack of vigilance can weaken our defenses. In Matthew 26:41, Jesus warned His disciples, "Watch and pray, lest you enter into temptation. The spirit indeed is willing, but the flesh is weak."

Jesus demonstrated what it means to be free from the enemy's grip. In John 14:30, He said, "I will no longer talk much with you, for the ruler of this world is coming, and he has nothing in Me." Because there was no sin in Jesus' life, Satan had no hold on Him—no open doors or legal right to attack. We should strive for the same standard, giving the devil no room to operate.

While the devil looks for opportunities, our job is to honor God. This involves not only repenting of sin and renouncing legal rights but also living with spiritual alertness and discipline. Becoming lukewarm in our walk with God is dangerous. We need to actively resist the enemy by aligning our hearts and actions with God's Word, shutting down the devil's schemes before they take root.

GENERATIONAL CURSES

Rev. Bob Larson neatly summarizes the common ways in which demons gain access as "ancestors, abuse, and actions."[1] We are about to explore these and other entry points more closely, starting with generational curses.

Generational curses are spiritual consequences passed down through bloodlines. When ancestors engage in witchcraft, idolatry, or other unrepented sins, the legal rights demons gain can extend to future generations, manifesting as patterns of chronic sickness, phobias, premature deaths, poverty, lack, repeated accidents, and broken family units. Exodus 34:7 reflects the serious generational impact of unrepented sin, stating that God "punishes the children and their children for the sin of the parents to the third and fourth generation" (NIV). This is not about God being unfair but about how sin's consequences often ripple through families until someone breaks the cycle.

You might say, "But that doesn't seem fair. Why should I suffer because of what my great-grandfather did?" Many things in life aren't fair. We unfairly inherited Adam's sinful nature, and sinfulness gets passed down until someone breaks the cycle. The good news is that Jesus came to set us free, and we will soon see how to break these generational curses through repentance and the power of Christ.

Generational curses are not rare. Consider James, who grew up in a family marked by generational curses and the lingering influence of Freemasonry. James was unaware that curses had formed in him a rigid and controlling mindset and an undercurrent of rage that he struggled to contain. The negative effects did not stop with James; they also impacted his wife and children, creating an atmosphere of fear and turmoil in their home.

At our church conference, James came seeking prayer but didn't realize what God was about to reveal. While James was in the prayer line, a minister declared over him a release from Freemasonry. He began wailing, crying, and shaking uncontrollably. Under the power of the Holy Spirit that spirit and a generational curse of rage and murder were exposed.

The minister proclaimed the name of Jesus over James and commanded the spirit of Baal—a spirit of destruction and bloodshed—to leave. A word of knowledge revealed that James' family had a history of violence, marked by the shedding of innocent blood. This resonated with James, who remembered his grandmother's story of meeting with a gunslinger known for his murderous ways. That same spirit had traveled through the generations, bringing chaos and rage into James' life.

James described how this rage spilled into his family. His autistic son, Benjamin, once told him, "I'm scared of you, Daddy." His wife noticed how their home environment changed when James returned home from work each day. James recognized that he struggled with uncontrollable anger at his job and even while driving. But it was years before he realized that his struggles had a spiritual source.

At the church conference all of that changed, and James experienced a profound release. The anger, hatred, and bottled-up rage that had controlled his life for so long completely lifted. For the first time in years, he experienced true peace.

No matter how deep generational curses run, God's power is greater. Through the blood of Jesus every curse can be broken, and God can turn it into a generational blessing. "Christ redeemed us from the curse of the law by becoming a curse for us" (Gal. 3:13, NIV). When we repent, renounce the sins of our ancestors, surrender to Christ, and remove demons that entered through curses, God transforms our families and establishes a legacy of freedom, peace, and righteousness for generations to come.

REJECTION IN THE WOMB AND BEYOND

When children are emotionally or verbally rejected by their parents, doors are opened to a spirit of rejection. Things said even during a pregnancy (i.e., "We didn't want this baby" or "This child is a mistake") can become gateways for demonic intrusion. This spirit of rejection often surfaces later in the child's life in the form of rebellion, addiction, or relational dysfunction.

In deliverance ministry, we've encountered countless adults who grapple with rejection that began in the womb. Freedom begins by breaking any word curses and renouncing the spirit of rejection. The Bible affirms that babies in the womb are deeply affected by their environment and spiritual influences. In Luke 1:41, John the Baptist leaped in Elizabeth's womb when he recognized Jesus' presence. If the Holy Spirit can affect an unborn child in such a profound way, negative spiritual forces can also exert influence.

Growing up fatherless is another significant source of trauma and rejection. In our society, countless homes lack fathers. The lack of a father's presence has far-reaching consequences. Tragically, statistics reveal that "criminal activity and fatherlessness are closely related."[2] The majority of school dropouts lack a father's presence, and most homeless families are fatherless. Yet while society punishes rebellion, it rarely addresses its root cause: rejection.

GROWING UP IN A BROKEN HOME

Broken homes provide fertile ground for demon activity. Divorce, domestic violence, and parental absence leave emotional scars and create vulnerabilities in which spirits of anger, fear, and rebellion frequently take root. Not everyone from a broken home has a demon, but the emotional wounds left by family brokenness can increase a person's susceptibility to spiritual oppression.

Demons are like vultures: They feed on what is already compromised, as Sarah's story powerfully demonstrates. As a mixed-race child, Sarah faced rejection even before her birth. Her grandmother was driven by prejudice and pressured Sarah's mother to abort her. Although her mother chose to give her life, the revelation of her grandmother's rejection sparked deep anger and pain in Sarah's soul. She continued to experience racism within her own family and suffered horrific abuse at the hands of her stepfather, who also abused her sisters and cousins.

Trauma silenced Sarah and bred bitterness within her. Desperate to cope, she turned to the occult. She and some friends made a Ouija board and cut their hands to use blood in their rituals. The darkness they invited quickly turned dangerous. The day after using the board, Sarah and her friends narrowly escaped a life-threatening car accident. But instead of turning to God, Sarah further immersed herself in darkness and invited demonic forces to guide her.

Years later, she knew she needed deliverance. During a prayer service she renounced her anger, pain, and ties to the occult. As she stood in worship, Sarah began manifesting signs of demonic oppression: Her body clenched; her hands tightened; and an uncontrollable scream erupted from within her. The spiritual battle peaked as deliverance prayers exposed the root causes. The demon spoke through Sarah, saying, "She wants to die." This revealed the spirit's assignment: to drive its host to hopelessness and despair. The demon also admitted that it had entered Sarah's life through the abuse, anger, and pain inflicted by her stepfather.

The demon resisted the deliverance fiercely, but the authority of Jesus Christ prevailed. As the prayers continued, Sarah felt a roar rise from deep within her as years of anguish were forced out of her body. When the evil spirit was finally expelled, Sarah fell to the ground, free for the first time in decades.

Demons exploit our deepest childhood wounds to establish their influence in places of pain and confusion. They dwell in brokenness and thrive there. But Jesus is greater! He frees and restores the captives, placing them in His spiritual home—the church—where healing and restoration are found.

SEXUAL ABUSE

Few things create spiritual wounds as deep as those caused by sexual abuse. Victims often experience years of torment as spirits of fear, anger, shame, and even self-hatred take root. Proverbs 18:14 asks, "A crushed spirit who can bear?" (NIV). The pain of sexual abuse often manifests in destructive behaviors like addiction or unhealthy relationships.

We ministered to a self-identified lesbian whose struggle began with the sexual abuse of a male relative. During deliverance, the demon declared that it had entered during that abuse. The woman's hatred for men and resulting same-sex attraction were fruits of the demonic presence. This demonic exploitation was brutal, but almighty Jesus brought healing and freedom nonetheless.

Another young lady attended our deliverance event seeking freedom. The spirit of lesbianism entered her life when she was molested at the age of four or five. Growing up, she was attracted only to girls. In high school she dated girls and considered it a normal lifestyle.

Not everything was normal, however. She started partying often and drinking heavily to numb her pain. Her nights were filled with such depression and anxiety that she contemplated suicide and obtained the pills that would end it all. But something inside her said there had to be more to life, and her praying parents did not give up on her. Seemingly out of the blue, she received a Facebook invitation to our deliverance conference, and her journey to freedom began.

Initially during the deliverance, she did not fully surrender. However, by the end of that night, she gave herself to God, and by the end of the weekend, she experienced complete deliverance. She felt an indescribable sense of peace, and her sexual perspective changed. Depression and anxiety no longer plagued her. She even cut off social media because it no longer held the same appeal. She had found her true purpose for living.

INVOLVEMENT IN THE OCCULT

Deuteronomy 18:10 warns, "Let no one be found among you who… practices divination or sorcery" (NIV). Occult practices such as witchcraft, astrology, tarot cards, and Ouija boards directly connect individuals to the demonic realm. Even seemingly harmless activities like reading horoscopes and practicing yoga have pagan roots that can open doors.

Isabella was born into a Christian family but struggled with demonic oppression that entered through her involvement in the occult. As a child she experienced disturbing bruises, cuts on her body, and unsettling visions. Seeking answers, she turned to New Age practices, including horoscopes, in hopes of finding healing and fulfillment. These activities offered fleeting moments of peace but ultimately left her feeling empty.

In 2020, Isabella realized that nothing truly fulfilled her. Encouraged by the prayers of her mother and grandmother, she began secretly reading her Bible and crying out to God for help. A pivotal moment came when God called her to choose between a toxic relationship and fully following Him. She ended the toxic relationship and attended our deliverance conference that weekend.

Initially, Isabella attempted to distract herself from heartbreak, but God had other plans. On the Saturday during the conference, she began manifesting demons and heard an audible voice saying, "I've been in your family for generations, and I'm not leaving you."

Terrified and desperate, Isabella returned the next day. At the Sunday service she experienced a powerful encounter with the Holy Spirit. As ministers prayed for her and demons were cast out, she manifested repeatedly and was delivered from a spirit of anger, generational curses of witchcraft, and a heavy spirit of depression. Afterward, she described feeling a profound sense of freedom and peace. She later joined our internship program, got married, and returned home to share the message of freedom with her family.

PARTICIPATING IN FALSE RELIGIONS

Involvement in false religions (including Freemasonry, Mormonism, Scientology, New Age practices, Jehovah's Witnesses, Buddhism, Hinduism, and Islam) opens the door to demonic influence. The Bible warns in 1 John 4:3, "Every spirit that does not confess that Jesus Christ has come in the flesh is not of God." False religions, including Mormonism and Islam, deny Jesus' true identity as the Son of almighty God and instead align with the spirit of the antichrist. Satan, "the god of this age," blinds the minds of unbelievers and "works in the sons of disobedience" (2 Cor. 4:4; Eph. 2:2), keeping them in spiritual darkness and rebellion against God.

Many false religions involve oaths, rituals, or practices that directly invite demonic forces. Freemasonry includes secret oaths and rituals in which participants symbolically "bind" themselves, invoking spiritual forces they might not fully understand. Similarly, New Age practices often encourage people to connect with spirit guides, channel energy, or meditate in a way that opens them to demonic influence. In Hinduism and Buddhism the worship of idols, the chanting of mantras, or the awakening of kundalini energy can invoke forces contrary to the Spirit of God, thereby inviting demonic oppression.

The Bible makes it clear that false worship is not benign but connected to demonic activity. First Corinthians 10:20 states that "the things which the Gentiles sacrifice they sacrifice to demons and not to God." People who worship idols are not bowing to lifeless objects; they are spiritually engaging with the demonic forces behind those idols.

False religions lead people to reject the sufficiency of Christ's sacrifice and replace it with works-based salvation, spiritual enlightenment through self-effort, or submission to false gods. Scientology focuses on self-empowerment and achieving spiritual clarity without God. Jehovah's Witnesses deny the divinity of Christ and redefine core biblical doctrines. These false beliefs might seem logical or harmless, but they create spiritual strongholds and give demons legal access to oppress, deceive, and bind people who submit to them.

Involvement in false religions aligns people with rebellion against the only true God. This gives demons a wide-open door! Jesus said in John 14:6, "I am the way, the truth, and the life. No one comes to the Father except through Me." Any system that denies this truth leads people away from God and into spiritual darkness. However, through repentance and faith in Jesus Christ as one's personal Savior, every chain can be broken. His sacred blood is sufficient to cleanse and deliver those bound by deception. As believers, we must pray for people in false religions, proclaim the truth of the gospel, and trust in the power of God to rescue spiritual captives.

BRINGING DEMONIC OBJECTS INTO YOUR LIFE

Certain objects such as charms, crystals, artwork linked to false gods, or books on witchcraft can act as spiritual conduits of demonic influence. These items are often dedicated to demons and can bring curses and oppression into people's lives.

The Bible teaches that spiritual power can flow through people, places, animals (such as the pigs in Matthew 8), and objects. God also used physical objects to display His power:

- Moses' rod became a symbol of God's authority. Moses used it to bring about miraculous signs. (See Exodus 4:3; 7:8–10.)

- In 2 Kings 5, God healed Naaman's leprosy through the waters of the Jordan River.

- In James 5:14, oil is mentioned for use in healing.

- In Mark 8:22–26, Jesus used His saliva to restore sight to a blind man.

- Even the hem of Jesus' garment carried divine power to heal a woman suffering from chronic bleeding. (See Matthew 9:20–22.)

- In Acts 19:11–12, handkerchiefs and aprons that Paul touched brought deliverance and healing.

The devil cannot create but only imitate, so he uses objects such as charms, dream catchers, and other items that are prayed over or dedicated to demonic powers. These objects can become portals for spiritual oppression and must be treated with caution.

A striking example of forbidden objects is found in Joshua 7. Following Israel's defeat of Jericho, Joshua ordered all accursed items from the town to be destroyed. But in Joshua 7:1 we read that Achan hid some valuables from among the spoils. His actions brought a curse on the entire Israelite camp, and Achan and his entire family perished.

Harboring objects tied to demonic or forbidden practices in your residence (or anywhere) is dangerous, as Deuteronomy 7:26 declares. This is why, during a revival in Ephesus, those who practiced the occult publicly burned their sorcery books and renounced their demonic practices. (See Acts 19:19.)

Witches and wizards often empower objects such as charms to imbue the items with spiritual influence. These items are often sold or gifted, bringing curses into unsuspecting people's lives. It is crucial to identify and remove any such objects from our homes to prevent demonic intrusion.

I was invited to pray for the sister of a church member who had been in a ten-year relationship she thought would last forever. When it ended abruptly, her life unraveled. She spiraled into deep depression, stopped eating, couldn't sleep, and even had to be hospitalized. Each day she would collapse onto her mother's couch in tears, unable to function on her own. Other family members were so worried that they called her daily to make sure she'd hold on.

Then her sister invited her to church. During worship, the troubled woman experienced God's presence for the first time. Overcome with emotion, she fell to her knees, sobbing uncontrollably as her sister held her. On the drive home, however, thoughts of worthlessness assaulted her: "You're ugly. No one will ever love you." She felt an unseen force crushing her spirit. At home, the atmosphere became oppressive and suffocating. She avoided staying there and spent most of her time with family.

Something felt deeply wrong, but she couldn't explain what it was. Then her sister asked us to come and pray over her house. When I arrived with two pastors and began to pray, the woman fell to her knees and began throwing up, something she said happened regularly at home. We noticed a sticker with writings above her door and two statues—gifts her in-laws obtained in Mexico. These items were meant to protect her home and relationships but became demonic footholds. I asked if we could remove and dispose of them, and she agreed.

What followed was miraculous. She immediately stopped vomiting and calmed down. We all felt the oppressive atmosphere lift, and her home became a place of peace again. She began spending time there, cooking meals, inviting friends over, and redecorating to make it her own. God also restored her joy and purpose!

We sometimes unknowingly own objects that serve as spiritual doorways for demonic influence—items such as voodoo dolls, depictions of snakes or dragons, Pokémon memorabilia, artwork tied to pagan worship, books on satanic horoscopes, and more. These items must be discarded, and any connection they have to Satan must be renounced.

We also need to avoid participating in events or holidays that clearly honor the devil. Whenever you move into a new residence or purchase a car, pray a prayer of dedication over it, asking God for His protection and blessing. Be intentional about steering clear of the "unfruitful works of darkness," and walk instead as a child of the light (Eph. 5:11).

ILLICIT SEXUAL ENCOUNTERS

Historically, sex has been a central element in pagan and occult practices, often serving to connect people with deities or spiritual power. Various cultures and traditions intertwine sexual acts with worship. Sex then becomes a sacred ritual that can bind participants to spiritual forces and create openings for demons.

In ancient Mesopotamia, some temples provided prostitutes for rituals of worship. We know this because of an ancient Nuzi tablet that reads:

> Let him burn his seven sons before the god Adad.
> Let him consign (*luramme*) his seven daughters to Ištar as whores (*harīmtu*).[3]

It seems that ancient Israel also had temple prostitutes, as 2 Kings 23:7 suggests: "Then [King Josiah] tore down the ritual booths of the perverted persons that were in the house of the LORD, where the women wove hangings for the wooden image."[4]

In Hindu Tantrism, sexual acts are used to awaken kundalini, a spiritual energy symbolized as a serpent coiled at the base of the spine. Ritual sex represents a union with cosmic forces and is believed to bring enlightenment and divine power. In modern Wiccan and neo-pagan traditions, rituals like the "Great Rite" use symbolic or actual sexual acts to represent the union of male and female divine forces. This is seen as a way to generate spiritual energy and connect with nature or supernatural realms.

In some African tribal religions, spiritual marriages (with spirits) are common. Through dreams or rituals, individuals engage in sexual acts with spiritual entities, hoping to acquire blessings or power. Similarly, Mesoamerican cultures such as the Aztecs and Mayans included sexual rites and often human sacrifices as part of their ceremonies to honor gods of fertility and agriculture.[5]

Satanism also integrates sexual rituals into its practices, often in deliberate defiance of Christian moral values. These acts are used to invoke demonic entities, blending sex and magic as a way to gain personal power or fulfill desires.

What ties these practices together is the belief in sex as a gateway to the spiritual realm. Unfortunately, these acts often result in spiritual bondage rather than liberation, creating soul ties and allowing demons to torment and oppress. The Bible warns us of the spiritual consequences of sexual sin, saying that "he who is joined to a harlot is one body with her" (1 Cor. 6:16). Many cases of deliverance I have seen involve people plagued by tormenting dreams or demonic oppression tied to sexual encounters.

Living a sexually pure life is a critical safeguard against demonic spirits. A condom might protect against physical disease, but it cannot shield you from spiritually transmitted demons that can be transferred through sinful sexual encounters.

I remember praying for a young man who had a demon enter him via sex with a witch. He didn't know she was a witch, but after that sexual encounter his manhood was compromised. He sought prayer because he felt something had entered him during that illicit experience. As I began to pray, a demon manifested violently. No one could restrain the man; he even broke a guitar belonging to the church. But he was finally set free from that powerful demon.

COMMITTING ABORTION

Abortion is an act of bloodshed that opens doors to curses and demonic oppression. Exodus 20:13 plainly says, "You shall not murder." Many women who have undergone abortions report feelings of guilt, shame, and torment that persist until they receive Christ's forgiveness and deliverance.

Throughout history, human sacrifice, and particularly child sacrifice, has been central to pagan civilizations. When a culture rejects God and elevates sex to the level of a deity, abortion becomes its ultimate sacrifice. Sadly, today's culture mirrors this pagan, post-Christian, idol-worshipping mindset. The same demonic forces that demanded child sacrifice in ancient times are active in contemporary society.

Psychologist and author Ginette Paris openly admits this in her book *The Sacrament of Abortion*. There she calls abortion a "sacred act" and even likens it to sacrifices made to the goddess Artemis.[6] Paris writes, "Our culture needs new rituals as well as laws to restore abortion to its sacred dimension...[as] simply another kind of morality, a pagan one."[7] Even The Satanic Temple has capitalized on this idea, offering religious abortion rituals it says will allow members to bypass certain abortion laws and regulations.[8] These chilling examples reveal that modern abortion is no different from the child sacrifices offered to ancient gods like Molech and Baal. (See 1 Kings 11:7; Leviticus 18:21; Jeremiah 19:4–5.)

Parents in ancient times sacrificed their children to gain favor with the gods, often with priests officiating. Today, physicians carry out this grim act under the guise of a medical procedure that is usually not medically necessary. Ancient children were pierced, cut, crushed, left to die, or burned. Today's abortions employ eerily similar methods in which children are torn apart, chemically burned, or dismembered. Ancient child sacrifices were considered holy and necessary for societal benefit. Modern abortions are often seen as a way to enable women to pursue their careers or gain so-called freedom from responsibility.

Even some Christians have followed King Solomon's example of building an altar to Molech. They do it by turning away from God's truth and advocating for abortion in the public square. The Bible gives us hope, however. When King Josiah led the nation of Israel back to God, he destroyed the altars of Molech and led his people to repentance. (See 2 Kings 23:10.) No matter how deep sin is today, the blood of Jesus is more powerful. Abortion opens doors to demonic habitation and spiritual bondage, but Jesus died to close the doors. His sacrifice breaks every curse, silences the voices of guilt and shame, and sets captives free.

UNGODLY ENTERTAINMENT

Movies, music, and TV shows influence us more than we realize. Content that glorifies immorality, violence, or the occult can open doors to demonic activity. Horror movies are often linked to tormenting dreams and spiritual oppression. Even the word *entertain* provides hints of influence. Coming from the Old French word *entretenir*, it is comprised of *entre* ("among") and *tenir* ("to hold").[9] Entertainment infiltrates our space and holds our attention while our eyes and ears serve as gates through which influences can travel. It stands to reason that if faith comes by hearing, other states of being can enter through what we hear or watch.

I met a pastor in Romania who was experiencing setbacks. He started watching my videos on YouTube and during one of them began manifesting demons and vomiting. Yet through that process he received deliverance. People watching videos can encounter God's power. But the opposite is also true: Demons can enter through the same forms of media.

I witnessed this firsthand at a youth rally where a girl behaved oddly during worship. Initially I assumed she was an exuberant worshipper. But when we invited the young people to surrender their lives to Christ, she came forward. As we pressed deeper into God's presence, her behavior turned violent, and demons began to manifest. When we asked her how this started, she revealed that something had come upon her after she'd watched a particular movie. Since then, she had been tormented in spiritual environments. After we cast out the demons, her torment stopped.

Music also affects the spiritual realm. As a harpist played, "the hand of the LORD came upon" Elisha, and the prophet received a word (2 Kings 3:15–19). Whenever distressing spirits affected Saul, David (who was filled with God's Spirit) played his harp, and "the distressing spirit would depart" from Saul (1 Sam. 16:23). Psalm 22:3 says that God "inhabit[s] the praises of" His people (WEB).

The spiritual world, including the occult, responds to sound, rhythm, and music. In occult and pagan circles, repetitive chants, drumming, and melodies are used to alter consciousness and summon spirits. In witchcraft, spells often include incantations to manipulate energies. Tibetan Buddhism uses mantras to connect with spiritual realms. Practices in voodoo and shamanism employ rhythmic drumming to enter trances and invite spirits to "possess" participants. Music and sound powerfully shape spiritual atmospheres.

Satan was a master of music in heaven. (See Ezekiel 28:13; compare Isaiah 14:12–17).[10] Today he distorts God's creation, using music to draw people into darkness. Cardi B, a popular rapper, once admitted that performing certain songs "activated demons" that she thought she had overcome.[11] Similarly, Flyysoulja from the Island Boys publicly claimed to have sold his soul to the devil.[12] If those creating music are under demonic influence, what impact does their music have on listeners?

Even influential artists like Taylor Swift weave themes of witchcraft and karmic ideology into their work. Her song "Willow" openly references casting spells, further normalizing occult practices in mainstream culture.[13] Reports of "post-concert amnesia" after her shows raise questions about the spiritual and psychological effects of consuming content steeped in ungodly themes.

Beyoncé has incorporated pagan and occult imagery in her work. She even described her onstage persona, Sasha Fierce, as something that "comes into [her]" during performances.[14] This alter ego appears more like a spiritual entity than a mere creative expression. Beyoncé has also popularized African spiritual traditions through projects like *Black Is King*, blending Christian symbols with pagan rituals. Some fans have created "Beyism," a religion that worships her.[15]

Travis Scott's 2021 Astroworld Festival tragically resulted in multiple deaths and injuries, with many describing the event as having a "demonic" atmosphere. The dark imagery in his promotional materials—depicting him as a demonic figure—reflects the spiritual influence embedded in modern media.[16]

We believers must be vigilant. Mark 4:24 warns, "Take heed what you hear"; Psalm 101:3 reminds us to "set nothing wicked before [our] eyes." We must guard our ear and eye gates carefully, ensuring that what we consume glorifies God and aligns with His truth. By doing so, we shut the door to the enemy and allow the light of Christ to fill our lives.

UNFORGIVENESS AND BITTERNESS

We have already seen how harboring unforgiveness gives demons a legal foothold. Jesus warned in Matthew 6:15, "If you do not forgive others their sins, your Father will not forgive your sins" (NIV). Unforgiveness is contrary to God's nature and limits His ability to operate freely in our lives. Bitterness is like poison, and demons thrive on its destructive power.

The apostle Peter addressed Simon the sorcerer in Acts 8:22–23, saying, "Repent therefore of this your wickedness, and pray God if perhaps the thought of your heart may be forgiven you. For I see that you are poisoned by bitterness and bound by iniquity." Simon was baptized and saved but had allowed bitterness to fester in his heart and become the root cause of his iniquity. This demonstrates how untreated bitterness can invite demonic forces to enslave even believers.

Jesus illustrates this truth through a parable in Matthew 18:21–35. A servant who had been forgiven of an enormous debt by his master refused to forgive a fellow servant who owed him far less. As a result, the master handed him over to the torturers (v. 34), which represent demons that gained access through offense and bitterness. When we receive forgiveness from God but refuse to extend it to others, we invite demonic torment.

Betrayal can happen to us, but bitterness doesn't have to follow. To walk in freedom, we must choose to forgive those who hurt us. This involves confessing our unforgiveness, resisting the enemy through prayer and repentance, confronting the offender with love, and surrounding ourselves with a community of believers who can support us. Counseling and time will help heal the wounds caused by betrayal and offense, but forgiveness is the first and most crucial step.

In Matthew 18:7, the Greek word for *offense* is *skandalon*, which refers to the trigger of a baited trap. When an animal attempts to snatch the bait, the trap snaps shut, catching the creature. Similarly, an offense is an enticement to destructive behavior, and it ensnares and ruins whoever takes the bait.

A few years ago, a mouse got into my office. I knew I wasn't fast enough to catch it, so I did what any good homeowner would do: I bought a mousetrap and let it do its work. I didn't force the mouse to take the bait. I wasn't even home when the poor creature was enticed. But its appetite triggered the trap, and the mouse was terminally ensnared.

Offense is the devil's bait. When someone hurts us and we take offense, the trap springs shut. Then the devil uses our anger, grudges, bitterness, and resentment to convince us that we're in control. We build walls to protect ourselves from others, but the walls isolate us. To avoid the devil's trap and further demonic influence, we must forgive quickly and refuse to let bitterness take root.

DRUGS AND ADDICTION

Substance abuse and addiction are open doors to spiritual oppression. *Pharmakeia* is the Greek word translated "sorcery" in Revelation 18:23, and it directly connects drug use to occult practices. For example, cannabis use in India dates back at least two thousand years.[17] Cannabis is mentioned in the early Vedas (Hindu scriptures) in the fourth book, the Atharvaveda,[18] likely written around 1500 to 1200 BC.[19] Cannabis is still today an important part of worship to the Hindu god Shiva, who is said to appreciate marijuana himself.[20] In modern India cannabis is used in the worship of a variety of gods, including Shiva, Vishnu, Kali, Kama, and Indra.[21]

Cannabis also grows wild in Nepal and has been cultivated in the country throughout history. As Westerners learned of the high-quality cannabis in Nepal, Kathmandu (the capital) became a sort of "hippie paradise." But in 1973, cannabis cultivation was forbidden, and in 1976, cannabis was made illegal in Nepal.[22] Nevertheless, it continues to grow in the wild and to be cultivated. The government does not interfere with its use in religious festivals such as Shivaratri, an annual festival in honor of Shiva.[23]

In Tibet, cannabis was traditionally considered sacred. It also plays a key role in the Tantric Buddhism of the Tibetan/Himalayan region.[24] In the words of a Hindu holy man, "That [smoking marijuana] makes us forget everything and we communicate with Shiva."[25]

From the perspective of deliverance ministry, communing or "communicating" with Shiva or any other pagan god, though masked as spiritual enlightenment, is in reality communicating with demonic powers and opening the door wide to demonic influence.

The use of substances such as cannabis not only increases the risk of psychosis and schizophrenia but also opens doors to evil spirits. Studies have shown that a drug-induced, altered state of mind can result in hallucinations or feelings of a higher power, which from our perspective, deceives individuals into interpreting a psychedelic condition as a divine encounter.[26] These so-called spiritual awakenings can feel euphoric, but they are deceptive and originate from demonic forces that lead people away from the truth and into the kingdom of darkness.

The demonic realm operates through deception. Demons offer a false sense of truth, love, peace, and enlightenment because Satan himself masquerades as "an angel of light" (2 Cor. 11:14). This false peace draws people deeper into addiction and occult practices. Satan offers temporary pleasures such as fame or wealth in exchange for people's souls, as he did when he tempted Jesus after His forty-day fast. (See Matthew 4:2–4.)

Obviously, not all addictions and demonic influences involve ancient rituals or religious practices. In modern times, substances like alcohol, hallucinogens, and even misused prescription drugs can cause spiritual vulnerabilities. Alcohol is often referred to as "spirits" and has long been associated with loosening inhibitions and opening the mind to harmful influences. The more a person loses control of their body and mind, the more access demonic forces can gain.

Addiction is more than a physical and mental struggle; it's a spiritual one. Romans 6:16 warns that we become slaves to whatever controls us. Paul also said, "You did not receive the spirit of bondage again to fear" (Rom. 8:15). There is a spirit of bondage that keeps people trapped in cycles of addiction. Addictive behaviors provide legal ground for demonic spirits to inhabit individuals. Not surprisingly, addicts often report feeling hopeless and unable to break free on their own.

These are signs of spiritual problems. We saw in chapter 5 that the demonic realm is real and Satan works to deceive, enslave, and destroy lives. Addiction is a spiritual battlefield. However, there is hope. In Luke 4:18, Jesus said He came to set the captives free. First John 3:8 explains that He came to "destroy the works of the devil." Jesus' sacrifice on the cross is the ultimate deliverance from sin and oppression. Through repentance, deliverance, and reliance on the power of the Holy Spirit, anyone bound by addiction can experience true freedom.

UNGODLY SOUL TIES

Soul ties are profound spiritual and emotional connections that bind you to another person, often influencing your thoughts, emotions, and spiritual life. Although they are not demons, soul ties can open doors for demonic oppression. So breaking these ties is a crucial step in deliverance and spiritual freedom.

Those who engage in occult and New Age practices widely acknowledge soul ties. Practitioners often describe spiritual connections that create lasting negative influence by binding individuals to others or to demonic spirits. Rituals, sexual encounters, and shared traumas are common gateways to these bonds.

The Bible provides various examples. One is the relationship between a parent and a child, as seen in Jacob's attachment to his son Benjamin after Jacob's beloved wife Rachel died in childbirth.[27] In Genesis 44, Judah pleaded with Joseph to release Benjamin, explaining that Jacob's "life [was] bound up in the lad's life" (v. 30). The bond between parent and child is natural but becomes unhealthy when it interferes with trusting God.

Another biblical soul tie is the friendship by which "the soul of Jonathan was knit to the soul of David" (1 Sam. 18:1). These two men shared a deep sense of love, loyalty, and godly friendship. Spiritual unity among believers can also form healthy soul ties, as Paul writes in Colossians 2:2 about hearts being knit together in love within the body of Christ.

Sexual relationships also create powerful soul ties. In marriage, God designed a holy, lasting soul tie by which two individuals become one flesh. But some sexually formed soul ties begin in ungodly contexts. In Genesis 34, Shechem violated Jacob's daughter Dinah and remained strongly attached to her, even asking for her hand in marriage. Ungodly soul ties from premarital or extramarital sexual relationships open doors to demons.

Emotionally or physically abusive relationships can bind a person to their abuser. Similarly, controlling spiritual leaders can form manipulative and oppressive ties. This often occurs through agreements or rituals performed in the occult, creating soul ties not only to religious leaders but also to institutions and demonic forces.

Many unhealthy attachments last long after a relationship has ended. You can become obsessed with a person and even adopt their addictions, attitudes, or mannerisms, as though part of their soul lives in you. Remaining in an abusive relationship and defending someone who is harming you is an abnormal attachment often fueled by (1) recurring dreams, thoughts, and fantasies about the past relationship or (2) keeping certain items or gifts they gave you.

Your soul is important, and God wants you to worship Him "with all your soul" (Matt. 22:37). This is difficult if your soul is broken into pieces belonging to other people. God desires to restore your soul, as Psalm 23:3 reveals. He longs for you to walk in freedom, unbound by the chains of past relationships or sinful agreements.

Let's always remember that demons are persistent, ruthless, and opportunistic, always watching for a chance to enter our unguarded open doors. Demons thrive on our pain, weaknesses, and sin. They seek to enslave us in deepening cycles of torment. But Jesus Christ is our Deliverer whose love knows no bounds. His power is unmatched, and His forgiveness is unfailing. No matter how deep our wounds, how great our mistakes, Jesus offers us freedom.

If you find yourself stuck in a cycle of emotional or spiritual bondage, remember that through repentance, you can receive restoration. The testimonies in this chapter (and countless others like them) remind us that the darkest battles are no match for the glorious light of Christ. Through His name every chain can break, every demon must flee, and every open door can be sealed shut *forever.*

CHAPTER 7

....

BREAKING BLOODLINE CURSES

CURSES ARE MORE than a Hollywood invention designed to spice up box-office receipts. Curses are very real, and Scripture frequently addresses them—not as abstract superstitions but as powerful spiritual forces that affect lives, families, and nations. A curse is like a shadow from the past that keeps someone from living in freedom or fulfilling their potential. It bends lives toward dysfunction and traps individuals in patterns of repeated struggle and failure.

The Bible doesn't shy away from curses, and neither should we. Understanding curses helps us to recognize any spiritual roots that might be animating our physical or emotional struggles. By identifying these roots, we can quit shadowboxing with surface-level problems and confront the deeper spiritual issues that are in play.

Ancient civilizations, pagan religions, and traditional cultures have had their ways of understanding and addressing curses and reflecting the broader spiritual worldview of their time. In the ancient Mesopotamian world, curses were often linked to divine punishment or the actions of malevolent spirits. People believed curses could come upon them for breaking sacred laws or offending the gods. To protect themselves, they relied on rituals and sacrifices conducted by priests who served as intermediaries between the human and spiritual realms. Protective charms and incantations were also widely used to ward off curses or reverse their effects.

Similarly, the ancient Egyptians saw curses as a means of protecting sacred spaces and objects, particularly tombs. Violating these spaces was thought to invoke the wrath of gods and bring curses upon offenders. Magic spells and amulets were standard in counter-acting these threats, and individuals sought the favor of their gods to cleanse themselves.

In ancient Greek and Roman traditions curses were often tied to *daimons*, which could be either helpful or harmful. Over time these entities came to be associated with illness, madness, and misfortune. Offending the gods and engaging in interpersonal disputes were believed to bring curses upon individuals and families. Priests, healers, and other spiritual figures performed ceremonies to drive out curses or appease the spiritual forces behind them.

Traditional African cultures often associated curses with ancestral spirits or witchcraft, believing that curses could result from angering the ancestors or violating tribal laws. Shamans and witch doctors addressed curses through rituals, sacrifices, and dances meant to restore harmony and appease the spirits.

In Eastern traditions such as Hinduism and Buddhism, curses were often linked to karma, with misfortune being seen as the result of wrong actions either in this life or in a previous one. People sought to reverse these effects through meditation, chanting, and performing acts of devotion thought to restore balance and harmony in their lives.

Although the methods for dealing with curses have varied from culture to culture, the underlying belief is universal: Curses are real and must be addressed. In many ways these beliefs reflect humanity's struggle to understand and confront suffering, misfortune, and the unseen forces that are believed to govern lives.

CURSES IN THE BIBLE

In contrast to these historical examples, the Hebrew Scriptures approached curses through the lens of a people's covenant relation-ship with God. Therefore, curses were understood as consequences of disobedience to divine commands. Deuteronomy 28 provided a clear framework for this teaching: Blessings follow obedience, and curses result from rebellion. Curses were not arbitrary or caused by spirits acting independently. They were tied directly to the moral and spiritual flaws of individuals or communities.

The ancient Jewish people believed that curses could be inherited through generational patterns based on the sins of ancestors. This belief is reflected in passages such as Exodus 20:5, in which God warns of "visiting the iniquity of the fathers upon the children to the third and fourth generations." However, curses could also result from personal actions such as idolatry, injustice, or the dishonoring of one's parents. Unlike many pagan traditions, Jewish culture placed responsibility for curses squarely on the shoulders of human beings.

God Himself pronounced some of the first curses recorded in Scripture. After the fall in the Garden of Eden, God told the serpent, "You are cursed" (Gen. 3:14). God also cursed the ground because of Adam's sin, declaring in Genesis 3:18 that it would "bring forth" thorns and require hard labor to produce food. After Cain murdered his brother Abel, God cursed Cain. (See Genesis 4:11.) Curses were a divine pronouncement of sin being judged. Later on, God promised Abram, "I will curse him who curses you" (Gen. 12:3). This divine protection over Israel extends to this day. History often shows how the nations and individuals opposing God's people have faced destruction.

This might come as a shock, but curses aren't initiated by demons. In Scripture they are often declared by God's people. Joshua cursed anyone who would rebuild Jericho, warning that they would do so at the cost of their children's lives. (See Joshua 6:26.) Elisha cursed his servant Gehazi for his greed and deceit, declaring in 2 Kings 5:27 that leprosy would come upon him. Even Jesus cursed a fig tree for its fruitlessness, and it withered immediately. (See Matthew 21:18–19.) When God's servants pronounced curses, heaven's authority backed them. The same is true of blessings: When Jesus cursed the tree, it withered, but when He blessed the loaves and fish, they multiplied.

Should we be cursing people? No. Romans 12:14 says, "Bless those who persecute you; bless and do not curse." Proverbs 18:21 says,

"Death and life are in the power of the tongue." As believers, we must use our words wisely to align with God's will.

Curses can also come from people in positions of authority, such as parents or leaders. In Genesis 9:24–25, Noah cursed his grandson Canaan because Canaan's father, Ham, dishonored Noah. Parents, grandparents, and even spouses can pronounce curses that have lasting effects on families. What we say matters. Speaking words of blessing over those under our care creates benefit in the spirit realm, but our words can also invoke harm.

Sometimes people bring curses upon themselves through their actions or words. In her determination to help Jacob deceive his father, Isaac, Rebekah told her son, "Let your curse be on me" (Gen. 27:13). Similarly, when Jesus was crucified, the crowd declared, "His blood be on us and on our children" (Matt. 27:25). Self-imposed spoken curses are real.

Finally, curses can come from agents of Satan. Balak hired Balaam to curse Israel, but Balaam couldn't do it because God turned the curse into a blessing. (See Numbers 23:8.) Later, Balaam advised Balak to lead Israel into sexual sin, which caused them to bring a curse on themselves. (See Numbers 31:16.) However, even when witches or warlocks try to curse God's people, those who obey God are protected because "a curse without cause shall not alight" (Prov. 26:2).

WORD, WORKS, AND WOVEN CURSES

Curses are like invisible chains that weigh heavily on lives and restrain blessing, progress, and joy. Blessings do the opposite: They open doors to expansion and divinely empower people to move forward. In Scripture, God often blessed those He called to multiply or advance. (See Genesis 12:1–3.) "The blessing of the LORD makes one rich, and He adds no sorrow with it" (Prov. 10:22). Blessings are like the wind at your back, pushing you forward, while curses are like headwinds, resisting and slowing you down.

Curses can be grouped into three main categories: spoken, earned, and generational. Let's explore all three.

Spoken curses

Spoken curses (or word curses) are declarations that invoke harm or limitation. God, individuals in authority, or agents of Satan speak most of the curses in the Bible. But we can speak curses over ourselves through negative words, often without realizing it. The tongue holds the power of "death and life" (Prov. 18:21). Until God's power breaks spoken curses, they create an atmosphere in which defeat thrives.

Recently a woman who worked as a nurse for thirty-five years shared her testimony at our church. From infancy she endured severe emotional and physical abuse. Many hateful spoken words, including curses such as "I wish you were never born" and "You're a burden" opened her to demonic oppression. For decades she was plagued by trauma, chronic illnesses, and cycles of abusive relationships. As a result, she lived with a medical condition known as "sympathetic shock."

At a young age she had been diagnosed with mental illness and was taking seven medications for it. She took additional medications for severe asthma and lung infections. She also endured the lingering effects of a traumatic brain injury from a car accident. The enemy tormented this woman with voices urging her to take her own life. She first attempted suicide at age sixteen and tried five more times after that. Twice she was legally dead! But God had not given up on her. Each time she died, God miraculously brought her back, even from a thirty-six-hour coma.

In April 2023, this woman attended our service, encountered the power of God, received deliverance from demons, and renounced all word curses spoken over her. As she grew in her identity in Christ, God healed her mind, heart, and body. The tormenting voices stopped, and God miraculously freed her from fifty-three years of asthma, her many medications, and her traumatic brain injury. During worship her balance and memory were also fully restored.

People's negative words imprisoned this woman in cycles of destruction, but Jesus came and set her free!

Earned curses

The second category of curses includes those resulting from actions contrary to God's laws and standards. Disobedience invites curses, as outlined in the Bible.

- Worshipping false gods brings a curse because it replaces God's rightful place in our lives. (See Deuteronomy 27:15.)

- Dishonoring parents invites curses by violating the commandment to honor those whom God has placed in authority. (See Deuteronomy 27:16.)

- Injustice toward the weak and helpless provokes God's judgment because it contradicts His heart for the oppressed. (See Deuteronomy 27:18–19.)

- Sexual practices outside of God's design (such as incest and other illicit acts) bring curses because they violate His standards for purity. (See Deuteronomy 27:20–23.)

- Anti-Semitism carries a curse because God has promised to bless those who bless His people and curse those who curse them. (See Genesis 12:3.)

- Stealing and perjury invite curses because they reflect dishonesty and greed, both of which God opposes. (See Zechariah 5:1–4.)

- Withholding one's tithes brings a curse since it reflects stinginess toward God and robs Him of what is rightfully His. (See Malachi 3:8–10.)

The first curse recorded in Scripture came when Adam disobeyed God. Nothing has changed since then. Heaven releases judgment on earth when God's laws are violated, and this judgment often takes the form of a curse.

The truth is that curses don't expire; they persist. This brings us to the third category of curses.

Generational curses

These are sometimes called "woven curses." They are deeply rooted in family bloodlines and passed down from generation to generation, becoming intricately "woven" into the fabric of a family's history. Generational curses create patterns of dysfunction, failure, or oppression that don't fade on their own. Whatever the recurring issues might be—poverty, addiction, broken relationships, or chronic illness—these curses continue to manifest unless they are dealt with spiritually. The good news is that they can be broken through God's intervention. We'll explore more about this later in this chapter.

CURSES ARE NOT DEMONS

Where do demons fit into all of this? How are curses related to deliverance? Demons are personal beings without bodies. They are intelligent and willful, always seeking to inhabit and influence human beings. By contrast, curses are impersonal, negative spiritual pronouncements that affect lives and sometimes span generations.

Although curses and demons are distinct, they are deeply interconnected. Curses provide legal ground for demons to enforce a curse's conditions. Demons don't initiate curses; they carry out the curses' effects. We know that disobedience brings judgment, and curses are often manifestations of such judgments, essentially granting demons permission to enforce the consequences of spiritual disobedience.

Deuteronomy 28 outlines about thirty manifestations of curses, which can be summarized by categories such as chronic sicknesses, ongoing mental health struggles, poverty and lack, loneliness, divorce, barrenness, premature death, and frequent accidents. These crises often persist from generation to generation, perpetuating a cycle of bondage until someone takes spiritual authority and breaks it.

When Jesus began His ministry, He quoted Isaiah 61:1: "The Spirit of the Lord God is upon Me...to proclaim liberty to the captives, and the opening of the prison to those who are bound." Notice how Jesus came to proclaim liberty to captives and freedom to those in prisons. Captives represent those enslaved by personal forces such as demons; prisons refer to spiritual confinements caused by curses. Both bondages can be broken when the anointing of the Holy Spirit brings freedom to the oppressed.

In the realm of spiritual bondage, curses and demons are two sides of the same coin. Curses are like unseen chains holding back affected individuals; demons are the active captors, ensuring that those chains remain in place. Deliverance addresses both: It expels demons in the name of Jesus and through the power of the Holy Spirit. Repentance and renouncement serve to break the curses. These dual actions bring the freedom that Christ offers to all who seek it.

THE REACH OF GENERATIONAL CURSES

Generational curses are powerful realities that shape lives and families in ways we often do not realize. Currently, the term *generational curse* has taken on a lighter, almost more humorous tone and is often used to describe quirky habits such as hoarding plastic grocery bags or following outdated traditions passed down from parents or grandparents. But generational curses carry far more weight when we consider their biblical meaning.

Western culture places a strong emphasis on individualism, unlike the biblical worldview, which is far more collective. In ancient Middle Eastern culture the family or tribe was often viewed as a single unit or "person." Romans 5:12 illustrates this perspective through Adam's sin, which carried consequences for him *and* all humanity. Later, when Achan sinned, God didn't say, "Achan sinned"; He said, "Israel has sinned" (Josh. 7:11). This collective view is essential to understanding how blessings and curses operate for individuals and entire households.

Scripture repeatedly shows that God deals with houses as well as individuals. In Genesis 7:1, God called Noah and his entire family to safety in the ark. In Genesis 19:12, God sought to save Lot's whole family from Sodom. To save His people in the first Passover, God instructed each family to take "a lamb for a household" (Exod. 12:3). In Joshua 6:23, Rahab's entire family was spared because she had spared Israel's spies in her house.

One person's faith often impacted an entire household, which was true of Cornelius, Lydia, and a certain jailer. (See John 4:46–53; Acts 10:44–48; 16:14–15, 26–31.) Paul even mentioned baptizing "the household of Stephanas" (1 Cor. 1:16). These stories show that blessings and curses have collective effects. Proverbs 3:33 confirms this, saying, "The curse of the Lord is on the house of the wicked, but He blesses the home of the just."

It's important to clarify that being part of a godly household does not guarantee salvation any more than coming from an ungodly household condemns someone to hell. Faith is an individual decision. Yet we cannot ignore how family dynamics influence our spiritual and personal lives. Paul reminded Timothy about the "genuine faith" that was in him, having "dwelt first" in his grandmother Lois and his mother, Eunice (2 Tim. 1:5). Timothy's family tree had more influence on his spiritual life than we might realize.

SCIENCE CONFIRMS SCRIPTURE

We are born with many traits that were passed down genetically. These include physical characteristics such as the color of our hair, eyes, and skin. However, traits are not limited to physical features. Character tendencies and behaviors are also transmitted. At least one study has shown that children of alcoholics are between two and ten times more likely to become alcoholics themselves.[1] This statistic aligns with the scriptural truth that both blessings and curses are passed down generationally.

Science provides compelling evidence that inherited traits extend beyond physical characteristics. Researchers at Emory University conditioned mice to fear a particular odor by pairing it with a mild electric shock. Later, the mice were allowed to mate, and their offspring exhibited a fear of the same odor, although they had never been exposed to it or experienced electric shock. Even more astonishing, the grandchildren of these mice inherited the same specific memory, demonstrating that experiences can be biologically passed down through generations.[2]

Similarly, studies on the children of survivors of the Holocaust and other traumatic events show the impact of generational inheritance. *The Guardian* states that among the many thousands of people directly exposed to the events of 9/11, approximately 1,700 were pregnant women.[3] Many of these women developed post-traumatic stress disorder (PTSD). Some of their children have also displayed heightened levels of fear and stress in response to loud noises, unfamiliar people, or new situations. The trauma that directly impacted these mothers appears to have been imprinted on their children.[4]

The scientific concept of inherited memory and traits mirrors the biblical concept of "the iniquity of the fathers," which influences subsequent generations (Num. 14:18). For example, both Abraham and Isaac struggled with fear and lying, and both lied about their wives (Abraham in Genesis 12 and 20; Isaac in Genesis 26). In Genesis 27, Jacob tricked his father into giving him the birthright of the firstborn son. This familial pattern of deception worked across the generations in Abraham's bloodline.

The good news is that inherited physical and spiritual traits do not have to define us. Although dormant tendencies can be activated by our wrong choices, associations, and circumstances, the opposite is also possible. Godly influences, meditation on God's Word, and choosing to honor God in thought, word, and deed can prevent these negative traits from taking root.

Most encouraging in this regard is knowing that through Christ, every negative cycle can be broken. Ezekiel 18:2–3 reminds us that even if we experience the consequences of our ancestors' sins, we are not doomed to repeat their mistakes. God offers us the power to resist these patterns and establish a legacy of blessings for future generations. We can replace the weight of inherited curses with the joy of inherited grace. This truth empowers us to take ownership of our lives and embrace the freedom God promises to His obedient servants.

WHAT IS NOT TRANSFORMED IS TRANSFERRED

A decade ago, I purchased a run-down rental property to generate passive income. The property needed significant renovations, and the yard was nothing but weeds. I didn't plant those weeds, but there they were, thriving. At first I felt frustrated by having to deal with the mess someone else left behind. But instead of blaming the previous owner, I rolled up my sleeves and got to work. Slowly but surely, the property's condition improved. When I sold it, the lawn was green and abundant, and the structure was greatly improved. The new owner inherited much more than a run-down building with a patch of weeds attached.

This experience mirrors how generational curses work. Maybe you're dealing with a mess because your parents didn't address specific issues such as addictions, anger, and financial instability. Scripture doesn't tell us to point fingers or play the blame game; it says to resist the devil and confront the problem at its root. All of us must face our families' generational patterns the same way I had to tackle those weeds around my rental property: We must face them and bring about lasting change.

When Solomon inherited his father's throne, he also inherited some unresolved issues, including enemies that David hadn't fully handled. I admire how David warned his son about these adversaries, but the responsibility to deal with them still fell to Solomon.

Demons and curses don't die with people. They continue operating and afflicting subsequent generations until someone confronts them. Solomon had to deal with his father's enemies before he could build the temple or establish his kingdom. Solomon exiled some enemies and executed others so they could no longer cause problems. Through Solomon's actions "the kingdom was established" (1 Kings 2:46).

What a powerful lesson this is! To establish God's blessings over our lives, we must confront and remove the generational curses passed down by our predecessors. Whatever the issues, they don't have to define our future. We have the authority to confront the "enemies" left behind and break their hold—on us and on the generations to come.

As Deuteronomy 23:5 says, "The LORD your God turned the curse into a blessing for you, because the LORD your God loves you."

WHEN CRAZY RUNS IN THE FAMILY

The contrasting legacies of two families vividly demonstrate the power of generational patterns: They are the Juke and Edwards families. Richard Dugdale, a late nineteenth-century social researcher, stumbled upon the tragic legacy of the Juke clan while visiting New York State prisons. There, he encountered numerous inmates who descended from Max Juke, a man born between 1720 and 1740 in New York, a British colony at that time.[5]

Max lived a rough life of hard drinking, hunting, fishing, and working when necessary. He was friendly enough and had many children by various partners. Two of his sons married two of their six sisters.[6] One of the sisters left the country, but Dugdale studied the remaining five sisters and five generations of their descendants.[7] Including Max Juke, his sons, the five sisters, and their descendants (all considered Juke clan members), seven generations amounted to about 1,200 people.[8]

The Jukes' lives were marred by poverty, crime, and dysfunction. Among the Juke descendants, 280 were poverty-stricken and 140 were criminals and offenders.[9] Juke clan members murdered at least seven people.[10] Dugdale estimated that the Juke family clan cost society $1,308,000 in the 1800s, an amount equivalent to about $53 million in today's money.[11]

In 1897 another researcher, A. E. Winship, was assigned to study the family of Jonathan Edwards, a devout Puritan preacher who raised eleven children with his wife, Sarah. Based in Northampton, Massachusetts, Edwards was a major leader in the First Great Awakening that swept through the American colonies in the mid-1700s. He is still remembered for his famous sermon "Sinners in the Hands of an Angry God."[12]

Though a great Christian leader, Edwards was eventually ousted by his church for standing his ground on spiritual matters.[13] Left virtually penniless, he took a post in a Native American village with 150 native families, where he spent the next eight years. Mere weeks before he died, he was appointed president of Princeton College.[14]

Despite the humiliation and poverty Edwards endured, God remembered the sacrificial and faithful way that he and his wife, Sarah, lived. Winship's research found that Edwards' family story differed drastically from that of the Juke family. From the Edwards line came extraordinary achievers: a US vice president, three US senators, three governors, thirteen college presidents, thirty judges, more than sixty-five professors, and one hundred lawyers.[15] Many became missionaries, pastors, and theologians, leaving a legacy of faith, leadership, and positive impact.[16] Edwards' descendants were also prominent in secular business, being in the upper management of steamship and railway companies, serving as directors of banks and insurance companies, and owning coal mines, iron plants, oil fields, and silver mines.[17]

The contrast between the Juke and Edwards families vividly underscores how generational choices shape future outcomes.

One such heartbreaking story in America and its politics is that of the Kennedy family, which has been shrouded in what many call the Kennedy curse. Despite their wealth and prominence, the family has endured many devastating tragedies over several generations. Rosemary Kennedy underwent a botched mental health surgery, leaving her severely disabled.[18] Her brother Joseph P. Kennedy Jr. died in a World War II plane explosion.[19] Another sibling, Kathleen (Kennedy) Cavendish, perished in a 1948 plane crash. Assassins murdered President John F. Kennedy and his brother Senator Robert F. Kennedy (in 1963 and 1968, respectively), leaving the nation in deep shock. JFK's son, John F. Kennedy Jr., his wife, Carolyn, and sister-in-law Lauren Bessette perished in a 1999 plane crash.

The Kennedy tragedies didn't stop there: drug overdoses, accidents, and untimely deaths have plagued the family. From skiing accidents to car crashes and even suicides, the Kennedys have endured loss after loss, fueling speculation about a curse on their lineage.[20]

Dwelling in the past is not necessarily helpful. However, our present often serves as a window into our past. Ignoring profound familial issues by declaring, "I'm a new creation," or adopting the "name it and claim it, blab it and grab it" approach that some faith preachers advocate will not produce lasting freedom. It is crucial that we acknowledge the patterns and scripts handed down to us because they have bearing on the roles we play in life.

Counselors often refer to these scripts as the unconscious patterns of thinking, feeling, and behaving that form in the early dynamics of our families and upbringing. These scripts are written long before we recognize them, and we follow them faithfully, clinging to what seems familiar. Yet such scripts can distort reality and guide us in deeply destructive ways.

Some argue that these patterns are purely psychological or habitual and have nothing to do with spirituality. But I believe both realities are involved. We can see our habits, behaviors, and emotions. They are like leaves on a tree. But the roots are the unseen spiritual influences that feed the outward manifestations. Counselors and disciplines can prune the branches, but breaking the root system requires spiritual intervention. Only by addressing both the natural and spiritual aspects of inherited patterns can we rewrite the script and walk in the freedom that Christ offers.

IT ENDS WITH ME

You are facing battles that didn't start with you. Some issues have been in your bloodline for generations, but they can end with you. You are called to be a bloodline curse–breaker. Let 1 Peter 1:18 remind you: "You were not redeemed with corruptible things, like silver or gold, from your aimless conduct received by tradition from your fathers." Whatever aimless conduct, sin, or struggle has come through your family tree, Jesus has redeemed you to bring its end.

The Book of Esther tells a powerful story of deliverance, not just for one person but for an entire people, and it shows that many of our battles have deep, generational roots. The conflict Esther faced started long before she was born—specifically, in the feud between Esau and Jacob.

After Jacob stole his brother's blessing, hatred for Jacob burned deep in Esau. Although he didn't act on his anger, his hatred took root in his descendants. Esau's grandson Amalek became the ancestor of the Amalekites, a nation that would later attack Israel without cause. Their cruelty was unmatched, targeting the weak and vulnerable Israelites who journeyed out of Egypt. In response to the Amalekites' unprovoked attack, God declared war on Amalek in Exodus 17:14, vowing to blot them out completely. The vow would take centuries to fulfill.

God eventually assigned Israel's first king, Saul, to finish off Amalek's bloodline. (See 1 Samuel 15:2–3.) He was to utterly destroy all Amalekites as punishment for their sin against Israel. But instead of fully obeying this order, Saul spared Agag, the Amalekites' king, and he kept the best of their livestock. This decision cost Saul his kingdom, but the repercussions went even further: Amalek's lineage continued, and generations later his descendant Haman rose to power in the Persian empire.

Haman harbored the same deep hatred for the Jewish people as his ancestors did, and he plotted to annihilate them. But God raised up Esther, a Jewish queen, and her cousin Mordecai, a descendant of Saul's family line, to stop Haman. Through their faith and courage,

Haman's plot was exposed, and he was executed. Amalek's bloodline ended, and God's promise was fulfilled.

Esther's story reminds us that battles left unfinished in one generation don't disappear but eventually resurface. Some of the battles we face today have been passed down through generations of past disobedience, sin, or struggles with poverty, addiction, sickness, and broken relationships. But that doesn't mean we're doomed to lose. With God's help we can break these cycles and pass victory on to the next generation.

Esther didn't let her family's history define her destiny. Instead she trusted God, stood firm, and left a legacy of triumph. Her story challenges us to do the same. No matter what battles you're facing, you can bring them to an end, in Jesus' name.

CURE FOR THE CURSE

Let's summarize what we've seen so far: Curses are real! They aren't demons but are more like spiritual contracts triggered when we disobey God. Demons then serve to enforce these contracts. Curses don't disappear; they must be broken. Because they are rooted in disobedience to God, curses can be broken when the disobedience is corrected.

Galatians 3:13 says, "Christ has redeemed us from the curse of the law, having become a curse for us (for it is written, '*Cursed is everyone who hangs on a tree*')" (emphasis added). Jesus didn't die on the cross just so we could live. He also took on sickness so we could be healed. He was rejected so we could be accepted. He was condemned so we could be justified. He bore poverty so we could receive His riches. He became sin so we could become God's righteousness. And He became a curse for us.

The method of crucifixion wasn't happenstance. The Bible declares that anyone who hangs on a tree is cursed. (See Deuteronomy 21:22–23.) Crucifixion was exceedingly painful and shameful. Hanging naked, nailed at the wrists and feet to a rough wooden cross, the victim had to push and pull himself up on the nails to breathe out the stale air in his lungs and inhale a bit of fresh air. He would then hang down until his lungs burned from the lack of oxygen, and he had to push and pull himself up again. This happened over and over again, hour after hour. Sometimes the sufferer's agony lasted for days until he finally died from exposure to the elements, shock, and suffocation.

The practice of crucifixion may have begun with the Assyrians and Babylonians. Starting in the sixth century BC, the Persians also used this method of torture, but their version included impalement directly through the body. The Romans practiced crucifixion until Constantine abolished it in the fourth century AD.[21] This form of execution was reserved for the worst offenders, including rebels and slaves.[22] Cicero said it was so barbaric that it was inappropriate even to discuss it among Roman citizens.[23] Yet this was the method God chose for His Son to bear the curse for us.

As Jesus hung on the cross, He bore the curse that sin carries. This is important to understand: Breaking the law brought a curse. Sin produced death or separation from God and also brought a curse—a spiritual verdict that allows demonic oppression. Jesus died to break this curse, offering us the blessing of Abraham. Jesus' sacrifice means we don't have to live in spiritual chains or generational cycles of bondage anymore.

However, while the cross broke the *power* of curses, the *presence* of curses has not yet been entirely removed from the world. The Book of Revelation tells us that curses won't be eradicated until Jesus returns. (See Revelation 22:1–5.) This raises a question for Christians: Does accepting Christ automatically remove all curses from our lives? Some people believe that when you're saved, all curses end. But while salvation makes us new creations (legally free), we are still called to walk out our freedom.

Think about it: When we are saved, we are declared righteous. That's our spiritual position. But in our daily lives we are called to *live* righteously. This is the process of becoming what we already are in Christ. In the same way, while the cross broke the power of curses, we must appropriate that victory through faith and action.

The Bible says Jesus redeemed us from the curse of the law. That means sin is removed when we trust in Him and repent. But the consequences of sin—sickness, hardships, and even generational patterns—don't vanish automatically. The cross dealt with the power and penalty of sin, but we must partner with the Holy Spirit to overcome its lingering effects. This applies to curses as well. The power of curses is broken, but we must renounce and remove them from our lives. It's like the Israelites in the Promised Land: God gave them the land, but they still had to fight enemies to possess it.

Similarly, our healing was purchased two thousand years ago. But does every believer experience physical healing the moment they're saved? No. The benefits of the cross must be appropriated by faith. Freedom from curses requires active engagement in a spiritual battle. So don't be discouraged if you recognize the presence of a curse in your life. The blood of Jesus is powerful. By faith, you can wage war against evil forces in the spiritual realm and walk in the freedom Christ purchased for you.

You are a bloodline curse–breaker, and you are called "for such a time as this"—just like Esther in her generation (Est. 4:14). What others have started, you are anointed to end. If curses have been spoken over you, now is the time to break them, in the name of Jesus. Chains are not stronger than Jesus, and no stronghold is mightier than the blood He shed for you.

First John 4:4 says that the One who is in you is greater than the one who is in the world. You don't have to live in repeated cycles of poverty, sickness, or loneliness. The cross has already broken the power of every curse. Stand firm in your identity as a child of God. Rise up in faith and declare that negative generational patterns are ending with you, and through Jesus you are stepping into a life of blessing, freedom, and victory. The time to act is now. So walk boldly into the fullness of God's promises for you and your family.

CHAPTER 8

....

SHADES OF WITCHCRAFT

WITCHCRAFT IS MORE than a shadowy idea. It's a dangerous force hiding in plain sight and disguising itself as harmless tradition, cultural ritual, and entertainment. But its goal is to enslave, destroy, and draw people away from God.

John Ramirez's story provides a firsthand glimpse into witchcraft's dark world.[1] The eldest of four sons, he was born in Puerto Rico but grew up in the Bronx. John's father treated his family terribly. He never kept his promises. He drank heavily. He physically beat and humiliated his wife, he discouraged his children, and he did not financially support the family. He was also involved in spiritism and routinely sent young John to purchase the ingredients necessary for witchcraft.

When a Christian revival tent came to the area, John saw people getting prayed for and blessed. But instead of praying for John, the minister passed him by. John assumed that God must not love him.

As a boy, John saw evil spirits and heard them speaking to him. When he was seven years old, a beaded necklace fell at his feet as he played outside. An evil spirit sent the necklace to initiate John into the spiritual world. He picked up the necklace, and the same spirit became his "father figure" and "protector."

When John was eight, his aunt Maria took him and his mother to a tarot card reading. The reader, a high priestess in the Santería religion, said John would lose his sight within thirty days unless he had a special cleansing that cost two hundred dollars. John's mother sold her bedroom set, returned to the tarot reader, and paid for the cleansing.

John then underwent a series of rituals and learned to worship the five main Santería gods. Two women performed the rites and became

John's godmothers in Santería. They took him to their Espiritismo churches, where expert practitioners taught him to cast spells, communicate with spiritual forces, and recruit new people into the religion. He also learned how to become demon-possessed.

Each day, John remained in the "church" from 7 p.m. until 5 a.m., and mediums gave readings and prophecies. John saw power being manifested and people being possessed by evil spirits. When other religionists told him he would become a significant figure in their religion, John felt wanted and accepted, something his father never gave him. By the age of thirteen John had become very proficient in Santería, and people were coming to him for readings. Even so, he continued longing for a father figure and lost his own father, who was brutally murdered.

John experienced much witchcraft. During one meeting, Aunt Maria became possessed and demanded that people come forward and be burned by a red-hot cigar. People screamed and fainted from the pain, but John steeled himself and endured it. Having passed this demonic test, he "graduated" into other, higher forms of satanism.

John was initiated into Palo Mayombe, sold his soul to the devil, and became a male leader called a Palero Tata. The morning after the ceremony, he went to a local diner for a donut and hot chocolate. The woman serving him caught his attention, and he sensed that she recognized the evil inside him. He boasted to her that he had just sold his soul to the devil. She let him know that she was a Christian and would be praying for him.

Nevertheless, John continued advancing in his religion. During a special ceremony the evil spirits gave him a good "report card," and Aunt Maria was very proud. Now he had money and power. He was paid to curse people, destroy marriages, and bring sickness, death, or chaos into people's lives. Using human bones, animal blood, and demonic contracts, he wreaked havoc, often on unsuspecting people. He learned to leave his body through astral projection, which allowed him to enter people's homes and curse their families. He could spiritually "size up" Christians, testing their faith and anointing. Those whose faith was weak were easy targets, but praying Christians were another story. John could not astral project where praying Christians were present. He hated those Christians.

Despite the power he possessed, John lived in constant darkness. He slept in cemeteries to increase his demonic strength. He drank blood and performed horrific sacrifices. He got married on Halloween amid blood rituals and demonic principalities that witnessed his union. His life was dedicated to serving the devil. He openly mocked God and cursed Christians, convinced that no one could ever stop him.

In the midst of John's deep darkness, God had other plans. John became interested in a young woman with Christian parents who prayed for him. While at home, John heard a voice say, "My son, I am coming soon. What are you planning to do with yourself?"

This was not a demon speaking. John felt an awesome peace, and within seconds he had a vision of "a blazing sky, like a ball of fire, while people on earth screamed and ran in fear for their lives."[2]

John attended church and started liking Sunday school and Bible study, which were so different from worshipping the devil and killing animals. He realized that although Satan had empowered him, Satan also kept him in bondage and spiritually possessed him. John wanted to be free but still practiced his dark religion during the week.

After years of serving Satan, John had a supernatural encounter that changed everything. He saw himself on a train heading straight for hell. The fear and despair on that train were overwhelming. The ground in hell breathed like a living creature, and the cries of torment were unlike anything he'd ever heard. Amid the chaos the devil himself appeared, reprimanding John and claiming ownership over him.

Then something extraordinary happened. A three-foot cross appeared in John's hand. The cross of Christ was there—in the middle of hell! Its power was so great it knocked the devil to the ground. The devil promised to keep John in hell and said he would be pronounced dead. John tried to convince the devil that he wouldn't leave him but was only confused.

The devil reached for John, but the cross reappeared in John's hand. John pushed it on the devil, and the devil fell to his knees. Then John woke up and realized that God really did love him. He heard the voice of Jesus saying, "I'm giving you one chance to repent and follow Me." That moment of grace broke through the chains of witchcraft and changed John's life forever.

John's story shows how real spiritual warfare is and exposes how witchcraft works through fear, manipulation, and deception. It also reveals the authority we have in Jesus when we pray—so much that no matter how hard John tried, he couldn't curse those who truly carried God's presence. It is also a powerful example of direct worship and dedication to Satan. John paints a vivid picture of the spiritual bondage that results from rituals and sacrifices that intentionally honor Satan.

Notice that John first became involved in witchcraft, which opens the door to demonic influence but does not always involve direct worship of Satan. Witchcraft can include spells, divination, or communication with spirits but is often used to seek personal power, healing, or enlightenment without declaring outright allegiance to Satan. This is where the two practices diverge: Satanists are explicit in their devotion to Satan. Witchcraft is found within satanism and on its own subtly draws people into practices that align with Satan's purposes. But practitioners of witchcraft don't necessarily acknowledge Satan consciously.

Neither modality is harmless. Both are deeply rooted in rebellion against God, and both lead to spiritual destruction. This chapter will dig into the many shades of witchcraft, which are not always as apparent as spells and curses. Sometimes witchcraft looks like astrology. Sometimes it involves "good luck" charms or cultural celebrations such as Halloween. Witchcraft sneaks into our lives through music, movies, and practices that seem innocent but are profoundly dangerous.

John's testimony proves that no one is too far gone for God. But it's also a wake-up call for the church. The enemy is not playing games, and we can't afford to play them either. The devil is organized, strategic, and relentless. But he is also defeated. The blood of Jesus is more powerful than any curse, spell, or demonic attack.

ANCIENT PRACTICES OF WITCHCRAFT AND SORCERY

While witchcraft and sorcery have distinct definitions—witchcraft involving innate magical abilities and sorcery relying on learned rituals—their practices have historically overlapped in various cultures. This convergence means that certain rituals and outcomes may be attributed to both, depending on the context.

The Bible addresses witchcraft and sorcery repeatedly, showing how widespread and dangerous these practices have been throughout history. Deuteronomy 18:10–12 warns Israel not to imitate other nations' divination, sorcery, and consulting of the dead. This was one reason why God commanded Israel to conquer and destroy Canaan, which was steeped in these abominations. Jezebel, Balaam, the magicians of Egypt, and even Simon the Sorcerer in the Book of Acts are examples of how detestable practices had infiltrated pagan and biblical history. King Saul's downfall is perhaps the most famous warning, as he sought guidance from a medium and ultimately lost his life and kingdom. (See 1 Chronicles 10:13–14.)

Witchcraft and sorcery were woven into the fabric of ancient cultures. In Mesopotamia, the cradle of world civilizations, the education of literate people (often called "scribes"—the equivalent of today's educated professionals and intellectuals) was fairly standardized and involved what could be called witchcraft. After completing his basic studies, a scribe had three options for further training: He could study divination (interpreting omens), lamentation (chanting to gods), or exorcism (neutralizing demons).[3]

In the sixth to fifth centuries BC, in the region of Sippar near the Euphrates River, a whole family of exorcists lived together in one house. Archaeologists have recovered their family library of three hundred cuneiform tablets. One-third of the tablets contained information about magic and medicine, with incantations, recipes, and prescriptions to fight natural sicknesses and demonic forces.[4]

Egyptian history reveals more than four thousand years of practicing magic. "Amulets date as far as the early fourth millennium BC; while magic texts occur from the late third millennium BC until the fifth century AD."[5] Ancient Egyptians believed in a supremely powerful force called *heka*, which could be understood as "magic" that was potentially helpful or harmful.[6] Heka operated in combination with two other forces: *hu* (divine utterance) and *sia* (divine omniscience).[7] Egyptians used heka in their funerals, temples, and everyday life.[8] However, ancient Near Eastern peoples viewed magic without the negative connotation it carries today.[9] Heka was also the name of the Egyptian "god of medicine and magic."[10]

"Another Egyptian word for magical power is *akhu*," which can sometimes be translated as "enchantments," "sorcery," or "spells."[11] It sometimes refers to deceased ancestors who have the power to effect change in the world of the living.[12] An akh could appear to a living human in physical form, and akhu required offerings from the living in exchange for protection.

> Oh, living ones who are upon the earth…may they say "1,000 bread and beer" for the owner of this tomb. Then I will watch over them in the necropolis. I am an effective and equipped *akh* and a lector priest who knows his spells. —From the tomb inscription of Harkhuf[13]

People also asked akhs for help, saying, "Remove the infirmity of my body. Become akh before me, that I may see you fighting on my behalf in a dream. I will (then) deposit offerings for you."[14]

Ancient Egyptians also valued exorcism. To remove a demon, one had to get the help of a more powerful spiritual being, such as a god, that would either cast out the demon or negotiate with it.[15] Ancient

Egyptians customarily used spiritual forces to achieve goals, enlist "helpful" spiritual beings to defeat evil spiritual beings, and consult with the dead.

In ancient Greco-Roman culture, people scratched curses on small, thin sheets of lead known as "curse tablets."[16] The University of Hamburg has assembled a database of 1,700 curse tablets.[17] People used them to request help from gods or spirits to win someone's love, harm a competitor or enemy, or take revenge. The tablet's creator would place it in a grave, a well, or the temple of an underworld god.[18] Below is the text from a curse tablet found in a grave in the city of Carthage:

> Bind the horses whose names and images/likeness on this implement I entrust to you: of the Red (team)...of the Blues.... Bind their running, their power, their soul, their onrush, their speed. Take away their victory, entangle their feet, hinder them, hobble them, so that tomorrow morning in the hippodrome they are not able to run or walk about, or win or go out of the starting gates, or advance on the racecourse or track, but may they fall down with their drivers.[19]

Witchcraft was often personal. Public worship focused on gods like Zeus, or Jupiter, but privately, individuals often turned to the sorcery of love potions, curses, and fortune-telling. In Rome, sorcery (known as *venefici* or *veneficium*) was both feared and sought after, with texts like *The Magical Papyri* detailing spells to summon spirits or influence other people.[20] Sacrifices, both animal and symbolic, were offered to appease spiritual forces.

African traditions of witchcraft are among the oldest, and many of them continue to this day. Traditional healers, often called witch doctors or shamans, served as mediators between the spiritual and physical realms. They healed sickness, broke curses, and invoked ancestral spirits using rituals, herbs, and dances.

Societies have not always seen witchcraft and sorcery as evil; their morality depended on their use for healing or harm. Indigenous cultures in the Americas also embraced sorcery. Native American tribes relied on medicine men and women to cure illnesses and connect with the spiritual world. In Central and South America, civilizations like the Mayans and Aztecs practiced human sacrifices, believing that spilled blood kept the gods appeased and the universe in balance. These rituals were not isolated acts but part of a complex belief system combining astronomy, mathematics, and spirituality.

In Asia, sorcery blended with religion and philosophy. In India, tantric practices called on spirits for destructive or manipulative purposes. Chinese culture incorporated sorcery into feng shui, ancestor worship, and astrology. These traditions blurred the lines between spiritual guidance and magic, emphasizing balance and energy rather than God's sovereignty.

Striking in all these ancient cultures is how witchcraft and sorcery were seen as serious, essential tools for survival and control. People used them to explain droughts, sickness, and disasters when other answers could not be found. They used these tools in hopes of gaining power amid chaos by securing blessings, warding off harm, or exacting revenge.

Witchcraft didn't disappear with the rise of technology or scientific discovery. It simply evolved into new forms and expressions. While ancient practices may have involved chants and amulets, they manifest today through modern tools like tarot cards, crystals, and spiritual "wellness" trends. The Bible's warnings are as relevant today as in millennia past: Witchcraft and sorcery are demonic deceptions that lead to destruction.

THE RISE OF "WITCHTOK"

Witchcraft is no longer hidden in the shadows but is mainstream, celebrated, and trendy. From social media platforms like TikTok to books, movies, music, and everyday products, witchcraft has been repackaged as something harmless and empowering. But it remains dangerous, and many don't realize its lasting consequences.

Consider TikTok. A growing trend called WitchTok has millions of young people sharing videos about casting spells, reading tarot cards, and performing rituals. The videos present witchcraft as being fun and creative. Tutorials teach how to clear bad energy, heal with crystals, and chant affirmations to get what you want. Even more concerning is how these practices are disguised as forms of self-care or wellness.

Books, movies, and music also normalize witchcraft. Popular novels feature witches as heroes who use magic to overcome challenges. Movies and TV shows make witchcraft exciting and relatable. Music often glamorizes the summoning of spirits, the chanting of spells, or a reliance on mystical forces, and many performers use occult symbols in their work. It is no longer shocking because it's so common in the industry.

Witchcraft has permeated everyday life. In addition to sage burning to "cleanse energy," mainstream media address the wearing of crystals for healing and the use of tarot cards for daily guidance.[21] Meditation practices that involve chanting or emptying the mind are presented as being pure, yet they are rooted in evil and open the unsuspecting participants to spiritual danger. Such ideas were once treated with caution, but dream catchers, charms, and even Ouija boards are now sold as decorations or party games.

Practices tied to witchcraft are even creeping into some Christian circles. So-called "Christian yoga" blends faith with techniques from Eastern mysticism. Instead of seeking God, some people call on angels for guidance. These are demonic spirits hiding behind a "Christian" mask.

THE ROOTS OF WITCHCRAFT AND SORCERY

Sorcery is more than spells, curses, and spiritual practices—it is deeply tied to the human desire for control. It is an expression of rebellion against God, a work of the flesh that reflects humanity's fallen nature.

Sorcerers attempt to gain power, manipulate others, or control circumstances apart from God's authority.

First Samuel 15:23 plainly says, "Rebellion is as the sin of witchcraft, and stubbornness is as iniquity and idolatry." This verse shows that witchcraft is a condition of the heart. When we reject God's Word and try to control our lives ourselves, we embrace the very root of witchcraft. Witchcraft is called the "religion of fallen humanity" because it thrives wherever rebellion exists.[22]

In Galatians 5:19–20, Paul lists sorcery as one of the works of the flesh alongside sins like idolatry, hatred, jealousy, and selfish ambitions. More than rituals or supernatural power, sorcery is about the sinful nature that seeks to dominate and defy God's authority.

Years ago I learned from Derek Prince that witchcraft—a work of the flesh—can reveal itself in three ways:

1. Manipulation: Using deception or emotional tactics to control others is a form of witchcraft. It is the subtle twisting of truth to serve personal agendas.

2. Intimidation: Any attempt to instill fear to gain control is rooted in witchcraft. Intimidation is rebellion in action, seeking to overpower others through force or fear.

3. Domination: The desire to dominate and control others, whether through authority or coercion, is another expression of witchcraft. It is rebellion disguised as leadership or power.[23]

Witchcraft also operates as a spiritual power. It is the side most people recognize—spells, curses, and rituals aimed to influence the spiritual realm. Witchcraft uses spiritual forces to gain control, while sorcery often works through physical objects like charms, potions, or talismans. Both are rooted in the same rebellion: rejecting God's authority and seeking power from other sources.

Ultimately, witchcraft and sorcery are the fruit of a rebellious heart. They offer a counterfeit power, promising control and independence but producing spiritual bondage. They are humanity's attempt to appropriate the authority and control that belong to God alone.

WITCHCRAFT IN CHURCH

Witchcraft is often associated with crystals, horoscopes, and spells, but its essence—control, manipulation, and domination—can manifest in churches. This becomes evident when churches are run more like cults than Christ-centered communities. Even without any occult symbols or practices, cultlike behaviors in the church are demonic in nature and deeply harmful to everyone involved.

Dictionary.com defines a cult as "great veneration of a person, ideal, or thing, especially as manifested by a body of admirers... a religion or sect considered to be false, unorthodox, or extremist, with members often living outside of conventional society under the direction of a charismatic leader."[24] Cults such as Jim Jones' Peoples Temple or David Koresh's Branch Davidians have caused tragic losses of life and mass destruction. But cultlike tendencies are also found in less conspicuous and infamous environments, including churches that claim to follow Christ.

Cults often reject orthodox biblical teaching. Jehovah's Witnesses and Mormons openly reject key Christian doctrines such as the Trinity and the sufficiency of Christ's sacrifice, for example. Cults also discourage critical thinking and frequently operate through authoritarian leaders who demand loyalty, suppress dissent, and punish anyone who dares to leave.

Spirits of control and manipulation can operate even in churches that hold to sound doctrine. When leaders act like lords rather than servants, exercising control over people's lives and decisions, they enter into witchcraft. Churches then function like cartels that demand absolute loyalty and punish or curse detractors. Their leaders use fear and intimidation to maintain control; isolate members from their families; and cross boundaries of morality, financial accountability, and personal freedom. They bombard followers with excessive lectures, obsessive praying, and even sleep deprivation to keep their minds in a weakened, compliant state. Brainwashing techniques and the use of short mantras (such as "Just obey your leaders" or "Doubt your doubts") substitute critical thinking with blind submission. Members are often required to make significant sacrifices, yet they are kept in the dark about how their money or efforts are being used.

Whether control is subtle or overt, it is demonic. The Bible teaches *self*-control as a fruit of the Spirit, not control over others. Manipulation is not the way of Jesus; servant leadership is. Jesus never dominated His disciples; He knelt to wash their feet. Authentic Christian leadership reflects humility and empowers others to freely choose their path in following Christ.

People are not demons to be subdued. They are made in the image of God and have free will. If they choose to leave a church or ministry, they should be free to do so without being threatened or shamed. If you find yourself under this kind of leadership, get out. The Spirit of Christ leads with love, not fear. Freedom in Christ means submitting to God, not being enslaved to human leaders. Manipulation, intimidation, and domination are signs of witchcraft. The only dominion we are called to exercise is over sin and demons, not people. Let us follow the example of Jesus, who came to serve rather than control.

NEW AGE BELIEFS AND PRACTICES

Another shade of witchcraft emerges from New Age spirituality, the "eclectic mixture of concepts and practices drawn from Eastern mysticism" and other influences.[25] New Age proponents adopt ideas such as reincarnation, enlightenment, and transcendental meditation. This belief system distorts the truth and attempts to manipulate the spiritual realm while rejecting a living relationship with God through faith in Christ.

A core New Age deception is the belief in multiple lifetimes, known as reincarnation. This gives people the false sense that they have end-less opportunities to "get it right." This lie removes the urgency of repentance and accountability before God. Another significant New Age deception is one Satan sold to Eve: It's the idea that humans are gods who need to remember or be reminded of their godhood.

New Age spirituality promotes the idea that humans are inher-ently good and should avoid negative thoughts. This belief denies the reality of sin and our need for the Savior. It attempts to reduce Christ to an enlightened teacher who achieved "Christ consciousness," and it rejects His deity and role as Savior of the world. Furthermore, it presents the Creator God as an impersonal energy detached from humanity. In the New Age, all religions are valid paths to God, attesting ultimately to a "religion of self" by which we create a false god in our image.

This incredibly dark deception blinds people to the truth. Then bondage traps them in practices that seem harmless or even benefi-cial. Activities such as energy healing, crystal use, tarot reading, yoga, meditation, angel worship, manifestations, and more are now widely normalized in our culture, increasing spiritual confusion.

NEW AGE TO NEW LIFE

My friend Everett's story reveals how New Age spirituality can start as a genuine search for truth but lead to even greater darkness. Everett grew up in an atheist family that never discussed religion and spiri-tuality. Not until high school, after a back injury ended his football career, did Everett begin to ask more profound questions about life.

Everett began studying psychology, philosophy, and meditation. This journey led him to Eastern practices such as Buddhist meditation and transcendental meditation, which were taught at his high school. Seeking to heal his back and improve his mental health, Everett experimented with yoga and dabbled in New Age ideas like the Law of Attraction. His intentions were good: He wanted to find healing for himself and help others overcome their struggles. But he unknowingly entered a tangled spiritual web.

Everett delved deeper and explored supernatural phenomena. He studied energy healing, chakras, and Taoist philosophies about life force energy (known as *chi*). He was fascinated by monks who claimed to channel energy into supernatural feats, even lighting fires with their minds. This eventually led Everett to experiment with psychedelics, including LSD, DMT, and mushrooms, which he believed opened doors to other dimensions and levels of consciousness.

While attending college in the New Age hub of Boulder, Colorado, Everett immersed himself in yoga studios, psychics, and New Age philosophies and became convinced that he would bring healing to humanity and awaken human consciousness. He believed he was fighting an unseen evil force that kept people in bondage, sickness, and despair. Despite Everett's intense spiritual pursuits, however, he felt empty and unfulfilled.

Everett's experiences brought him face-to-face with the dark side of the spiritual realm, including encounters with demonic entities. This led him to seek guidance from a well-known exorcist, Rev. Bob Larson. While Everett was initially skeptical of Christianity, his interactions with Larson and his witnessing of a powerful deliverance challenged his beliefs. Everett ultimately encountered the gospel and came to believe in Jesus Christ. After his conversion, he also experienced deliverance.

NEW AGE WAYS

What makes New Age spirituality so deceptive and attractive is that it looks like Christianity but without the perceived rules and restrictions. Followers feel free to believe whatever they choose as they delve deep into supernatural realms. Although many Christian churches shy away from spiritual topics, the New Age draws people who are spiritually unaware or unrenewed.

Exploring New Age beliefs is like drinking from a toilet—the water looks OK, but it's filthy. Consider what Jesus told the Samaritan woman at the well: "Whoever drinks of this water will thirst again" (John 4:13). The promises of New Age spirituality don't only fail to satisfy; they leave you spiritually sick, bound to lies, and parched.

Only Jesus offers us living water that satisfies completely. (See John 4:14.) And only He is "the way, the truth, and the life" (John 14:6). For our good and the good of others, let's identify some of the New Age's counterfeit tools and practices.

Healing crystals

The use of crystals for "healing" or "positive energy" dates back thousands of years to ancient civilizations including the Egyptians, Greeks, and Romans. These cultures used gemstones for various purposes, including medicinal and spiritual practices.

The Bible mentions crystals but never assigns them mystical properties. Job 28:17 references their value, and Ezekiel 1:22 describes their beauty. The breastplate worn by the Levitical high priest contained twelve stones, each engraved with the name of a tribe of Israel and symbolizing God's covenant with His people. (See Exodus 39:10–13.) Revelation 22:1 reveals that the river described in the new heaven and new earth is as transparent as crystal, showcasing the purity and majesty of God's creation.

Scripture is clear: We do not need crystals or any object to attract wealth, rekindle romance, ward off evil spirits, or connect to the Holy Spirit. Deuteronomy 18:10–12 plainly shows that manipulating the spiritual realm through objects such as crystals amounts to witchcraft and is explicitly condemned by God.

Tarot cards

Tarot cards are also very prominent New Age tools of divination, self-discovery, and guidance for the future. Tarot cards are seen as a gateway to the spiritual realm and are used to connect people with supposed "higher powers," spirit guides, or the user's inner self.

In the New Age, tarot is marketed as a harmless activity involving intuition, energy alignment, and spiritual awakening. The cards' popularity has grown significantly in recent years, partly due to their media portrayal and accessibility through social media and apps. They are intentionally being normalized as a form of spiritual guidance, especially among young people. But behind the colorful artwork and mystique lies a deeper, darker reality.

Tarot cards are an occult method of accessing forbidden spiritual knowledge apart from God. The cards provide more than a "reading" or insight; they invite spiritual entities to operate in the user's life. Deuteronomy 18:10–12 explicitly condemns divination and the seeking of guidance from spiritual sources other than God. Many individuals who have dabbled in tarot experience nightmares, spiritual torment, or oppression until they turn to Christ and sever their occult ties.

Yoga

Yoga is popular today, not only among New Agers but also in mainstream culture. Amazingly, it is one of the most debated topics among Christians. While many people practice yoga for physical fitness or stress relief, its origins and spiritual connections are deeply concerning.

Yoga means "to yoke" or "to unite."[26] The word originates from ancient Hindu texts known as the Vedas, which describe yoga as a spiritual discipline designed to merge one's soul with the universal consciousness, or Brahma, a concept central to Hinduism. Physical poses and strict yoga disciplines were created to facilitate this spiritual union. Their origins were influenced not by divine revelation, as Hindus believe, but by spirits that we recognize as demonic.

Many yoga poses are acts of worship dedicated to Hindu gods and goddesses such as Shiva, Shakti, and Ganesha.[27] While Westernized yoga often presents the poses as mere stretches, the practice remains deeply spiritual. Yoga also heavily incorporates meditation, seeking to connect individuals with their "inner light" or higher consciousness.[28]

Engaging in yoga can open doors to spiritual deception and demonic influence. Practices like Kundalini yoga aim to awaken an "energy force," activate chakras, and achieve enlightenment.[29] This energy is not neutral—it is a spiritual entity. Many who practice Kundalini yoga report manifestations of a snakelike spirit, which brings to mind the demonic imagery often associated with the serpent in the Bible.

Certain types of yoga, such as Bhakti yoga, go even further by requiring participants to chant and summon Hindu gods, which is outright idolatry. Whether or not those involved in this yoga form consciously worship these deities, their willing participation grants demonic spirits the legal right to operate in their lives. What often starts as a search for peace, healing, or self-discovery can result in spiritual bondage or oppression. This is the danger of seeking from demonic spirits what only Jesus Christ can provide.

Hanna has experienced the effects of yoga's deceptions firsthand.[30] The first time I saw her was at a deliverance meeting where she manifested the Hindu goddess Kali, a demon of destruction and death. Hanna's arms flailed, her tongue stuck out, and she lost control of her body as the unclean spirit was exposed. Even en route to the meeting Hanna experienced a sudden suicidal impulse, attempting to open the door of a moving car. She later realized this was the demon's last-ditch effort to prevent her deliverance.

Hanna was raised in a family with roots in Taoism and Buddhism. She was unaware of the spiritual impact of the family's practices, which included visiting fortune tellers and Buddhist temples. For approximately fourteen years Hanna also practiced yoga almost daily and taught it professionally for much of that time, instructing as many as eighteen classes per week. Trained in various yoga styles, including Bikram (hot yoga), Ashtanga, and Sattva, yoga was more than an exercise for Hanna—it was her identity.

However, after being baptized in the Holy Spirit, Hanna began losing her passion for yoga, something she couldn't explain initially. Eventually the Holy Spirit prompted her to throw away her yoga books and materials, which represented a significant financial and emotional investment.

Since her deliverance, Hanna has experienced a profound transformation. She no longer suffers from anxiety attacks. She walks in her God-given authority, enjoys a deeper hunger for Him, and lives a disciplined spiritual life. She fasts, prays, and is fully aware of who she is and whose she is. Hanna's story is a powerful example of how Jesus can redeem and restore even those who become deeply rooted in spiritual darkness. Her testimony also highlights how practices such as yoga lead to demonic oppression.

Meditation

Another form of modern witchcraft is Eastern meditation. Meditation is marketed as a cure-all for stress, anxiety, and even physical health. From apps to corporate wellness programs, everyone seems to be practicing meditation. But the kind of meditation that dominates our culture has roots in Eastern practices (mainly Buddhist meditation). It is spiritually dangerous and entirely at odds with biblical meditation.

According to my count, the Bible speaks about meditation at least twenty-three times, with nineteen mentions found in the Book of Psalms. David, a man after God's heart, knew the power of meditating on God's Word and works, a spiritual practice that focuses the heart and mind on God Himself. (See Isaiah 26:3; Joshua 1:8; Psalm 119:15.)

Buddhist meditation and its modern adaptations take you in the opposite direction, encouraging you to *empty your mind*. The goal is detachment from thoughts, emotions, and even reality itself. Practices like mindfulness and transcendental meditation teach people to focus on breathing, repeating mantras, or becoming "one with the universe."[31]

This might seem harmless and relaxing, but a passive, empty mind is an open door. As Christians, we know that if we don't actively fill our minds with God's truth, the enemy will offer his lies. The

Bible therefore urges us to meditate on God's Word and attach ourselves to Him. Philippians 4:8 instructs us to focus on what is true, noble, right, pure, lovely, and admirable (NIV). Biblical meditation engages the mind and heart in a way that glorifies God and strengthens our faith.

Buddhist meditation shifts worship away from God and turns it inward toward the *self*. It replaces confession and repentance with rituals such as burning candles or focusing on nature. It replaces Scripture with mantras that often take biblical truths out of context. For example, phrases like "I am enough" or "I am loved" are repeated mindlessly and divorced from the reality of God's identity and role in our lives. This self-centered focus feeds the lie that peace can be found apart from God.

Buddhist meditation isn't spiritually empty. It's spiritually dangerous. Many who practice Eastern meditation report altered states of consciousness, out-of-body experiences, or encounters with spiritual entities. This is not a matter of relaxation but of demonic activity. The Bible warns us in 1 Peter 5:8 to be alert and sober-minded because the devil prowls around "like a roaring lion," looking for someone to devour. Meditation that empties the mind invites that lion to come inside.

Biblical meditation is active and intentional. Psalm 119:15 says, "I meditate on your precepts and consider your ways" (NIV). This practice engages the mind in spiritual warfare, strengthens our faith, renews our minds, and draws us closer to God. The world's version of meditation is a counterfeit that offers a peace it cannot deliver. True peace comes from being filled with the Holy Spirit and anchored in God's Word.

Spirit guides

In New Age spirituality, angels (spiritual guides and messengers of light) play a significant role. New Age practitioners frequently claim to communicate with angels for guidance, protection, and enlightenment. Practices like angel card readings, invoking angels during meditation, and calling on "guardian angels" for help are common.

The obsession with angels is not new. Islam began when the prophet Muhammad claimed to receive revelations from the angel Jibril (Gabriel). Similarly, Mormonism started with Joseph Smith's alleged encounter with the angel Moroni, who revealed the supposed location of the Book of Mormon. Both of these religions preach messages that contradict the gospel of Jesus Christ. The apostle Paul warned against this danger, saying, "Even if we or an angel from heaven should preach a gospel other than the one we preached to you, let them be under God's curse!" (Gal. 1:8, NIV).

Hebrews 1:14 says angels are servants of God who minister to His people. As spiritual beings, they assist God, especially in the work of salvation, conveying His word to human beings and attending to the needs of His flock. They always do God's bidding. New Age spirituality distorts this role, turning angels into independent, omniscient beings who can be summoned at will, bypassing God's authority. This approach opens the door to demonic spirits masquerading as angels of light. (See 2 Corinthians 11:14.) Many who seek angelic communication unknowingly welcome spirits that draw them away from God's truth.

An excessive focus on angels distracts us from the centrality of Christ. Angels are not objects of worship. They are created beings who worship and serve God. Satan exploits any misplaced devotion to angels and leads people astray. We must heed Paul's warning about "anyone who delights in false humility and the worship of angels" (Col. 2:18, NIV). Our focus should remain on Christ, the only Mediator between God and humanity. (See 1 Timothy 2:5.) Angels are real and play a role in God's plan, but they are not the source of truth or salvation.

Horoscopes

Astrology might seem purely entertaining, but it veils spiritual dangers. Social media and celebrity endorsements have normalized and marketed zodiac predictions, but astrology is neither fun nor insightful. It is deception, pure and simple.

Seeking guidance from the stars is nothing new. For centuries pagan cultures believed that celestial movements could shape human destiny. The Babylonians were among the earliest practitioners who charted the skies and attributed divine power to the stars. They believed that the alignment of celestial bodies dictated the fate of nations and individuals. Ancient Egyptians linked their agricultural cycles and their concept of the afterlife to the stars, particularly the movements of Sirius and Orion. The Greeks formalized astrology, weaving it into their mythology and shaping the zodiac system, which is still used today. People from Mesopotamia to India venerated the stars as guides.

Because of its association with celestial movements, astrology often masquerades as science. But it differs starkly from astronomy, which studies the planets and stars as God's creation. Astrology uses celestial bodies to predict events and determine personalities, a practice rooted in ancient pagan beliefs.

The word *zodiac* is derived from the Greek *zodiakos kyklos* (meaning "circle of animals").[32] It symbolizes the constellations that are believed to influence human destiny. Such beliefs cause individuals to trust in the creation rather than the Creator.

Scripture explicitly warns against such practices. In Isaiah 47:13–14, God condemns Babylon's reliance on astrologers, stating that their predictions cannot save them from judgment. Deuteronomy 18:10–12 categorizes astrology with detestable practices such as witchcraft and divination. Second Chronicles 33:1–6 ties King Manasseh's engagement with astrology and the worship of heavenly bodies directly to evil. These scriptures make clear that astrology is not an innocent, neutral pastime but a spiritual counterfeit. It manifests spiritual danger in three major ways:

- It diverts trust from God, violating the command to worship Him alone.

- It fosters a fatalistic mindset, convincing people that their lives are predetermined by the stars (contrary to the Bible's teaching that God's will and our choices shape our destiny).

- It aligns with occult practices, which can open portals to demonic oppression.

I was privileged to interview Angela Ucci, a former astrologer and "star seer" whose life has been completely transformed by the power of Jesus Christ.[33] Angela became deeply entrenched in New Age practices in 2014, when her beloved grandmother suddenly died. Overcome by grief, Angela sought to connect with her grandmother's spirit, which led her to psychic mediums and a spiral into New Age practices.

Angela's testimony is shocking and powerful. Through years of tarot cards, crystals, and spirit channeling, she was deceived into believing that she was communicating with her grandmother. Not recognizing the deception, Angela became engrossed in astrology, even creating a podcast to share her astrological insights.

Despite her outward success and spiritual pursuits, Angela felt emptier than ever, culminating in a moment of despair where she almost ended her life. At her lowest point, Angela cried out to Jesus, saying, "Jesus, save me." Immediately she experienced an overwhelming peace that she had never known.

Years of torment had ended, but Angela's journey didn't end there. Led to repent, she gave up her New Age practices, burned her tarot cards and crystals, and abandoned her astrology podcast. Angela experienced deliverance, even casting out the spirit that masqueraded as her grandmother. Today she boldly proclaims the gospel and exposes the lies of the New Age through her podcast, *Heaven and Healing*.[34]

Necromancy

In the current culture, talking to the dead has been broadly normalized. From TV shows like *Long Island Medium* and *Crossing Over with John Edward* to celebrities openly discussing their visits to psychics and mediums, the idea of communicating with deceased loved ones is portrayed as comforting and empowering. Hollywood has made necromancy seem like an innocent way to gain closure, guidance, or reassurance from beyond the grave. However, what is marketed as harmless entertainment or exploration is dangerous and rooted in witchcraft.

The human desire to communicate with the dead has a long history. Ancient cultures often used necromancy to seek power, knowledge, or comfort. Ancient Egyptian priests conducted rituals to interact with spirits, believing the dead could influence the living world. The Greeks consulted oracles, who claimed to channel the spirits of the dead to predict the future or offer divine advice. These practices were always tied to the occult, involving rituals, invocations, and sacrifices that opened spiritual doors to dark forces. What many saw as wisdom or power often led to fear, chaos, and bondage because they had unknowingly invited demonic influences into their lives.

God's stance on necromancy is unambiguous. In Deuteronomy 18:10–12, He condemns it along with other "abominations." This warning is protective. Such practices are forbidden because they invite darkness and oppose God's order.

One of the most striking examples of necromancy in Scripture is the story of King Saul. When Saul's disobedience interfered with his ability to hear from God, he asked a medium to summon the prophet Samuel. (See 1 Samuel 28:3–19.) Saul sought direction concerning the ongoing warfare. What he received was a harsh rebuke and message of judgment, confirming that his life and reign were about to end in spiritual ruin.

Today's culture might treat necromancy as entertainment or self-help, but it remains a form of witchcraft, a counterfeit that offers hope but delivers only spiritual darkness.

Ouija boards

The Ouija board is specifically designed to act as a medium for contacting the spirit world, including the dead. Today, the Ouija board represents casual entertainment. It is marketed as a harmless party game, a way to dabble in what is mysterious or supernatural. Movies like *Ouija* and *Ouija: Origin of Evil* glamorize its use, portraying dramatic spirit encounters as fun, spooky activities. However, this playful packaging conceals a far darker history of opening dangerous spiritual doors.

The Ouija board was first marketed in 1890, at the height of the Spiritualist movement. It was created to connect people with the spirit realm. Designed as a flat board with letters, numbers, and words like *yes*, *no*, and *goodbye* printed on it, the board was paired with a movable planchette on which participants placed their fingers while asking questions. They then waited for answers to be spelled out as the planchette was allegedly guided by unseen forces.

The use of Ouija boards continues to yield disturbing outcomes. In March 2023, twenty-eight Colombian schoolgirls were hospitalized after playing with a Ouija board and experiencing symptoms of anxiety and fainting.[35] Similarly, thirty-six students suffered "convulsions, temporary loss of sight and anxiety after reportedly using a Ouija board."[36] The most infamous incident occurred between 2006 and 2007 at a Catholic girls' school near Mexico City, where hundreds of students suffered from unexplained symptoms such as difficulty walking and recurring trance states after using Ouija boards.[37] These incidents are not coincidences—they reveal the dangerous spiritual reality behind what many consider to be a harmless activity.

The Bible is unequivocal in its warnings about such practices.

Isaiah 8:19 asks, "Should not a people seek their God? Should they seek the dead on behalf of the living?" Scripture warns that in the latter days people will be drawn to "deceiving spirits and doctrines of demons" (1 Tim. 4:1). The use of Ouija boards is a deception that offers insight but delivers spiritual darkness.

Instead of seeking the dead, God calls us to seek Him, the living God, who holds all wisdom, truth, and comfort. True peace and guidance cannot be found in the occult or through tools like the Ouija board. They are found only in a relationship with our Creator, who loves us and desires to lead us in paths of righteousness and safety. The thrill of the unknown is never worth the risk of spiritual harm.

Dream catchers

Dream catchers are rooted in Native American spirituality and traditionally thought to filter out bad dreams as a person sleeps. Each catcher is crafted from a willow hoop, is adorned with feathers and other decorations, and has a woven web or net inside the hoop.[38] According to legend, a spider gifted the web as a protective charm to a grandmother, promising to catch any bad thoughts that came as she slept. This deeply cultural practice is also tied to occult beliefs, making it spiritually dangerous.

People often hang dream catchers above their beds. This attempt to manipulate the spiritual realm aligns with idolatry and witchcraft rather than reliance on God. The Bible strongly warns against bringing objects associated with pagan or occult practices into our homes. Deuteronomy 7:25–26 states, "You shall burn the carved images of their gods with fire; you shall not covet the silver or gold that is on them, nor take it for yourselves, lest you be snared by it; for it is an abomination to the LORD your God. Nor shall you bring an abomination into your house, lest you be doomed to destruction like it." This passage reminds us that objects tied to false spiritual beliefs can act as snares and open doors to demons.

While dream catchers are often marketed as benign decorations or cultural artifacts, their roots and intended purpose are far from harmless. They do not protect their users but can invite nightmares, demonic attacks, and spiritual darkness.

Amulets and talismans

Amulets and talismans are often worn as jewelry and are believed to provide protection or luck, with symbols such as the "evil eye" commonly featured. Similarly, zodiac symbols, such as necklaces or bracelets displaying astrological signs, are thought to harness celestial power and influence fate. Lucky charms such as rabbits' feet, four-leaf clovers, or specific stones are often marketed as tools for gaining prosperity or protection.

Like all items and practices that attempt to manipulate the spiritual realm, amulets and talismans can serve as demonic traps. As Psalm 91:1 declares, "He who dwells in the secret place of the Most High shall abide under the shadow of the Almighty." We are not called to seek luck but to seek God's favor, which is granted when we humble ourselves before Him and trust in His sovereignty. Relying on occultic objects denies the sufficiency of God and opens us to spiritual deception.

SANTERÍA

Earlier in this chapter we read how John Ramirez became involved with Santería, a religion blending African spiritual practices and Roman Catholicism.[39] *Santería* means "the way of the saints." While this seemingly indicates something harmless, Santería is inseparable from witchcraft and revolves around worshipping powerful spirits called orishas.[40] Followers believe these spirits control aspects of life but also depend on human worship and sacrifices (often through animal rituals) for survival.

Santería began in Cuba when enslaved Africans merged their outlawed spiritual beliefs with Catholicism to protect their traditional practices. Orishas were disguised as Catholic saints such as Saint Barbara and Our Lady of Charity, creating a false sense of religious legitimacy. Today, followers use rituals, charms, and animal sacrifices to gain the favor of orishas, hoping for blessings in health, prosperity, or guidance. But the Bible warns against such practices, calling them abominations in passages like Deuteronomy 18:10–12.

Santería's use of Catholic imagery misleads many people into thinking the religion is aligned with Christianity. However, its focus on gaining power and blessings from spirits rather than God's grace separates Santería from Christianity and aligns it with witchcraft. Therefore, Santería rituals are not harmless traditions. In a 1993 Supreme Court case, Justice Kennedy described the religion's practice of animal sacrifice as a key part of its worship.[41] Those who have left Santería reveal the darkness behind its practices. Many people report spiritual torment, nightmares, and demonic oppression that only lifted when they turned to Jesus Christ.

As Jesus said when He was tempted by Satan, "You shall worship the LORD your God, and Him only you shall serve" (Luke 4:8). Santería and all forms of witchcraft are counterfeits of God's truth. Jesus' sacrifice is enough, and He alone holds the power to bring lasting peace and purpose.

WAR ON WITCHCRAFT

Witchcraft ensnares souls and is aligned to the devil's mission to steal, kill, and destroy. (See John 10:10.) Witchcraft works to snatch the human mind, will, and emotions and drag us into darkness masked as enlightenment.

Out of love for His people, God has declared war against dark practices. He spoke through His prophet Ezekiel words that reverberate to this day: "Behold, I am against your magic charms by which you hunt souls....I will tear them from your arms, and let the souls go, the souls you hunt like birds. I will also tear off your veils and deliver My people out of your hand" (Ezek. 13:20–21). This prophecy declares God's heart. He is 100 percent opposed to the works of witchcraft, and He is 100 percent for us. He fights to liberate us from occult snares and deliver us into His marvelous light.

Jesus Christ didn't come to help us cope with the enemy's grip. He came to utterly destroy the works of darkness, redeem what was lost, break every chain, and set captives free. Witchcraft is real, and it's deadly, yet whatever power it boasts pales in comparison to the authority of Jesus Christ. His light dispels every shadow, His truth silences every lie, and His Spirit breaks every curse.

If you feel trapped by the snares of the occult, please hear this: God's power is greater. His love is deeper. And His deliverance is here. Today is the day to renounce every connection to witchcraft and receive the freedom only Jesus can give. Come into the light. Let go of the veils, charms, and bondage. There is a Savior who is stronger than any spell—a Shepherd who rescues souls from the lion's mouth. He is Jesus, and He is calling you to freedom.

CHAPTER 9

DON'T DOMESTICATE DEMONS

Deliverance hinges on a simple but powerful truth: You can't conquer what you won't confront. The enemy thrives in the shadows of denial, secrecy, and compromise. Making covenants with what we're called to conquer only domesticates demons, allowing them to live with us, manage us, and influence our lives. Instead of walking in victory, we become entangled in agreements that weaken our authority. Yes, God will deliver us from our enemies. But He will not deliver us from our "pet friends."

Consider the story of Joshua and the Gibeonites in Joshua 9. Joshua was anointed to conquer the land and eliminate Israel's enemies. Through deception, however, the Gibeonites tricked him into a covenant of protection. They disguised themselves as harmless travelers from a faraway land. Believing the lie, Joshua made a covenant with them—without first consulting God. When he discovered the true identity of the "travelers," it was too late. The covenant had already bound him to protect what God had told him to destroy.

For many of us, this story mirrors reality. Through ignorance, fear, or deception we allow sin, compromise, and even demonic influences to infiltrate our lives. Instead of confronting these intruders, we make room for them. We justify the habit, excuse the relationship, or rationalize the mindset. And like Joshua, we find ourselves tied to what we were called to conquer.

THE DANGER OF DOMESTICATION

Domesticating demons means normalizing dysfunction. Instead of addressing spiritual roots, we accommodate torment, oppression, or addiction. A person battling pornography might justify their struggle as something "everyone deals with." They try to manage it through willpower, but the spiritual root remains. This was my own story for years. I prayed, fasted, and repented, yet the bondage persisted. It wasn't until I recognized the spiritual nature of the struggle and confronted it through deliverance that true freedom came.

Some believers tolerate a spirit of fear, labeling it "anxiety" or "nervousness." They live with chronic worry, nightmares, or phobias, believing it's part of their personality. Fear becomes a squatter in their soul. Instead of terminating fear, they tolerate it.

Whatever you tolerate, you permit to stay. You might recognize generational patterns of divorce, poverty, or addiction but chalk them up to bad luck or genetics. Instead of addressing the spiritual roots, you accept the issue as your portion. Like the Kennedy curse, these patterns persist until someone stands up and confronts the enemy. Someone needs to cancel curses rather than justifying them.

GOD CAN'T HEAL WHAT YOU HIDE

Deliverance is for the desperate. Just as the Holy Spirit fills those who thirst, God delivers those who cry for freedom. But as long as you give your demons cover, you'll live in bondage. Consider the man at the pool of Bethesda. Jesus asked him, "Do you want to be made well?" (John 5:6). That question cuts through every excuse, justification, or temptation to surrender. Deliverance begins when we answer, "Yes, Lord."

Downplaying an issue, rationalizing our sin, or refusing to acknowledge spiritual strongholds ties God's hands. Deliverance requires transparency and confrontation. We have to face life's losses and disappointments, not bury them in graveyards that conceal them from our conscious view. Avoidance strategies only invite demonic spirits to exploit and oppress us.

- A woman holding on to bitterness after a betrayal might feel justified in her pain. But unforgiveness opens the door to torment, as Jesus warned in Matthew 18:34. Until she releases the bitterness, the "torturers" (demons) maintain legal access to her life.

- A man who experienced abuse as a child might unknowingly harbor a spirit of rejection or fear. Instead of seeking healing, he builds emotional walls, isolating himself and perpetuating the enemy's hold.

- Families bound by cycles of poverty, sickness, or addiction often fail to recognize the spiritual component of their struggles. They fight the symptoms (financial lack, medical bills, etc.) but never address the curse that keeps the cycles alive.

Deliverance is a divine exchange. Jesus came to "destroy the works of the devil" (1 John 3:8). He delivers us not so we can manage our demons but so we can live in victory. Just as He drove the merchants out of the temple in Matthew 21:12, Jesus cleanses every corner of our lives. But He won't force His way in—we have to open the door.

Let's not repeat Joshua's mistake by making covenants with our enemies. Let's confront and conquer the enemy by walking in the authority and freedom Christ purchased for us. What we tolerate, we empower. But what we confront, we conquer. The choice is ours.

DELIVERANCE STARTS WITH REVELATION: GOD WANTS TO HELP YOU

Freedom begins with the revelation that *God wants to set you free more than you want to be free.* He sees your pain and the cycle that has you stuck, He understands the hopelessness you feel, and He loves you.

God's desire for your deliverance is rooted in His compassion, justice, and promise to war against the enemy of your soul.

When humanity first sinned, God didn't curse Adam and Eve directly. Instead, He cursed the ground and childbearing as consequences of sin. He did, however, directly curse Satan. In Genesis 3:15, God declared war on the serpent, promising that the Seed of the woman (Jesus) would crush his head (NIV). From the beginning God has been on the side of freedom, redemption, and restoration. He is at war with the devil and his schemes, and His heart is for His people to be free so they can serve Him fully. (See Exodus 8:1.)

While we must repent of sin and get right with God, we must also understand that our God is for us. He is on the side of freedom, not bondage. He fights for our deliverance because He loves us and longs for us to live in the fullness of His purpose.

GOD, THE DELIVERER; DEMONS, THE "AMALEKITES"

Israel's deliverance from Egypt provides a powerful picture of God's heart for freedom. When His children were enslaved, God destroyed Egypt's gods through signs and wonders. (See Exodus 3:20; Psalm 135:8–9.) Finally, in Exodus 14:27–28, God crushed Pharaoh and his entire army in the Red Sea. The Israelites didn't have to fight for their deliverance because God fought for them. (See Exodus 14:14.)

After the exodus, a new enemy arose against Israel: the Amalekites. This opportunistic, ruthless tribe attacked Israel's rear guard, preying on the weak and weary, according to Deuteronomy 25:17–18. But God didn't let this assault go unpunished. Joshua defeated the Amalekites in battle, and Moses built an altar, declaring the name of the Lord as Jehovah Nissi, "The-Lord-Is-My-Banner" (Exod. 17:15). God vowed to blot out the memory of Amalek from under heaven and declared that He would be at war with Amalek from generation to generation. (See Exodus 17:14, 16.) God is passionate about defending, delivering, and restoring His people.

Demons are also passionate, but about attacking God's people. In

Deuteronomy 25:18, the Amalekites attacked Israel from behind and picked off the stragglers. Demons are equally opportunistic and ruthless in exploiting weaknesses. They target the weary, discouraged, vulnerable, isolated, and defenseless. They prey on unresolved trauma, bitterness, or unchecked sin. They thrive in the shadows of our pain and vulnerabilities, seeking to destroy us from the inside out.

Thankfully, God is better at delivering us than we are at getting bound! He doesn't abandon His children to their enemies. As He did with the Amalekites, He will conquer the demons that attack His people. Psalm 52:5 declares that God will uproot evil from its place. Psalm 37:9 promises that evildoers will be cut off. God is actively engaged in the battle against evil and committed to setting His people free.

JESUS CAME TO SET THE CAPTIVES FREE

Jesus Christ is the ultimate proof of God's desire to deliver. Jesus is God in the flesh, and His mission on earth was to set the captives free. (See Luke 4:18.) Wherever He went, Jesus healed the sick, delivered the oppressed, and broke the power of sin and Satan. Acts 10:38 declares that He healed "all who were oppressed by the devil." He ultimately "disarmed principalities and powers," making "a public spectacle of them" through His victory on the cross (Col. 2:15). And He declared, "If the Son sets you free, you will be free indeed" (John 8:36, NIV).

Jesus wasn't worried about His deliverance ministry upsetting religious leaders. When He set free the man plagued by a legion of demons, the entire city asked Jesus to leave. (See Mark 5:16–17.) Their rejection did not bother Jesus, however. He remained focused on freeing the man who desperately needed Him.

On the cross, Jesus took the curse upon Himself to free us. (See Galatians 3:13.) He paid the ultimate price so we could walk in freedom from sin and from every form of oppression. Our hope in Christ is clear in Romans 8:11: The same delivering, victorious power that raised Him from the dead now works in us!

Because of what Jesus did, there is hope and help for you. No matter how deep the bondage or how relentless the attack, God is greater. Psalm 34:17 promises, "The righteous cry out, and the LORD hears, and delivers them out of all their troubles." Deliverance isn't for a select few; it's the inheritance of every child of God. So, take heart and let Jesus be the Lord your Banner, Healer, and Deliverer. He is mighty to save.

GOD'S MERCY IN OUR WEAKNESS

Remember that God personally declared war on the Amalekites, yet Saul disobeyed the order to totally annihilate them. At Ziklag they mercilessly attacked the people of God. At the time, David had reached a breaking point after being pursued by King Saul for years. Convinced that Saul would kill him, David sought refuge in enemy territory, saying, "The best thing I can do is to escape to the land of the Philistines" (1 Sam. 27:1, NIV). Turning to the Philistines brought temporary relief from Saul's threats, but the compromise exacted a high cost for David, his family, and God's people.

While in Philistine territory, David made decisions that led him further away from God. He aligned himself with Achish, an uncircumcised ruler of Gath, and became a mercenary, fighting not for God's glory but for personal benefit. To maintain his position, David even resorted to lies and deceit. There are no recorded psalms from David during this time, which speaks to how far he had drifted.

The consequences of David's compromise came crashing down in 1 Samuel 30, when the Amalekites attacked Ziklag while David and his men were away in battle. The marauders burned the city to the ground, taking everything—all their wives, children, and possessions. The destruction David feared did not come from Saul but from his own choices. What David thought would bring peace brought unimaginable pain.

Yet David's story reveals God's incredible mercy, which shines brightest in our darkest moments. Faced with the devastation of

Ziklag, David could have remained paralyzed by shame or despair. But he didn't. He "strengthened himself in the LORD his God" (1 Sam. 30:6). Despite his long drift, David knew where his help came from. He sought God's guidance, asking, "Shall I pursue this raiding party? Will I overtake them?" (1 Sam. 30:8, NIV). God's response was full of mercy and power: "Pursue, for you shall surely overtake them and without fail recover all" (1 Sam. 30:8).

God didn't just forgive David; He empowered him. David's failures didn't disqualify him from receiving God's deliverance. Instead, God used David's repentance and reliance on Him to bring a miraculous victory. David pursued the Amalekites, defeated them, recovered everything that had been stolen, and took additional plunder.

DON'T QUIT—PURSUE, OVERTAKE, AND RECOVER

David's story reminds us of God's heart for restoration. Even when we compromise and bring trouble upon ourselves, God stands ready to intervene. He doesn't excuse our sins but saves us from them. He doesn't overlook our bondage; He breaks the chains. God's mercy is available, and His power is sufficient.

Many of us have had our "David moments." Consider the father who struggled with addiction, losing his family in the process. When he finally cried out to God, he experienced personal freedom and the restoration of his relationship with his children. The same is true of the wife who suffered betrayal in her marriage and felt that her life was over. When she turned to God for healing, she found the strength to fight for her family—and her marriage was restored. Don't forget the young man caught in the grip of pornography. He believed he could never break free, but through deliverance and God's grace he overcame and discovered a new purpose for his life.

The same God who delivered David also promises to restore what has been lost in our lives. Joel 2:25 declares, "I will restore to you the years that the swarming locust has eaten." So take heart! God's word to you is the same as it was to David: "Pursue, overtake, and recover all." This is not a time to give up, accept defeat, or believe the lie that you are too far gone. Strengthen yourself in the Lord. Seek Him with all your heart. His mercy is endless, His power is unmatched, and His desire for your freedom never wavers. He will empower you to rise up and reclaim what the enemy has stolen.

THE POWER IS AVAILABLE TO YOU NOW

The biblical model for deliverance is most powerfully demonstrated in the ministry of Jesus, who set the captives free with a word, breaking the chains of darkness and restoring lives. (See Matthew 8:16; Luke 4:18.) But here is the truth that you need to hold on to today: *That same power is available to you, right where you are, right now.* He has provided everything your victory requires. Consider it your spiritual arsenal.

The name of Jesus

Jesus' name is mighty, not only in the mouth of a seasoned preacher but also in your mouth. Demons tremble at Jesus' name because it carries the full authority of heaven to break chains and shatter the works of darkness. (See Philippians 2:9–11.) You can call on that name right now and experience the power of His deliverance.

The blood of Jesus

Also in your spiritual arsenal is the blood of Jesus. Revelation 12:11 declares, "They [God's people] overcame him [the accuser] by the blood of the Lamb and by the word of their testimony." The blood Jesus shed on the cross didn't lose its power after the resurrection. It remains as potent today as it was when He cried, "It is finished!" (John 19:30). Jesus' blood has already paid for your deliverance. Hebrews 12:24 says His blood speaks a better word over your life—a word that silences the enemy's accusations. When you apply Jesus' blood by faith, the devil must flee.

The Word of God

God's Word is your sword—sharp and powerful, able to pierce the darkness and dismantle strongholds. (See Hebrews 4:12.) When Jesus was tempted by Satan in the wilderness, He wielded the Word, countering every lie of the enemy with "It is written" (Matt. 4:4, 6, 7, 10). That same Word becomes a weapon of light against the powers of darkness when you speak it. Declare it boldly over your life, and watch it break through the enemy's lies.

The Holy Spirit

The Holy Spirit is not a weapon but God Himself, who empowers and equips you for the battle. He is the commander of the Lord's armies, the One who brings the kingdom of God to bear on the enemy's kingdom. His power sets free "those who are bound" (Isa. 61:1). Remember, the same power that raised Jesus from the dead lives in you—here and now. Through the Holy Spirit the authority of Jesus is enforced in your life. His presence within you guarantees victory.

Please hear this, loud and clear: *You can experience freedom today.* The power of Jesus' name, His blood, His Word, and His Spirit are fully available to you. Right now you can take a step of faith and declare, "In the name of Jesus, I renounce every lie of the enemy. I apply the blood of Jesus over my life. I speak the Word of God, which declares that I am free. And I welcome the power of the Holy Spirit to fill every part of me."

Imagine someone who is locked in a prison cell but also has the key. That cell door will open when the person inside the cell turns the key in the lock. That's how deliverance works. God has provided the name and blood of Jesus, His Word, and His Spirit. But you must step out in faith to use it.

I once met a woman who had been tormented for years by fear and depression. She felt helpless, as though nothing could break the cycle of darkness. One day, as she listened to a sermon about the power of Jesus' name, something clicked. She didn't wait for someone to pray over her. She simply declared the name of Jesus over her mind and emotions—right there in her living room! She applied the blood of Jesus to her life, spoke scriptures about freedom and peace, and invited the Holy Spirit to take control.

That day, the torment lifted, and she experienced the peace of God for the first time in years. What changed? She realized that the power wasn't only available to someone else—it was available *to her*.

You don't have to wait for the perfect moment or setting. The power of God is here now, and it is sufficient. Jesus said in John 8:36, "If the Son sets you free, you will be free indeed" (NIV). You don't have to earn that freedom or beg to experience it. You receive it by faith. The prison doors are open, and the chains are broken. So step into the freedom Jesus paid for you to experience.

WHEN SELF-DELIVERANCE IS NOT ENOUGH

Self-deliverance is a wonderful tool that God has made available to His people. It allows us to experience freedom from demonic oppression through personal repentance, prayer, and submission to the Holy Spirit. The same power that raised Jesus from the dead empowers us to confront the enemy directly. Many people experience significant breakthroughs through self-deliverance, testifying to the authority believers have in Christ.

We will explore self-deliverance in chapter 10, but before we do, let's establish some key points. First, self-deliverance is powerful, but it won't always be enough to fully resolve demonic strongholds. In cases where strongholds are deeply entrenched (as with generational curses, trauma, or deeply rooted sin) people often need the help of an anointed minister to facilitate their deliverance.

The biblical pattern frequently involves someone with spiritual authority to cast out demons. For example, Jesus delivered the Gadarene demoniac, who was powerless to free himself from the legion of spirits tormenting him. (See Mark 5:1–20.) Similarly, Paul cast the spirit of divination out of the slave girl in Acts 16:16–18. Jesus never instructed people to cast demons out of themselves; in

Mark 16:17, He commissioned His followers to cast demons out of other people.

Several signs can reveal when self-deliverance is not enough. Persistent demonic manifestations (despite personal prayer), recurring torment (such as nightmares or physical sensations), the inability to break free from addictions or sin (despite genuine repentance), and resistance to spiritual growth often point to deeper spiritual hindrances that require the intervention of someone with authority in deliverance ministry.

Our ministry has seen many people attempt self-deliverance and experience some level of breakthrough. However, they often discover that their efforts prepared them for the complete freedom they later experienced while working with an anointed minister. Some people break through surface-level oppression through fasting and prayer but discover that the root cause stubbornly remains. Their attempts at self-deliverance are not wasted; by the time they seek ministerial assistance, they are more spiritually open and desperate for freedom, which creates fertile ground for God's power to move.

Every situation is unique. Imagine a soldier on the battlefield who's been shot in the leg. His training might help him to stop the bleeding with a tourniquet. He might even be able to extract the bullet. But if the bullet is in too deep, has struck an artery, or is too close to vital organs, that soldier will need an experienced medic to perform surgery, prevent infection, control bleeding, and possibly save him from perishing.

Someone struggling with demonic oppression can pray, fast, rebuke spirits, or use Scripture as a kind of tourniquet. These efforts might bring a measure of relief. But for more profound spiritual issues, using self-deliverance is like trying to perform surgery on yourself. You're in no position to see the full picture or address the root problem. You need an anointed deliverance minister, a spiritual "surgeon" who can do what you cannot do for yourself.

There is no shame in seeking help. Dentists don't fill their own cavities. Eye surgeons wouldn't dream of operating on their own eyes. When the Israelites were enslaved in Egypt, they needed Moses. Those oppressed by demons in the Gospels needed Jesus to bring them freedom.

If you've attempted self-deliverance and experienced some level of breakthrough, don't just try harder—seek help. It takes humility to ask another person to guide you through deliverance. Even deliverance ministers sometimes need the help of other ministers. There should be no regret or shame in seeking the help Jesus offers. Your freedom is worth it!

....

CHAPTER 10

SELF-DELIVERANCE PRAYERS AND DECLARATIONS

A s WE HAVE seen, you can experience healing without having someone else pray for you. You can even receive the precious gift of salvation without a preacher or another believer physically present. Deliverance can happen through a video, a phone call, or even a book. The power of deliverance doesn't rely on methods but on our mighty, God-given spiritual arsenal: the name of Jesus, the blood of Jesus, the Word of God, and the Holy Spirit. (See chapter 9.) These are available to every believer and are able to break the chains of demonic oppression.

Remember that deliverance is not a passive experience; it is a face-to-face confrontation with the devil. This chapter is designed to guide you through the process, equipping you with prayers and steps to confront the enemy and walk in the freedom Christ has already won for you. So let's enter into the deliverance God has promised by taking our first step.

STEP 1: RECOGNIZE THE NEED FOR DELIVERANCE

First, you must recognize your need. As believers, we can normalize demonic influence to the point that we fail to detect the strongholds fighting us. Jesus addressed this oversight with people who believed in Him and claimed they had "never been in bondage to anyone" (John 8:33). They had faith, but their history was filled with bondage. Deception clouded their judgment, as it often clouds ours.

When you need freedom, realizing that you need it is the most challenging part. But once you take that step, you are halfway to deliverance. Acknowledging demonic activity or open doors is vital to breaking free.

Prayers for recognizing the need for deliverance

"Search me, O God, and know my heart; try me, and know my anxieties; and see if there is any wicked way in me, and lead me in the way everlasting" (Ps. 139:23–24).

Lord Jesus, I acknowledge that You are my Deliverer. I believe You came to set the captives free and destroy the works of the enemy. I place my trust in Your power to break every chain in my life.

Father, I ask You to reveal anything in my life that has opened a door to the enemy. Shine Your light into the hidden places of my heart and show me where I need Your deliverance. I repent of any sins, actions, or agreements that have allowed darkness to take root in my life. Help me to close these doors and walk in freedom.

Lord, I humble myself before You and admit that I cannot fight this battle alone. I surrender every part of my life to You. Teach me to trust in Your strength, for Your Word says that where Your Spirit is, there is freedom (2 Cor. 3:17, NIV). *Set me free and lead me to live in Your truth.*

STEP 2: REPENT OF ANY KNOWN SINS

Repentance is one of the most powerful tools God has given us, the key to closing doors that sin has opened to the enemy. If sin opens a door to hell beneath you, repentance opens heaven's windows above you. Repentance is not simply saying "I'm sorry"; it involves a heartfelt turning away from sin and a turning toward God. It means acknowledging your wrongdoing, renouncing it, feeling genuine sorrow for it, and committing to walk in obedience to God.

Repentance was the cornerstone of John the Baptist's message, the essence of Jesus' preaching and His command to His disciples. In Matthew 3:2, John declared, "Repent, for the kingdom of heaven is at hand!" Jesus echoed this in Mark 1:15, saying, "Repent, and believe in the gospel." Repentance is not a mere moment but a lifestyle that keeps the windows of heaven open over your life.

Prayers of repentance

Lord Jesus, I come before You in humility, acknowledging my sin. I have fallen short of Your glory and walked in ways that grieved Your heart. I confess my sins to You, and I ask for Your forgiveness. Wash me clean with Your blood and renew my spirit. I turn away from my sin and turn toward You. Help me to walk in obedience and live a life that honors You. In Jesus' name, amen.

Lord Jesus, I confess that I am a sinner in need of Your grace. I believe You died on the cross for my sins and rose again to give me new life. I confess You as my Lord and Savior. I surrender my life to You and ask You to come into my heart. Lead me, guide me, and fill me with Your Holy Spirit. Thank You for saving me and making me Your child. In Your name I pray. Amen.

Father, I come before You, confessing the sins of my ancestors. I repent of any wickedness, idolatry, or rebellion they committed that opened doors to the enemy in my family line. I renounce every generational curse and sinful pattern passed down to me. I plead the blood of Jesus over my life and my family. Lord, let Your forgiveness flow and break every chain. Set me and my household free. In Jesus' name, amen.

Lord Jesus, I confess and repent of any involvement in the occult, whether through curiosity, ignorance, or deliberate actions. I renounce every pact, ritual, or agreement made with darkness. I renounce all practices of witchcraft, divination, astrology, and anything that dishonored You. I plead the blood of Jesus over my life, breaking all ties with the kingdom of darkness. Forgive me, Lord, and cleanse me completely. I declare You as my Lord and Savior. In Jesus' name, amen.

Father, I come before You to confess [name the specific sin]. *I recognize how it has grieved Your heart and opened doors to the enemy. I renounce this sin and ask for Your forgiveness. Close every door this sin has opened in my life. Please strengthen me to resist temptation. I thank You for Your mercy and grace, which restore me to You. In Jesus' name, amen.*

STEP 3: RENOUNCE CURSES, OATHS, COVENANTS, AND SOUL TIES

Renouncing is a critical step in breaking free from demonic influence and severing ties with the kingdom of darkness. To renounce means to cancel a contract or disown a connection. Spiritually, it means declaring that you are cutting off every agreement or bond that has connected you to demonic forces. Exodus 23:32 says, "You shall make no covenant with them, nor with their gods." Renouncing fulfills this command by canceling any spiritual covenants that have given the enemy access to your life, whether you entered them knowingly or not.

In 2 Corinthians 4:2, Paul says, "We have renounced the hidden things of shame, not walking in craftiness nor handling the word of God deceitfully, but by manifestation of the truth commending ourselves to every man's conscience in the sight of God." The Greek word for *renounce* means to forbid, give up, disown, or "say off for oneself" something that was previously agreed to and brought harmful consequences.[1] It is a spiritual declaration that you are no longer in partnership with what opposes God. Renouncing severs connections with the demonic, revokes any access the enemy had, and allows you to reclaim your freedom in Christ.

Prayers of renunciation

In the name of Jesus, I renounce all agreements I have made with Satan and his demons. I cancel every pact, contract, or covenant made knowingly or unknowingly, and I declare that I am free by the blood of Jesus. I reject all allegiance to the kingdom of darkness and declare my allegiance to Jesus Christ alone. Amen.

In the name of Jesus, I renounce all lust, sexual perversion, immorality, unclean conversations, fantasies, tormenting dreams, and every unclean spirit with which I have made a pact. I break every connection with pornography, fornication, adultery, and every form of sexual sin. I reject and renounce every spirit of incubus, succubus, and all spirits tied to sexual immorality. I declare myself free by the power of the Holy Spirit. Amen.

I renounce and rebuke all witchcraft, sorcery, divination, tarot cards, astrology, Ouija boards, séances, spiritism, and occult practices. I reject all curses, spells, incantations, rituals, and ceremonies. I cancel every connection with the demonic through these practices and declare that the blood of Jesus covers me. All ties to the occult are severed in Jesus' name. Amen.

In the name of Jesus, I renounce every ungodly soul tie I have formed through relationships, emotional bonds, or sexual activity. I break every unhealthy connection and release myself from every person with whom I have formed these ties. I ask the Holy Spirit to cleanse my emotions, mind, and spirit and fully restore me to wholeness. I return any part of others that has remained with me and reclaim all parts of myself that I have lost through ungodly soul ties. I seal this with the blood of Jesus. Amen.

Father, in the name of Jesus, I renounce all hatred, anger, bitterness, envy, resentment, and unforgiveness in my heart. I release everyone who has wronged me, and I forgive them fully as You have forgiven me. I reject every spirit of offense, division, and hostility, and I declare freedom in my relationships. Fill me with Your peace and love. Amen.

I renounce every spirit of addiction in my life. I reject the demonic influence behind alcohol, drugs (both prescription and illegal), nicotine, gambling, pornography, and any other substance or behavior that has enslaved me. I sever every chain of bondage and declare myself free in Jesus' name. Lord, help me to walk in self-control and the fullness of Your Spirit. Amen.

In the name of Jesus, I renounce all generational curses passed down through my family line. I break every curse of sickness, disease, poverty, broken relationships, infertility, and premature death. I cancel every agreement made by my ancestors with the enemy, and I plead the blood of Jesus over myself and my family. Every chain is broken, and the power of the cross reverses every curse. Amen.

Lord, I renounce every word curse spoken over my life, whether by others or by me. I cancel all negative declarations, inner vows, and bitter-root judgments that have given the enemy legal ground in my life. I break the power of these curses in Jesus' name and declare that I am blessed, favored, and free. Amen.

In the name of Jesus, I renounce all fear, including fear of death, darkness, failure, rejection, and the future. I reject every spirit of timidity, torment, and anxiety. I declare that God has not given me a spirit of fear, but of power, love, and a sound mind (2 Tim. 1:7). I walk in confidence and courage through the Holy Spirit. Amen.

I renounce every spirit of heaviness, depression, hopelessness, despair, and suicide, in the name of Jesus. I reject every lie of the enemy that says I am worthless, and I declare that I am chosen, loved, and valuable in God's sight. I receive "the oil of joy" and "the garment of praise" in place of "the spirit of heaviness" (Isa. 61:3). Amen.

I renounce every spirit of infirmity and sickness that has attacked my body. I declare that my body is the temple of the Holy Spirit and no disease has the right to remain in me. I reject all generational sicknesses, chronic diseases, and afflictions. By the stripes of Jesus, I am healed and declare total restoration in my health. Amen.

I renounce every spirit of bondage and slavery to sin. I reject all forms of idolatry, addiction, and compulsive behaviors. I declare that there is freedom where the Spirit of the Lord is. I am no longer a slave but a child of God, walking in liberty through Christ. Amen.

I renounce every spirit-husband/spirit-wife in the name of Jesus. I break every covenant made with these spirits through dreams or sexual encounters. I reject their influence in my relationships, health, and spiritual life. I declare my freedom and restoration through the power of Jesus Christ. Amen.

STEP 4: RELINQUISH UNFORGIVENESS AND BITTERNESS

Unforgiveness and bitterness create legal grounds for the enemy to operate in our lives. We give the devil a foothold when we hold on to offense, resentment, or grudges. Hebrews 12:15 warns us about the danger of allowing bitterness to take root, saying we should be "looking carefully lest anyone fall short of the grace of God; lest any root of bitterness springing up cause trouble, and by this many become defiled." Bitterness doesn't just hurt the one who is bitter; it poisons others. It binds us in spiritual chains, making deliverance more difficult and blocking the flow of God's grace in our lives.

Without forgiveness, there is no freedom. Forgiveness is one of the most powerful tools God has given us. It is not optional for a believer; it is essential. Jesus made this clear in Matthew 6:14–15 when He said, "If you forgive men their trespasses, your heavenly Father will also forgive you. But if you do not forgive men their trespasses, neither will your Father forgive your trespasses." The enemy loses his grip over your life when you forgive.

Forgiveness does not change the past, but it does enlarge the future. It does not justify what was done to you or pretend that it didn't hurt. Forgiveness is not a feeling but a decision. It is a choice to release someone from the debt they owe you and release yourself from the trap of offense. It means surrendering your desire for revenge and trusting God to handle justice. Forgiveness does not excuse the offense or require immediate reconciliation. It does not erase the memory of the pain, but it removes the power of that pain to control your life. As theologian Lewis B. Smedes said, "To forgive is to set a prisoner free and discover that the prisoner was you." When you forgive someone, you set a prisoner free—only to discover the prisoner was you.[2]

Forgiveness is a vital step in deliverance from demonic strongholds. Demons thrive on our unresolved pain and bitterness. They use these open wounds as entry points to oppress and torment us. Often deliverance begins as we release those who have hurt us and surrender our pain to God. The absence of forgiveness hinders complete deliverance because unforgiveness protects the enemy's legal right to operate in our lives.

Prayers of forgiveness

Dear Lord, I thank You for forgiving me through Jesus Christ. Today, I choose to forgive [name anyone who has wronged you]. I release them from any debt they owe me, and I surrender my desire to see them suffer for what they did. I bless them and ask that You guide them in Your righteousness, peace, and joy.

Lord, I also forgive myself for the mistakes and failures I have held against myself. Thank You for Your forgiveness and grace, which set me free. I let go of any offense I have held against You for not meeting my expectations. I trust Your plans and Your love for me. Help me to walk in freedom and wholeness through the power of the Holy Spirit. In Jesus' name, amen.

Lord Jesus, I renounce all bitterness, resentment, and unforgiveness that have taken root in my heart. I break every curse of rejection, whether verbal, relational, or perceived. I renounce rejection from the womb, from word curses, and from inner vows I have spoken over myself.

I forgive those who rejected, abandoned, or abused me physically, mentally, verbally, sexually, or in any other way. I release them into Your hands, Lord, and I declare freedom from all bitterness, anger, jealousy, envy, and shame resulting from rejection.

Holy Spirit, pull up every bitter root in my heart and replace it with the fruit of Your Spirit. Heal my heart and renew my mind so that I may walk in love, peace, and joy. In Jesus' name, amen.

Lord, I refuse to let bitterness control my life any longer. I declare that I am free from all anger, unforgiveness, and resentment. By the blood of Jesus, I am cleansed, and I walk in freedom and forgiveness. Amen.

Father, I ask You to bless those who have wronged me. Bless their lives with Your presence, provision, and peace. Lead them to repentance and a relationship with You. I speak life and blessing over them, and I surrender my pain to You. Heal my heart and fill it with Your love. In Jesus' name, amen.

STEP 5: RELEASE YOURSELF IN THE NAME OF JESUS

Now that you have recognized the spiritual issue and have taken the crucial steps of (1) repenting of any sin that opened doors to the demonic, (2) renouncing any oaths, covenants, contracts, or connections to demons, and (3) releasing unforgiveness and bitterness toward anyone who has wronged you, you are ready to be set free.

Deliverance is a spiritual act of warfare as you stand in the authority of Jesus Christ to command unclean spirits to leave. As a child of God, you have been given power through the name of Jesus to break the chains of oppression and take back what the enemy has stolen.

Prayers for spiritual warfare and deliverance

In the name of Jesus Christ, I command every unclean, familiar, or ancestral spirit that has entered through open doors in my life to come out of me now! You have no authority in my life because I have repented, renounced, and surrendered to the lordship of Jesus. I command you to leave me right now, in Jesus' name!

In Jesus' name, I come against every spirit of witchcraft, occultism, sorcery, and false religion. I renounce every ritual, incantation, spell, hex, and connection to these practices. I break every chain and destroy every stronghold of witchcraft, and I command you to leave me now, in Jesus' name!

Every spirit of killing, stealing, and destruction—I rebuke you and command you to come out in the name of Jesus! Every demonic spirit assigned to bring chaos and destruction to my life, family, health, or purpose—I cancel your assignments right now in the name of Jesus Christ. I declare freedom and peace over every area of my life!

In Jesus' name, I break every curse spoken over my life, whether generational, ancestral, or self-imposed. I destroy every hex, vex, spell, and incantation, and I cancel their legal right to operate. I come against the curse of Leviathan and break it, going back ten generations on both sides of my family. Every demonic spirit tied to my bloodline, you are cast out now, in Jesus' name!

In Jesus' name, I bind every spirit connected to sexual, physical, emotional, and mental abuse. I command every unclean and foul spirit associated with these traumas to leave now. You have no place in my body, mind, or emotions. I declare healing and restoration over every area of my life that was broken by abuse.

I come against every spirit of sexual immorality, lust, pornography, and perversion, in Jesus' name. I command you to leave my body, mind, and spirit right now! I renounce all unholy ties, fantasies, or addictions, and I declare freedom and purity, in Jesus' name.

In the name of Jesus, I dispel every spirit of fear, anxiety, and worry. I declare that I am not a slave to fear, because I am a child of God (Rom. 8:15). Every giant of intimidation, every wall of oppression, and every root of fear planted by the enemy must fall now, in Jesus' name. I walk in boldness, confidence, and victory!

I command every mountain in my life and every obstacle hindering my freedom and purpose to be removed and cast into the sea, in Jesus' name (Mark 11:23). The power of the Holy Spirit destroys every demonic stronghold that has taken root in my life.

Spiritual declarations

I declare that I am free because the Son has set me free, and I am free indeed (John 8:36).

No weapon formed against me shall prosper, and in Jesus' name, I condemn every tongue that rises against me in judgment (Isa. 54:17).

I plead the blood of Jesus over my mind, body, and spirit. I am covered, protected, and sealed in Christ.

STEP 6: REMOVE ANY DEMONIC OBJECTS

Now that you have repented, renounced, and released yourself in the name of Jesus, it is time to take the next step in your journey to freedom. Remove anything from your life that might still be connected to your old ways or to the enemy's influence. This is an essential act of spiritual warfare. Holding on to objects, symbols, or items tied to darkness gives the enemy a foothold in your life. God's Word shows us the seriousness of dealing with such things. In Joshua 7:24–25, the Israelites destroyed accursed items that had brought trouble upon them. In Acts 19:19, those who turned to Christ burned their magic books publicly, entirely severing their ties to witchcraft. Similarly, in Exodus 32:20, Moses destroyed the golden calf the Israelites had worshipped.

You must do the same. Ask the Holy Spirit to reveal anything that could be causing a spiritual hindrance. Start with the obvious, then allow Him to bring hidden things to light. Go through your closets, office, basement, backyard, storage areas, and even your car. Don't overlook your digital space, as this can also contain spiritually harmful items.

Look for objects that represent or are tied to the occult, idolatry, or demonic practices. This could include Native American artifacts such as thunderbird jewelry, pottery that serves as a spirit guide, or totem poles. Remove symbols such as bear tracks, feathers, crows, dragonflies, or rainbows tied to spiritual mysticism. Objects associated with New Age practices—crystals, astrology charts, incense for spiritual purposes, or anything tied to yoga poses (which are offerings to Hindu gods)—must be discarded.

If you have items connected to witchcraft (including Ouija boards, tarot cards, ritualistic cups, or books about spells and magic), destroy them. Even seemingly innocent good luck charms (rabbits' feet, four-leaf clovers, lucky horseshoes, etc.) carry a spiritual weight that must be eliminated.

Also be sure to remove any religious objects or symbols tied to false gods or idolatry. This includes statues of Mary holding Jesus, crucifixes with Jesus still on them, Mormon books, the satanic bible, swastikas, pentagrams, or anything connected to Freemasonry (such as pyramids or the all-seeing eye). These objects might seem harmless or decorative, but they carry a spiritual influence that can hinder your walk with God.

Also examine your entertainment choices. Certain movies, music, and video games glorify violence, witchcraft, horror, or immorality and can open doors to the demonic. This includes games like Dungeons & Dragons, The Witching Hour, and video games with dark spiritual themes. Movies and media with extreme violence, pornography, or depictions of satanic rituals must also be removed from your life.

Remember the biblical instruction to eradicate accursed things as you go through this process. Joshua and the Israelites burned such items with fire, and in the Book of Acts, those who practiced magic did the same, counting their value as worthless compared to the freedom they found in Christ. This is about more than the physical removal of objects; it is a spiritual declaration that you are cutting ties with the enemy and dedicating yourself fully to God.

Prayer of cleansing

As you remove these items, pray this prayer to invite the Holy Spirit to cleanse your home and life:

> *Heavenly Father, I come to You in the name of Jesus. Thank You for revealing anything in my life that does not honor You. I repent for allowing these things into my home and heart. I renounce these objects' connection to darkness, the enemy, and any demonic influence.*
>
> *In the name of Jesus, I now command every spirit tied to these objects to leave my life and home right now! You have no authority here. I break every curse, spell, and legal right of the enemy to operate. I dedicate my life and my home to You, Lord. Holy Spirit, fill every space with Your presence, peace, and power. Cleanse my environment and set me apart for Your purposes. In Jesus' name, amen.*

By removing these objects and committing yourself to Christ, you are closing doors to the enemy and opening yourself to experience the fullness of God's freedom and blessing. Remember that these steps are acts of obedience and worship, and God honors those who fully surrender to Him. As you walk in freedom, fill your life with His Word, prayer, and worship to ensure that no space is left for the enemy to return. "If the Son sets you free, you will be free indeed" (John 8:36, NIV).

STEP 7: RESIST THE DEVIL BY SPEAKING GOD'S WORD

Even after your deliverance, the devil will try to attack you from the outside. He will lie and claim that he is still operating from within you. You cannot agree with those lies or allow them to take root in your heart. Reject them and resist the devil by submitting to God, and the devil will flee from you, according to James 4:7. Demons on the inside are removed, but you must resist demons on the outside with firm faith.

When God supernaturally delivered Israel from Egypt, the blood of the Passover lamb brought the final breakthrough for their freedom. Their joy was short-lived, however, and fear overtook them not long afterward when the enemy who had oppressed them came after them again.

That's often how it works with demons. Even after someone becomes free, demons try to regain entry. Notice that God didn't tell the Israelites to be afraid or go back for another deliverance; He told them to go forward. They were free, but not yet free indeed. However, their obedience in moving forward led to Pharaoh and his army being drowned in the sea, never to be seen again.

Deliverance doesn't eliminate battles; it removes bondage. When the Israelites left Egypt, they were freed from oppression but still had to learn to fight in the Promised Land. God didn't drive out their enemies for them; He empowered them to take dominion over the land. Similarly in the story of Esther, even after Haman was hanged, his plot to destroy the Jews remained in place. The king didn't end the threat outright. Instead, he empowered the Jews to rise up and defend themselves. (See Esther 8:11.) Deliverance is the first step, but dominion requires stepping into the authority God has given.

James 4:7 commands us to submit to God and resist the devil, who will then flee. The devil on the inside torments, but the devil on the outside tempts. He seeks to regain access through our agreement with his lies. Satan is like a snake. A snake needs no arms or legs; its power is in its mouth—its venom. Similarly, Satan's power isn't physical but verbal. His venom consists of lies, accusations, fear, confusion, and panic, as well as bitterness, offense, and unforgiveness. (See John 8:44; Genesis 3:1–5; Revelation 12:10; 2 Timothy 1:7.) He uses lies to poison our minds and hearts, and he gains access through the agreement believers give him. To stand against Satan, we must reject his lies and stand firm on the truth of God's Word.

Sometimes you must speak God's Word aloud to combat the enemy. Jesus did this in the wilderness, declaring, "It is written" (Matt. 4:4, 7, 10).

Jesus also rebuked Peter in Matthew 16:23 after Peter tried to dissuade Him from going to the cross. The Word of God is our weapon. When spoken in faith, it silences the enemy's lies and pushes him back.

Declarations and prayers of resistance

> *I reject every lie of the enemy. I declare that I am free indeed, for whom the Son sets free is free indeed* (John 8:36). *The truth of God's Word is my foundation, and I will not waver.*

> *There is "no condemnation to those who are in Christ Jesus"* (Rom. 8:1). *I am forgiven, redeemed, and clothed in the righteousness of Christ.*

> *The accuser of the brethren has been cast down* (Rev. 12:10). *I silence every voice that rises against me in judgment, for this is my heritage in the Lord* (Isa. 54:17).

> *"God has not given [me] a spirit of fear, but of power and of love and of a sound mind"* (2 Tim. 1:7). *I will not fear, for "the LORD is my light and my salvation"* (Ps. 27:1).

> *Though the enemy might attack from the outside, I resist him in the name of Jesus. "Greater is he that is in [me], than he that is in the world"* (1 John 4:4, KJV). *I stand firm, clothed in the full armor of God* (Eph. 6:10–18).

STEP 8: GIVE GOD WHAT THE DEVIL USED TO TAKE

All of this brings us to the real purpose of deliverance: devotion to God. God delivers us so that we can belong to Him. When Moses confronted Pharaoh, he repeated versions of God's central reason for the Israelites' deliverance: "That they may serve Me." (See Exodus 3:18; 5:1, 3, 8; 7:16; 8:1, 20; 9:1, 13; 10:3, 7.)

For the Israelites, deliverance meant relief from harsh labor, but the ultimate goal was for the people to fully belong to God and serve Him without constraints. I believe the Israelites missed this point.

Their idea of freedom was incomplete and revolved around being freed from Pharaoh's oppression.

Deliverance must move us *from* a life enslaved to sin and Satan *to* a life of service to God. If it doesn't, we've missed the point. We are not truly free until we serve God with at least the same passion and dedication we once gave to sin. In essence, deliverance doesn't give us more of God; it allows God to have more of us. Repenting, renouncing, releasing ourselves, and resisting the devil are critical. But there's more: We need to use our freedom not as an excuse to do whatever we choose, but to serve God. We were freed to live *for Him.*

Israel's journey reflects a progression: The Israelites' departure from Egypt represents deliverance. Their wilderness journey represents discipleship, through which character develops and obedience is learned. The Promised Land represents destiny and walking in dominion. We must follow the same journey, realizing that unless deliverance leads to discipleship, it will never lead to dominion. This is the reason so many people go from deliverance to deliverance without stepping into the full purpose of their freedom. Deliverance is not an ending but a starting point. The real goal is for us to live as God intended, reigning in life through the abundance of grace and the gift of righteousness—not only surviving but thriving.

To fully experience this progression, we need to replace the empty spaces in our lives with God's Word and power. Where there was demonization, we need to develop discipline. Where there was bondage, we need to establish boundaries. Where demons once ruled, our devotion to God should take over. God didn't set us free so we could spend all our time and resources on ourselves. He set us free so we could give them to His kingdom. The purpose of freedom is to serve Him.

Prayers of dedication and surrender

Father God, I come before You with a heart of surrender. Thank You for delivering me from bondage and setting me free through the power of Jesus Christ. I lay my life before You, holding back nothing. I now completely give You the areas where I was once bound. I surrender my heart, mind, will, and every part of my life to Your purpose.

Lord, where I once served sin and Satan, I now choose to serve You. I renounce all lies of the enemy and declare that I belong to You alone. My time, energy, talents, and resources are Yours. Use me for Your glory and Your kingdom. I will not use my freedom as an excuse to live for myself but as an opportunity to walk in obedience and devotion to You.

Holy Spirit, help me to replace the emptiness my deliverance left behind with a complete devotion to You. Fill me with Your Word, power, and presence. Where there was chaos, let there be peace. Where there was bondage, let there be discipline and boundaries. Where darkness reigned, let Your light shine. Teach me to love and serve You with the same passion I once gave to sin. I declare that my life is Yours, and I will live it for Your glory.

Lord Jesus, thank You for breaking my chains and setting me free. I promise to follow You wherever You lead. I commit to serving You in every area of my life, especially in the places where I was once in bondage. I will no longer allow the enemy to take ground in my heart. Instead, I give that space to You. I declare that my past will no longer define me; my identity is in You.

Lord, I surrender to You again today. Where bondage was, I now commit to serving You. Help me to walk in Your truth, stand firm in my freedom, and live for Your glory. Teach me to honor You in every area of my life. I promise to follow You and use my freedom to serve Your kingdom. Thank You for setting me free. I belong to You, Lord.

STEP 9: RENEW YOUR MIND WITH GOD'S WORD

After deliverance, some people struggle with the same old thoughts and feelings they had before they were delivered. It's not that the demon is still there, but it shows that a stronghold in the mind was built over time.

A demon is often called a "strong man," and a stronghold can be described as the house of thoughts constructed by the demon to hide itself. You cannot take what belongs to the strong man without binding him first. (See Mark 3:27.) Deliverance binds and removes the demon. But the stronghold of lies left behind must be pulled down. These thought patterns of fear, anger, rejection, depression, or self-hatred give demons protection and a place to stay.

Unlike open doors, which can be shut instantly through repentance, strongholds are layered with lies, feelings, and habits. It takes time to tear them down. These demonic spiritual fortresses must be demolished with the truth of God's Word. You don't remove them by casting them out; you must cast them down by renewing your mind with the truth of God's Word and consistently resisting the enemy's lies. This process requires intentional effort, but remember that the battle is spiritual. God has given you mighty weapons with which to fight.

When writing to the Corinthians, Paul used the image of a fortress to explain the spiritual warfare in which he engaged. He spoke in 2 Corinthians 10:4–5 about the "weapons of our warfare," the pulling down of strongholds, the destruction of arguments, and the taking captive of every thought to obey Christ. The dismantling of strongholds requires us as believers to abide in the truth and let it transform our thinking. As Jesus said in John 8:32, "You shall know the truth, and the truth shall make you free." Not only must the truth be present, but we must also know the truth. Then, as the truth replaces the enemy's lies, the stronghold comes down—brick by brick.

So fill your mind with Scripture and reject the devil's lies. Ensure lasting freedom and victory by consciously aligning your thoughts with God's Word. This will demolish the devil's strongholds and ensure that demons cannot regain control.

Prayers to pull down strongholds

> *Heavenly Father, I come before You acknowledging that there are strongholds in my mind. These patterns of thinking do not align with Your truth, so I surrender them to You and ask for Your help in tearing them down. Lord, reveal every lie I have believed and every argument that has exalted itself against the knowledge of You. Open my eyes to see the truth in Your Word, as well as the lies I must renounce. I submit my mind to You and ask that Your Spirit would guide me into all truth. In Jesus' name, amen.*

> *Lord Jesus, thank You for setting me free through Your death and resurrection. I know that the truth of Your Word transforms my mind and brings me lasting freedom. Right now, I declare that I no longer agree with the enemy's lies, whether they are rooted in fear, rejection, anger, or shame. I replace them with the truth of Your Word: I am loved (Jer. 31:3). I am chosen (Eph. 1:4). I am a new creation in Christ (2 Cor. 5:17). I have been given the mind of Christ (1 Cor. 2:16). I choose to think on what is true, noble, and pure (Phil. 4:8). Thank You for renewing my mind and helping me to walk in Your freedom. In Your name, I pray. Amen.*

> *I renounce the stronghold of fear in my mind. I reject the lies that have made me feel powerless, anxious, or afraid. Your Word says that You have "not given [me] a spirit of fear, but*

of power and of love and of a sound mind" (2 Tim. 1:7). *I declare that You are my "refuge and strength," my "ever-present help in trouble"* (Ps. 46:1, NIV). *I speak peace over my thoughts and invite Your presence to fill every place where fear once ruled. I choose to trust in You completely, knowing that Your "perfect love casts out fear"* (1 John 4:18). *In Jesus' name, amen.*

I renounce the stronghold of rejection that has taken root in my mind and heart. I declare that I am not rejected but accepted in Christ (Eph. 1:6). *I am Your child, loved unconditionally and chosen by You. I break every lie that tells me I am unworthy or unloved, and I replace it with the truth that "I am fearfully and wonderfully made"* (Ps. 139:14). *Lord, heal every wound caused by rejection and fill those places with Your love and acceptance. I walk in the truth that I am Yours, and nothing can separate me from Your love* (Rom. 8:35–39). *In Jesus' name, amen.*

Holy Spirit, I ask You to renew my mind daily with the truth of God's Word. Where there was once darkness, let there be light. Where there was confusion, bring clarity. I bring "every thought into captivity to the obedience of Christ" (2 Cor. 10:5). *I reject every argument, lie, and imagination that "exalts itself against the knowledge of God"* (2 Cor. 10:5). *Teach me to meditate on Your Word day and night so that my mind will be transformed and strongholds will be demolished. I declare that my mind belongs to You, and I will stand firm in Your truth. In Jesus' name, amen.*

Father, I know that breaking strongholds takes time and persistence. I ask for Your strength to continue this battle. Help me to resist the lies of the enemy and to stand firm on the promises in Your Word. I declare that the weapons of my warfare are mighty in You, and I will not grow weary in pulling down strongholds (2 Cor. 10:4). *Thank You for empowering me to replace every lie with truth and to walk in the freedom You have already given me. I trust You to finish the good work You have begun in me* (Phil. 1:6). *In Jesus' name, amen.*

STEP 10: REMAIN ROOTED IN THE LOCAL CHURCH

The final step in deliverance is to move from freedom to dominion, which happens through discipleship. Discipleship is where strongholds are confronted, healing takes place, and we are taught how to fight spiritual battles. This crucial process happens most effectively within the context of a local church. This is not just a place where we gather; it's the environment God designed for our growth, healing, and transformation. It's where demons are removed, character is formed, and faith is strengthened. It's where iron sharpens iron and we are refined to become more like Christ.

The original Greek word for *church* is ἐκκλησία (*ekklēsia*), which originally referred to a public assembly or gathering of citizens. In a Christian context it means the congregation or assembly of believers in Christ. (See Matthew 16:18.) The church is not a mere collection of disconnected individuals. So stop saying, "I am the church." That's like a bolt claiming to be a building, a leg claiming to be a whole body, or a single justice claiming to represent the entire Supreme Court. The church is an assembly of believers. If it never assembles, it is not a church. Gathering is more than something we do; it is the essence of the church. God has saved us as individuals to become part of a corporate assembly.

Just as the human body functions through the interconnection of its many parts, the church thrives when believers come together in unity, each playing their unique role in service to God and one another. God uses this community to teach us His ways, confront strongholds in our minds, and equip us to walk in dominion. Through sound teaching, accountability, and the fellowship of believers we grow in faith and maturity. The local church becomes the family where we are discipled, our character is shaped, and we learn how to wield the weapons of our warfare. It's also where we find healing—not just from spiritual oppression but also from the wounds of life.

When you are planted in a local church, God is able to pour blessings into your life. Psalm 92:13 reminds us, "Those who are planted in the house of the LORD shall flourish in the courts of our God." In the local church context, discipleship leads to flourishing. It moves us from deliverance to dominion and from freedom to fruitfulness. This is God's design for every believer—to be delivered, discipled, and empowered to reign in life through His grace.

As you embrace the local church and allow God to work through it, your faith will deepen, your strongholds will be demolished, and your life will be transformed for His glory. This is the place where true dominion begins.

Remember as you pray the remaining prayers and reflect on all that we have explored together that deliverance is not meant to make you homeless; it's meant to make the devil homeless! Become planted in a home church so you can "flourish in the courts of our God" (Ps. 92:13).

Prayers for church hurts

Heavenly Father, I come before You with an open heart, acknowledging the hurt I've experienced within the church. I know the church is Your design, a place for healing and growth, yet sometimes people can cause pain. I release the offense, the disappointments, and the wounds I've carried from past experiences. I choose to forgive those who have hurt me, just as You have forgiven me. Heal my heart, Lord, and help me to trust again. Remove any bitterness or resentment that may have taken root, and restore my love for Your people. I ask for Your grace to move forward, to be planted in Your house, and to receive the blessings You've prepared for me in the community of believers. In Jesus' name, amen.

Lord Jesus, thank You for placing me in the body of Christ. I know that being in a community isn't always easy, and there are sometimes misunderstandings and conflicts. Help me to approach every situation with humility, love, and patience. Teach me to forgive quickly and to seek reconciliation where friction exists. I ask for Your wisdom in navigating diffi- cult relationships, and I ask for Your peace to rule in my heart. Remind me that although the church is not perfect, it is Your chosen vessel for my growth and discipleship. Help me to focus on serving You and loving others, even when it's hard. In Your name, I pray. Amen.

I renounce the lie that I don't need the church or that I can grow in my faith without being part of a community. I reject the thoughts that tell me I'm better off alone. Your Word says that we are one body, and we grow together as each part does its work. I ask You to renew my mind and align my thoughts with Your truth. Plant me firmly in a local church where I can be discipled, sharpened, and used for Your glory. Help me to see the value of gathering with other believers and embrace the joy of living in community. Thank You for the gift of the church. In Jesus' name, amen.

Lord, I pray for unity in the church. Help us to overcome differences, misunderstandings, and offenses so we can walk together as one body. Teach us to bear with one another in love and to strive for peace in every situation. Let the church be a place where Your Spirit dwells richly, we are built up in love, and our character is shaped to reflect You. Use every moment of friction or difficulty to refine us and make us more like Christ. Thank You for using the community to grow us and glorify Your name. In Jesus' name, amen.

Father, I commit myself to being planted in Your house. I choose to embrace the local church, not as an obligation but as a gift You've given for my growth and discipleship. Help me to stay rooted, even when it's challenging. Teach me to serve faithfully, love deeply, and grow in the fellowship of believers. I pray for Your blessings as I align my life with Your design for community. May I flourish in Your courts and bear fruit that glorifies You. In Jesus' name, amen.

A PERSONAL NOTE FROM THE AUTHOR

GOD LOVES YOU deeply. His Word is filled with promises that reveal His desire to bring healing, hope, and abundant life to every area of your being—body, mind, and spirit. More than anything, He wants a personal relationship with you through His Son, Jesus Christ.

If you've never invited Jesus into your life, you can do so right now. It's not about religion—it's about a relationship with the One who knows you completely and loves you unconditionally. If you're ready to take that step, simply pray this prayer with a sincere heart:

> *Lord Jesus, I want to know You as my Savior and Lord. I confess and believe that You are the Son of God and that You died for my sins. I believe You rose from the dead and are alive today. Please forgive me for my sins. I invite You into my heart and my life. Make me new. Help me to walk with You, grow in Your love, and live for You every day. In Jesus' name, amen.*

If you just prayed that prayer, you've made the most important decision of your life. All of heaven rejoices with you, and so do I! You are now a child of God, and your journey with Him has just begun. Please contact my publisher at pray4me@charismamedia.com so that we can send you some materials that will help you become established in your relationship with the Lord. We look forward to hearing from you.

NOTES

CHAPTER 1

1. Rebecca Brown, *He Came to Set the Captives Free* (Whitaker House, 1992).
2. Brown, *He Came to Set the Captives Free.*
3. Brown, *He Came to Set the Captives Free.*
4. Brown, *He Came to Set the Captives Free.*
5. I am aware of the controversy surrounding this book, and I don't necessarily encourage reading it if you are new to demon deliverance. You might want to start with my book *Break Free.*
6. Sam Kestenbaum, "The Demon Slayers," *Harper's*, August 2024, https://harpers.org/archive/2024/08/the-demon-slayers-sam-kestenbaum-exorcisms/.
7. "Competing Worldviews Influence Today's Christians," Barna, May 9, 2017, https://www.barna.com/research/competing-worldviews-influence-todays-christians/.
8. A. W. Tozer, *The Knowledge of the Holy: The Attributes of God; Their Meaning in the Christian Life* (HarperOne, 1961), 2.
9. Gregory A. Boyd, *God at War: The Bible and Spiritual Conflict* (InterVarsity Press, 2014), 56.
10. Obviously, John Calvin did not assert everything that now comes under the loose heading of "Calvinism." For a modern yet classic presentation of Calvinist theology, see Millard J. Erickson, *Christian Theology*, 3rd ed. (Academic, 2013). For a solid understanding of Arminianism, see Roger E. Olson, *Arminian Theology: Myths and Realities* (IVP Academic, 2009); and Thomas C. Oden, *Classic Christianity: A Systematic Theology* (HarperCollins, 2009).
11. "Omaha Beach," National Museum of the US Navy, accessed May 15, 2025, https://www.history.navy.mil/content/history/museums/nmusn/explore/photography/wwii/wwii-europe/operation-overlord/invasion-normandy/omaha-beach.html.
12. C. S. Lewis, *Mere Christianity* (HarperOne, 1952, 1980), 46.
13. Michael S. Heiser, *Reversing Hermon: Enoch, the Watchers, and the Forgotten Mission of Jesus Christ* (Defender, 2017), 96, 102; see Enoch 6:6–7:2.

14. Craig A. Evans, "Mark's Incipit and the Priene Calendar Inscription: From Jewish Gospel to Greco-Roman Gospel," *Journal of Greco-Roman Christianity and Judaism* no. 1 (2000): 73.

15. Evans, "Mark's Incipit and the Priene Calendar Inscription," 68–70.

16. John Francis Wilson, *Caesarea Philippi: Banias, the Lost City of Pan* (I. B. Tauris, 2004), 3.

17. Wilson, *Caesarea Philippi*, 3. For more recent archaeological work, see Marek Dospel, "Ruins at Banias—King Herod's Palace Identified at Caesarea Philippi," Biblical Archaeology Society, May 18, 2022, https://www.biblicalarchaeology.org/daily/biblical-sites-places/biblical-archaeology-sites/ruins-at-banias-king-herods-palace-identified-at-caesarea-philippi/.

18. George Eldon Ladd, *The Presence of the Future: The Eschatology of Biblical Realism* (Eerdmans, 1974); see the general concept on pages 10, 120, 141, 146.

CHAPTER 2

1. James B. Pritchard, ed., *Ancient Near Eastern Texts Relating to the Old Testament*, 3rd ed. (Princeton University Press, 1969), 109; Joel Soza, "Lilith in the Bible," in *The Lexham Bible Dictionary*, ed. John D. Barry et al. (Lexham Press, 2016).

2. Avigail Manekin Bamberger, "Naming Demons: The Aramaic Incantation Bowls and Gittin," TheGemara.com, accessed May 15, 2025, https://thegemara.com/article/naming-demons-the-aramaic-incantation-bowls-and-gittin/.

3. The Ancient Egyptian Demonology Project, led by Dr. Kasia Szpakowska at Swansea University, UK, proposed that ancient Egyptians were aware of more than four thousand demons. Eric A. Powell, "The World of Egyptian Demons," accessed May 15, 2025, https://archaeology .org/collection/the-world-of-egyptian-demons/; "Ancient Egyptian Demonology," Swansea University, accessed May 15, 2015, https://www .swansea.ac.uk/arts-and-humanities/arts-and-humanities-research/our-recent-research-projects/ancient-egyptian-demonology/.

4. Werner Foerster, "Daimon, Daimonization, Daimonizomai, Daimoniodis, Deisidaimon, Deisidaimonia," in *Theological Dictionary of the New Testament*, eds. Gerhard Kittel, Geoffrey W. Bromiley, and Gerhard Friedrich (Eerdmans, 1964), 8.

5. Don Richardson, *Eternity in Their Hearts* (Bethany House, 2005), 77.

6. Indlieb Farazi Saber, "Jinn: Who Are the Supernatural Beings of Arabian and Islamic Tradition?," Middle East Eye, September 20, 2022, https://www.middleeasteye.net/discover/jinn-islamic-arabian-tradition-supernatural-beings.

7. Fouad Masri, *Connecting with Muslims: A Guide to Communicating Effectively* (IVP Books, 2014), 85. For statistics on belief in jinn among Muslims today, see "Chapter 4: Other Beliefs and Practices," Pew Research Center, August 9, 2012, https://www.pewresearch.org/religion/2012/08/09/the-worlds-muslims-unity-and-diversity-4-other-beliefs-and-practices/.

8. *The Exorcist*, Warner Bros., 1973; *The Conjuring*, New Line Cinema, 2013; *Paranormal Activity*, Paramount Pictures, 2007.

9. *Hellboy*, Revolution Studios, 2004; *Lucifer*, Aggressive Mediocrity, 2016–2021.

10. David P. Wright, "Azazel," in *The Anchor Yale Bible Dictionary*, ed. David Noel Freedman (Doubleday, 1992), 536.

11. See Michael S. Heiser's discussion of 1 Enoch and the Dead Sea Scrolls in his book *Demons: What the Bible Really Says About the Powers of Darkness* (Lexham Press, 2020), 137–138.

12. Flavius Josephus, "Concerning the Wife of Solomon; Concerning His Wisdom and Riches; and Concerning What He Obtained of Hiram for the Building of the Temple," in *Antiquities of the Jews*, trans. William Whiston, book 1, *Containing the Interval of One Hundred and Sixty-Three Years—From the Death of David to the Death of Ahab* (Project Gutenberg), chap. 2.

13. D. C. Duling, "Testament of Solomon: A New Translation and Introduction," in James H. Charlesworth, *The Old Testament Pseudepigrapha*, vol. 1 (Yale University Press, 1983), 935–987.

14. Peter W. Flint, "Psalm 151 and the Dead Sea Scrolls," Bible Odyssey, accessed May 15, 2025, https://www.bibleodyssey.org/articles/psalm-151-and-the-dead-sea-scrolls/.

15. J. A. McGuire-Moushon, "Divine Beings," in *Lexham Theological Wordbook*, ed. Douglas Mangum et al., Lexham Bible Reference Series (Lexham Press, 2014).

16. For further reading, see Gerhard Kittel, ed., *Theological Dictionary of the New Testament* (Eerdmans, 1964), under "δαίμων κτλ"; Eric Sorensen, *Possession and Exorcism in the New Testament and Early Christianity* (Mohr Siebeck, 2002), 84.

17. David Brown, "Chronological Table of the Miracles of Christ," Jamieson, Fausset & Brown, Blue Letter Bible, accessed May 15, 2025, https://www.blueletterbible.org/Comm/jfb/misc/miracles.cfm.

18. Vlad Savchuk, "50,000 Exorcisms: The Life and Lessons of the World's Top Exorcist," December 20, 2024, YouTube video, 1:18:53, https://www.youtube.com/watch?v=mQu6-Gi03uM.

19. Justin Martyr, *The Second Apology* (Fig, 2012), 4.

20. Justin Martyr, *"The Second Apology 6.6,"* in Kyle Pope, *The Second Apology of Justin Martyr with Text and Translation* (Ancient Road Publications, 2001), 25.

21. Tertullian, *Apology*, trans. S. Thelwall, from *Ante-Nicene Fathers*, vol. 3., eds. Alexander Roberts, James Donaldson, and A. Cleveland Coxe (Christian Literature Publishing Co., 1885), revised and edited for New Advent by Kevin Knight, http://www.newadvent.org/fathers/0301.htm.

22. Origen, *"Against Celsus,"* in *The Ante-Nicene Fathers: Translations of the Writings of the Fathers Down to A.D. 325*, eds. Alexander Roberts and James Donaldson, book I, chapter LXVII, 734.

23. R. H. Charles, *The Apocrypha and Pseudepigrapha* (Clarendon Press, 1913), 198; Heiser, *Demons*, 137–138.

CHAPTER 3

1. Merrill Frederick Unger, *Demons in the World Today: A Study of Occultism in the Light of God's Word* (Tyndale House, 1971); Merrill F. Unger, *What Demons Can Do to Saints* (Moody Bible Institute, 1977).

2. Bible Study Tools, s.v. *"diamonizomai,"* accessed May 15, 2025, https://www.biblestudytools.com/lexicons/greek/kjv/daimonizomai.html#:~:text=dahee%2Dmon%2Did'%2D,13.

3. Derek Prince, *They Shall Expel Demons*, exp. ed. (Chosen Books, 2020), 21.

4. Prince, *They Shall Expel Demons*, 21.

5. Frank and Ida Mae Hammond, *Pigs in the Parlor: A Practical Guide to Deliverance* (Impact Books, Inc., 2010), 9.

6. Neil T. Anderson, *The Bondage Breaker* (Harvest House Publishers, 2019), 122.

7. "FAQ," Spiritual Freedom Church, accessed May 15, 2025, https://boblarson.org/about-bob/faq/.

8. Clinton E. Arnold, *Three Crucial Questions About Spiritual Warfare* (Baker Academic, 1997), 112–113.

9. "The Temple Mount," Temple Institute, accessed May 15, 2025, https://templeinstitute.org/illustrated-tour-the-temple-mount/#:~:text=At%20the%20beginning%20of%20the,acres%20(150%2C000%20square%20meters.

10. "The Temple Mount," Temple Institute.

11. For more teaching on this point, see Sam Storms' detailed articles: Sam Storms, "Can a Christian Be Demonized? Part One," *Enjoying God*, February 16, 2017, https://www.samstorms.org/enjoying-god-blog/post/can-a-christian-be-demonized-part-one; Sam Storms, "Can a Christian Be Demonized? Part Two," *Enjoying God*, February 17,

2017, https://www.samstorms.org/enjoying-god-blog/post/can-a-christian-be-demonized-part-two.

12. "Unless Scripture explicitly tells us we must do something, what is only narrated or described does not function in a normative (i.e. obligatory) way—unless it can be demonstrated on other grounds that the author intended it to function in this way." Gordon D. Fee and Douglas Stuart, *How to Read the Bible for All Its Worth*, 4th ed. (Zondervan, 2014), 124.

13. See, for example, Grant R. Osborne, *The Hermeneutical Spiral: A Comprehensive Introduction to Biblical Interpretation*, rev. ed. (IVP Academic, 2010), 207.

14. If you want to learn more about Roman stories and examples, read Matthew B. Roller, *Models from the Past in Roman Culture: A World of Exempla* (Cambridge University Press, 2018); Rebecca Langlands, *Exemplary Ethics in Ancient Rome* (Cambridge University Press, 2018); Sinclair Bell and Inge Lyse Hansen, *Role Models in the Roman World: Identity and Assimilation* (University of Michigan Press, 2008); William Kurz, "Narrative Models for Imitation in Luke-Acts," in *Greeks, Romans, and Christians: Essays in Honor of Abraham J. Malherbe*, eds. David L. Balch, et al. (Augsburg Fortress Press, 1990); Jane D. Chaplin, *Livy's Exemplary History* (Oxford University Press, 2000); Jane D. Chaplin, "Livy's Use of Exempla," in *A Companion to Livy*, ed. Bernard Mineo (John Wiley & Sons, 2015); Marc van der Poel, "The Use of Exempla in Roman Declamation," *Rhetorica: A Journal of the History of Rhetoric* 27, no. 3 (2009): 332–353, https://doi.org/10.1525/rh.2009.27.3.332. For practical application of examples to the Bible, see also David John McCollough, *Ritual and Religious Experience in Early Christianities: The Spirit In Between* (Mohr Siebeck Ek, 2022).

15. Titus Livius (Livy), *The History of Rome, Book 1*, ed. Rev. Canon Roberts, preface 10, Perseus Digital Library, accessed May 15, 2025, https://www.perseus.tufts.edu/hopper/text?doc=Perseus%3Atext%3A1999.02.0026. For a story of a Roman hero told as an example of courage, see Polybius, *Histories*, Perseus Digital Library, accessed May 15, 2025, https://www.perseus.tufts.edu/hopper/text?doc=Perseus%3Atext%3A1999.01.0234%3Abook%3D6%3Achapter%3D55.

16. Tertullian, "De Spectaculis," New Advent, accessed May 15, 2025, https://www.newadvent.org/fathers/0303.htm; Cyril of Jerusalem, "Catechetical Lecture 19," New Advent, accessed May 15, 2025, https://www.newadvent.org/fathers/310119.htm.

17. "When entering the water, we make profession of the Christian faith in the words of its rule; we bear public testimony that we have

renounced the devil, his pomp, and his angels." Tertullian, "*De Spectaculis*," in *Ante-Nicene Fathers*, vol. 3, eds. Alexander Roberts and James Donaldson (Wm. B. Eerdmans, 1885), 81. Tertullian's noted lifespan is approximate.

18. "First you entered into the vestibule of the Baptistery, and there facing towards the West you listened to the command to stretch forth your hand, and as in the presence of Satan you renounced him." S. Cyril, *The Catechetical Lectures of S. Cyril, Archbishop of Jerusalem*, trans. Edwin Hamilton Gifford, in *Nicene and Post-Nicene Fathers*, Second Series, vol. 7, eds. Philip Schaff and Henry Wace (Christian Literature Publishing, 1894), Catechetical Lecture 19.2. The original English translation text has updated the pronoun *ye* to *you*. Cyril of Jerusalem also explains the idea of "pomp": "Now the pomp of the devil is the madness of theatres, and horse-races, and hunting, and all such vanity. Be not interested in madness of the theatre, where you will behold the wanton gestures of the players, carried on with mockeries and all unseemliness, and the frantic dancing of effeminate men...the things...hung up at idol festivals, either meat or bread, or other such things polluted by the invocation of the unclean spirits, are reckoned in the pomp of the devil." S. Cyril, *The Catechetical Lectures*, 6–7.

19. Paul F. Bradshaw, *Apostolic Tradition: A New Commentary* (Liturgical Press Academic, 2023), 9, 59.

20. Bradshaw, *Apostolic Tradition*, 65.

21. "We have the case of the woman—the Lord Himself is witness—who went to the theatre, and came back possessed. In the outcasting, accordingly, when the unclean creature was upbraided with having dared to attack a believer, he firmly replied, 'And in truth I did it most righteously, for I found her in my domain.'" Tertullian, "*De Spectaculis*," 90.

22. "And, on the other hand, some of those who are baptized in health, if subsequently they begin to sin, are shaken by the return of the unclean spirit, so that it is manifest that the devil is driven out in baptism by the faith of the believer, and returns if the faith afterwards shall fail." Cyprian of Carthage, "Epistle 75: To Magnus on Baptizing the Novatians," in *Ante-Nicene Fathers*, vol. 5., ed. Philip Schaff, 946.

CHAPTER 4

1. Thomas Aquinas, *The Summa Theologiæ of St. Thomas Aquinas*, 2nd ed., trans. Fathers of the English Dominican Province (R. & T. Washbourne, 1914), 201. (See Part 3, Question 41.)

2. James Swanson, *Dictionary of Biblical Languages with Semantic Domains: Hebrew (Old Testament)* (Logos Research Systems, 1997), s.v. "8069 יְקָב."

3. Also in the NIV, see Genesis 49:9 ("crouches") and Isaiah 11:6 ("will lie down").

4. E. A. Speiser, *Genesis: Introduction, Translation, and Notes*, vol. 1, Anchor Yale Bible Commentaries (Yale University Press, 2008), 33; Roy Gane et al., *Genesis, Exodus, Leviticus, Numbers, Deuteronomy: Zondervan Illustrated Bible Backgrounds Commentary (Old Testament)*, vol. 1, ed. John H. Walton (Zondervan, 2009), 38.

5. Swanson, *Dictionary of Biblical Languages with Semantic Domains*, s.v. "9592 הַקּוּשֶׁת."

6. Terry L. Laughlin, "Enemies Exposed," Sermons by Logos, accessed May 15, 2025, https://sermons.logos.com/sermons/122514-enemies-exposed.

7. "Traitor's Gate," Spain, accessed May 15, 2025, https://www.spain.info/en/places-of-interest/portal-traicion/.

CHAPTER 5

1. Maverick Moves, "Is General Butt Naked a Hero? Conversations with a Man That Used to Eat Children," *Maverick's Substack*, July 21, 2024, https://maverickmoves.substack.com/p/is-general-butt-naked-a-hero.

2. Joshua Blahyi, *The Redemption of an African Warlord: The Joshua Blahyi Story: A Modern Day Conversion from Saul to Paul* (Destiny Image, 2013), 44–47.

3. Blahyi, *The Redemption of an African Warlord*, 63–72.

4. Blahyi, *The Redemption of an African Warlord*, 84.

5. Moves, "Is General Butt Naked a Hero?"

6. Moves, "Is General Butt Naked a Hero?"

7. Blahyi, *The Redemption of an African Warlord*, 100.

8. Blahyi, *The Redemption of an African Warlord*, 101–102.

9. Blahyi, *The Redemption of an African Warlord*, 103.

10. Blahyi, *The Redemption of an African Warlord*, 103–104.

11. Blahyi, *The Redemption of an African Warlord*, 108, 110, 112.

12. Blahyi, *The Redemption of an African Warlord*, 121.

13. Blahyi, *The Redemption of an African Warlord*.

14. Bob Larson, "Worst Demon You've Never Heard Of," *Bob Larson Blog*, April 18, 2022, https://boblarson.org/worst-demon-youve-never-heard-of/. I highly recommend Dr. Bob Larson University to those who want to learn more about deliverance. Visit https://boblarsonuniversity.org/.

15. Larson, "Worst Demon You've Never Heard Of."

16. Paolo Carlin, "Vexation, Obsession, and Possession: The Extraordinary Ways the Devil Attacks," Catholic Exchange, August 16, 2021, https://catholicexchange.com/

vexation-obsession-possession-the-extraordinary-ways-the-devil-attacks/. The four descriptions noted here are based on Fr. Carlin's article.

17. Christianities?, "Tucker Carlson: I Was Mauled by a Demon! Exclusive Clip from Christianities Documentary," October 31, 2024, YouTube video, 3:59, https://www.youtube.com/watch?v=LDIqoPKNhgo.

18. Walter Bauer et al., *Greek-English Lexicon of the New Testament and Other Early Christian Literature*, 3rd ed., ed. Frederick William Danker (University of Chicago Press, 2000), s.v. "ἐνοχλέω."

19. Timothy Friberg and Barbara Friberg, "ἐνοχλέω," in *Analytical Lexicon of the Greek New Testament* (2023).

20. Francis Brown et al., *Enhanced Brown-Driver-Briggs Hebrew and English Lexicon* (Clarendon Press, 1977), s.v. "תִּלֵיל."

21. Vocabulary.com, s.v. "succubus," accessed May 15, 2025, https://www.vocabulary.com/dictionary/succubus#.

22. Saint Augustine, *The City of God* (bk. 5, chap. 23), Christian Classics Ethereal Library, accessed May 15, 2025, https://www.ccel.org/ccel/schaff/npnf102.iv.XV.23.html#:~:text=There%20is%2C%20too%2C%0a%20very,lust%20upon%20them%3B%20and%20that.

23. Juliana Menasce Horowitz and Nikki Graf, "Most U.S. Teens See Anxiety and Depression as a Major Problem Among Their Peers," Pew Research Center, February 20, 2019, https://www.pewresearch.org/social-trends/2019/02/20/most-u-s-teens-see-anxiety-and-depression-as-a-major-problem-among-their-peers/.

24. "Adolescent Health," Centers for Disease Control, accessed May 15, 2025, https://www.cdc.gov/nchs/fastats/adolescent-health.htm#:~:text=Leading%20causes%20of%20deaths%20among,Suicide.

25. Oren Miron et al., "Suicide Rates Among Adolescents and Young Adults in the United States, 2000–2017," *Journal of the American Medical Association* 321, no. 23 (June 2019), https://pmc.ncbi.nlm.nih.gov/articles/PMC6582264.

26. Mahita Gajanan, "The Story Behind *The Sons of Sam*, Netflix's True Crime Docuseries About David Berkowitz," *Time*, May 5, 2021, https://time.com/6046079/the-sons-of-sam-true-story-david-berkowitz/.

27. Michael A. Caparrelli, *Monster Mirror: 100 Hours with David Berkowitz, Once Known as Son of Sam* (n.p., 2023), 161.

28. Caparrelli, *Monster Mirror*, 164.

29. Caparrelli, *Monster Mirror*, 34–35.

30. Gabriella Miller, "The Devil Made Me Do It: The Viability of Demonic Possession as a Murder Defense," *Vermont Law Review*, March 27, 2024, https://lawreview.vermontlaw.edu/

the-devil-made-me-do-it-the-viability-of-demonic-possession-as-a-murder-defense/; *The Conjuring: The Devil Made Me Do It*, New Line Cinema, 2021.

CHAPTER 6

1. Bob Larson, *Dealing with Demons* (Destiny Image, 2016), 161.
2. Jack Brewer, "Issue Brief: Fatherlessness and Its Effects on American Society," America First Policy Institute, May 15, 2023, https://americafirstpolicy.com/issues/issue-brief-fatherlessness-and-its-effects-on-american-society.
3. Marten Stol, *Women in the Ancient Near East* (De Gruyter, 2016), 421–422.
4. There is great debate on the meaning of the Hebrew word for *perverted person* (*qedeshim*). Were they male prostitutes? Pimps controlling the women? Were they all just sacred functionaries? For several views, see Edward Lipinski, "Cult Prostitution in Ancient Israel?," *Biblical Archaeology Review* 40, no. 1 (January/February 2014): 49–56; Joan Goodnick Westenholz, "Tamar, Qĕdēšā, Qadištu, and Sacred Prostitution in Mesopotamia," *Harvard Theological Review* 82, no. 3 (July 1989): 245–265, http://www.jstor.org/stable/1510077.
5. Deborah Van Hoewyk, "Social Class, Politics, Economics, and Religion: A Brief History of Aztec Sex," *The Eye*, June 29, 2024, https://theeyehuatulco.com/2024/06/29/social-class-politics-economics-and-religion-a-brief-history-of-aztec-sex/.
6. Ginette Paris, *The Sacrament of Abortion* (Spring Publications, 1998), 34, 51, 57.
7. Paris, *The Sacrament of Abortion*, 56.
8. John Ferrer, "The Satanic Temple Abortion Clinic: A Critical Assessment," *Christian Research Institute*, January 17, 2024, https://www.equip.org/articles/the-satanic-temple-abortion-clinic-a-critical-review/. See also Joseph P. Laycock, "How the Satanic Temple Is Using 'Abortion Rituals' to Claim Religious Liberty Against the Texas 'Heartbeat Bill,'" The Conversation, September 22, 2021, https://theconversation.com/how-the-satanic-temple-is-using-abortion-rituals-to-claim-religious-liberty-against-the-texas-heartbeat-bill-167755.
9. Online Etymology Dictionary, s.v. "entertain," accessed July 11, 2025, https://www.etymonline.com/word/entertain.
10. On the surface, these two references seem to refer to the human kings of Tyre and Babylon. However, the worldview of Ezekiel and Isaiah is supernatural. Ezekiel begins with a vision of awesome supernatural creatures and the chariot of YHWH. The Spirit of YHWH is personified in Ezekiel 8:1–3. Isaiah includes the specific mention of the demonic. For example, Isaiah 34:14 includes a vivid description of

demon activity, including mention of the famous ancient Near Eastern demon Lilith. This is sometimes translated as "night creature"—but check your Bible's footnotes. The Hebrew is תִיִליִל (*Lilit*, (f(em).), a demon connected with sexual relationships (incubus–succubus) (Hebrew and Aramaic Lexicon of the Old Testament (HALOT)). Isaiah 13:21 likewise mentions various kinds of demons (often translated as "desert creatures" and "wild goats"; however, these refer to demons). See, for example, J. Alec Motyer, *The Prophecy of Isaiah* (InterVarsity Press, 1993); George Buchanan Gray, *A Critical and Exegetical Commentary on the Book of Isaiah 1–27* (T & T Clark, 2001). The Bible uses concepts and terminology from the cultures surrounding Israel. That does not mean the Bible is glorifying or approving of demons or other foreign concepts; the Bible simply spoke the language of the day. So while clearly referring to human kings, Ezekiel 28:13 and Isaiah 14:2–17 can also be read as having a double meaning. The writers of the prophecies were referring to the spiritual power that lay behind these human rulers. That is not at all strange for the ancient world, which viewed its kings as sons of the gods.

11. Isaiah Saldivar, "Cardi B Admits Her Song Activates Demons! She Is Crying Out for Help!," April 30, 2022, YouTube video, 7:22, https://www.youtube.com/watch?v=f4Ph3G-jAUg.

12. Isaiah Saldivar, "Island Boy Flyysoulja Admits to Selling His Soul to the Devil," November 20, 2021, YouTube video, 11:04, https://www.youtube.com/watch?v=USNzwUpDMw0.

13. Taylor Swift, "Willow," Universal Music Group, 2020.

14. OWN, "Beyonce on Her Alter Ego, Sasha Fierce, The Oprah Winfrey Show, Oprah Winfrey Network," August 17, 2019, YouTube video, 1:36, https://www.youtube.com/watch?v=4AA5G8vCl9w; Wikipedia, s.v. "I Am…Sasha Fierce," accessed May 15, 2025, https://es.wikipedia.org/wiki/I_Am…_Sasha_Fierce.

15. Georgia Hadjis, "Beyism: A Religion," *Medium*, October 15, 2016, https://medium.com/@georgiahadjis/beyism-a-religion-1f21bc767c66.

16. EJ Dickson, "Tiktok Isn't Stopping Astroworld Demonic Conspiracy Theories," *Rolling Stone*, November 9, 2021, https://www.rollingstone.com/music/music-news/tiktok-astroworld-conspiracy-theories-satanism-1255358/.

17. Prakat Karki and Madhavi Rangaswamy, "A Review of Historical Context and Current Research on Cannabis Use in India," *Indian Journal of Psychological Medicine* 45, no. 2 (August 2022): 105–116, https://journals.sagepub.com/doi/10.1177/02537176221109272.

18. Ernest L. Abel, *Marihuana: The First Twelve Thousand Years* (McGraw-Hill, 1982), 19.

19. *Britannica*, s.v. "Atharvaveda," accessed May 15, 2025, britannica.com/topic/Atharvaveda.

20. For a description of a visit to a Hindu temple in Nepal, see Danielle Preiss, "Shiva Is a God Who Likes Marijuana—And So Do Many of His Followers," NPR, March 7, 2016, https://www.npr.org/sections/goatsandsoda/2016/03/07/469519964/shiva-is-a-god-who-likes-marijuana-and-so-do-many-of-his-followers#:~:text=Both%20are%20symbols%20of%20religious,of%20a%20relaxed%20music%20festival.

21. Mia Touw, "The Religious and Medicinal Uses of *Cannabis* in China, India and Tibet," *Journal of Psychoactive Drugs* 13, no. 1 (January–March 1981): 23–34, https://citeseerx.ist.psu.edu/document?repid=rep1&type=pdf&doi=e3a536c619f8de0266fd3f5d017d762d2c6d4893.

22. Dhana Ratna Shakya et al., "Cannabis Use and Abuse in Nepal: A Review of Studies," *Journal of the Nepal Medical Association* 59, no. 241 (September 2021): 954–961, https://pmc.ncbi.nlm.nih.gov/articles/PMC9107886/.

23. Shakya et al., "Cannabis Use and Abuse in Nepal," 956.

24. Touw, "Religious and Medicinal Uses of *Cannabis* in China, India and Tibet," 25.

25. Preiss, "Shiva Is a God Who Likes Marijuana—And So Do Many of His Followers."

26. Ari Brouwer et al., "The Trajectory of Psychedelic, Spiritual, and Psychotic Experiences: Implications for Cognitive Scientific Perspectives on Religion," *Religion, Brain & Behavior* (July 2024), 1–17.

27. Jacob was also deeply tied to his son Joseph, who was sold into slavery by his brothers.

CHAPTER 7

1. Daniel Z. Lieberman, "Children of Alcoholics: An Update," *Current Opinion in Pediatrics* 12, no. 4 (August 2000): 336–340, https://journals.lww.com/co-pediatrics/abstract/2000/08000/children_of_alcoholics__an_update.9.aspx.

2. "Mice Can Inherit Learned Sensitivity to a Smell," Emory News Center, December 2, 2013, https://news.emory.edu/stories/2013/12/smell_epigenetics_ressler/index.html; Brian G. Dias and Kerry J. Ressler, "Parental Olfactory Experience Influences Behavior and Neural Structure in Subsequent Generations," *Nature Neuroscience* 17, (2014): 89–96; see especially page 3.

3. Mo Costandi, "Pregnant 9/11 Survivors Transmitted Trauma to Their Children," *The Guardian*, September 9, 2011, https://www.theguardian

.com/science/neurophilosophy/2011/sep/09/pregnant-911-survivors-transmitted-trauma.

4. Costandi, "Pregnant 9/11 Survivors Transmitted Trauma to Their Children"; Rachel Yehuda et al., "Transgenerational Effects of Posttraumatic Stress Disorder in Babies of Mothers Exposed to the World Trade Center Attacks During Pregnancy," *Journal of Clinical Endocrinology and Metabolism* 90, no. 7 (2005): 4,115–4,118, https://pubmed.ncbi.nlm.nih.gov/15870120/.

5. R. L. Dugdale, *"The Jukes": A Study of Crime, Pauperism, Disease and Heredity* (G. P. Putnam's Sons, 1877), 14. "Max Juke" was a pseudonym Dugdale devised to protect the innocent.

6. Dugdale, *The Jukes*, 14.

7. Dugdale, *The Jukes*, 14.

8. Dugdale, *The Jukes*, 15.

9. Dugdale, *The Jukes*, 68.

10. Dugdale, *The Jukes*, 68.

11. Dugdale, *The Jukes*, 70.

12. You can read the sermon as printed in 1741 at Jonathan Edwards, "Sinners in the Hands of an Angry God: A Sermon Preached at Enfield, July 8, 1741," ed. Reiner Smolinski, Digital Commons University of Nebraska-Lincoln, accessed May 15, 2025, https://digitalcommons.unl.edu/cgi/viewcontent.cgi?article=1053&context=etas.

13. One of the young men in his church found a midwife's manual with illustrations of the female anatomy and passed it around to nine of his friends. Edwards tried to discipline the young men but lost his job. For more details, see "Jonathan Edwards Loses His Pulpit Over Bad Books," New England Historical Society, accessed May 15, 2025, https://newenglandhistoricalsociety.com/jonathan-edwards-loses-his-pulpit-over-bad-books/.

14. A. E. Winship, *Jukes-Edwards: A Study in Education and Heredity* (R. L. Myers, 1900), 30.

15. Winship, *Jukes-Edwards*, 43, 54, 58.

16. Winship, *Jukes-Edwards*, 57.

17. Winship, *Jukes-Edwards*, 60.

18. "Rosemary Kennedy, the Eldest Kennedy Daughter," National Park Service, accessed May 15, 2025, https://www.nps.gov/articles/000/rosemary-kennedy-the-eldest-kennedy-daughter.htm.

19. Faith Karimi, "Death Is the Latest in a Long List of Tragedies for the Kennedy Family," CNN, August 2, 2019, https://www.cnn.com/2019/08/02/us/kennedy-family-tragedies/index.html.

20. Karimi, "Death Is the Latest in a Long List of Tragedies for the Kennedy Family."

21. F. P. Retief and L. Cilliers, "The History and Pathology of Crucifixion," *South African Medical Journal* 93, no. 12 (2003): 938–941, https://pubmed.ncbi.nlm.nih.gov/14750495/.

22. Retief and Cilliers, "Pathology of Crucifixion," 939. See also this easy-to-read article: Cahleen Shrier, "The Science of the Crucifixion," Azusa Pacific University, March 1, 2002, https://www.apu.edu/articles/the-science-of-the-crucifixion/.

23. M. Tullius Cicero, *Pro Rabirio Perduellionis Reo* (English), 5.16; M. Tullius Cicero, *The Orations of Marcus Tullius Cicero*, trans. C. D. Yonge and B. A. London (Henry G. Bohn, 1856); M. Tullius Cicero, *For Rabirius on a Charge of Treason*, chapter 5, section 16.

CHAPTER 8

1. Details of John's story are taken from John Ramirez, *Out of the Devil's Cauldron: A Journey from Darkness to Light* (Heaven and Earth Media, 2012).

2. Ramirez, *Out of the Devil's Cauldron.*

3. Philip Boyes, "Scribes and Spooks: Exorcists in Ancient Mesopotamia," *CREWS*, October 31, 2018, https://crewsproject.wordpress.com/2018/10/31/scribes-and-spooks-exorcists-in-ancient-mesopotamia/#:~:text=Once%20trainee%20scribes%20had%20mastered,additional%20years%20of%20advanced%20study. The *CREWS* blog is from Contexts of and Relations between Early Writing Systems, a European Research Council–funded project hosted at the Faculty of Classics, Cambridge.

4. Boyes, "Scribes and Spooks."

5. Geraldine Pinch, *Magic in Ancient Egypt* (British Museum Press, 1994), 9.

6. Pinch, *Magic in Ancient Egypt*, 9.

7. San, "Sia, Hu, and Heku—Intelligence, Power and Magic," Iseum Sanctuary, January 9, 2022, https://iseumsanctuary.com/2022/01/09/sia-hu-and-heku-intelligence-power-and-magic/.

8. Flora Brooke Anthony, "Heka: Understanding Egyptian Magic on Its Own Terms," TheTorah.com, accessed May 15, 2025, https://www.thetorah.com/article/heka-understanding-egyptian-magic-on-its-own-terms.

9. Anthony, "Heka."

10. Joshua J. Mark, "Heka," World History Encyclopedia, February 23, 2017, https://www.worldhistory.org/Heka/.

11. Pinch, *Magic in Ancient Egypt*, 12.

12. Julia Troche, *Death, Power, and Apotheosis in Ancient Egypt: The Old and Middle Kingdoms* (Cornell University Press, 2021), 33–35.

13. Troche, *Death, Power, and Apotheosis in Ancient Egypt*, 33, 39.

14. Troche, *Death, Power, and Apotheosis in Ancient Egypt*, 43.

15. Pinch, *Magic in Ancient Egypt*, 45.

16. Pinch, *Magic in Ancient Egypt*, 91.

17. Tablet image from Universitat Hamburg, accessed May 15, 2025, https://www.thedefix.uni-hamburg.de/html/heurist/?db=The_dema&website&id=41774.

18. Christopher A. Faraone, "Ancient Greek Curse Tablets," Fathom Archive, accessed May 15, 2025, https://fathom.lib.uchicago.edu/1/777777122300/.

19. "Curse Tablets of Roman Britain," Centre for the Study of Ancient Documents, University of Oxford, accessed May 15, 2025, http://curses.csad.ox.ac.uk/; see also Charlotte Spence, "Curse Tablets and Our Understanding of the Ancient World," *Ekklesia Magazine*, accessed May 15, 2025, https://ekklesiamag.wordpress.com/curse-tablets-and-our-understanding-of-the-ancient-world/; see also "RIB 154. Curse upon Thief of 'Vilbia,'" Roman Inscriptions of Britain, accessed May 15, 2025, https://romaninscriptionsofbritain.org/inscriptions/154.

20. Hans Dieter Betz, ed., *The Greek Magical Papyri in Translation, Including the Demotic Spells* (University of Chicago Press, 1986).

21. Brooke Bobb, "How to Energetically Clear Your Space with Sage," *Vogue*, August 22, 2016, https://www.vogue.com/article/sage-how-to-cleanse-energy-home-office-smudging.

22. Derek Prince, "The Nature of Witchcraft (Part 1)," Derek Prince Ministries, accessed May 15, 2025, https://drive.google.com/file/d/1NyMzaGryC0XvoEe4VqjaDsed5Nk0XllK/view.

23. Derek Prince taught these three points many years ago. See Derek Prince, "Witchcraft in Disguise: Part 5—Seven Steps to Revival," April 2, 2015, YouTube video, 1:40:07, https://www.youtube.com/watch?v=3F90EVoni-Y&t=5s.

24. Dictionary.com, s.v. "cult," accessed May 15, 2025, https://www.dictionary.com/browse/cult.

25. "What Is New Age Spirituality?," Ligonier, July 2, 2023, https://learn.ligonier.org/articles/field-guide-on-false-teaching-new-age-spirituality.

26. Yogapedia, s.v. "Yoga," last updated December 21, 2023, https://www.yogapedia.com/definition/4/yoga.

27. Emma Newlyn, "Six Sacred Yoga Poses," accessed May 15, 2025, https://www.yogaeasy.com/artikel/6-sacred-yoga-poses.

28. Kate Holcombe, "Yoga Wisdom: How to Spark Your Inner Light + Share It with Others," Yoga Journal, last updated January 14, 2025, https://www.yogajournal.com/meditation/meditation-classes/let-shine/.

29. "Why Is Kundalini Yoga So Powerful?," Adwait, June 14, 2023, https://adwaityoga.com/why-is-kundalini-yoga-so-powerful/.

30. Hanna Yi's testimony is available online, including all the details set out here and more. See HungryGeneration, "Set Free from Demon of Death. Ex-Yoga Instructor Finds Freedom After Encountering God," April 1, 2022, YouTube video, 8:35, https://www.youtube.com/watch?v=xqQFJaySGzk.

31. Linden Thorp, "The Origin of Meditation: Making Bonds with the Universe," *Meditation Magazine*, March 9, 2017, https://www.meditationmag.com/blog/origin-meditation-making-bonds-universe/.

32. "The Twelve Zodiac Constellations," Centre of Excellence, accessed May 15, 2025, https://www.centreofexcellence.com/the-12-zodiac-constellations/.

33. For more of Angela's testimony, see Vlad Savchuk, "From Astrology, Tarot, and Occult to Jesus," April 19, 2023, YouTube video, 1:05:45, https://www.youtube.com/watch?v=7mWp1ZBbJ8o.

34. Angela Ucci, host, *Heaven and Healing*, accessed May 16, 2025, https://heavenandhealing.com/.

35. Ben Cost, "Twenty-Eight Girls Hospitalized with 'Anxiety' After Playing with Ouija Board," *New York Post*, last updated March 8, 2023, https://nypost.com/2023/03/07/28-girls-hospitalized-for-anxiety-after-ouija-board-game/.

36. Antony Clements-Thrower, "Hysteria at School as Thirty-Six Students Hospitalized After 'Playing with Ouija Board,'" *Mirror*, July 8, 2023, https://www.mirror.co.uk/news/world-news/hysteria-school-36-students-hospitalised-30421723.

37. Daniel Hernandez, "The Haunting of Girlstown," Vox, May 20, 2020, https://www.vox.com/c/the-highlight/21242299/outbreak-girlstown-chalco-world-villages-villa-de-las-ninas.

38. Caitlin Berve, "Catching Dreams: Dream Catcher Origins and How to Make One," Caitlin Berve Author, June 5, 2020, https://www.caitlinberve.com/blog/catching-dreams-dreamcatcher-origins-and-how-to-make-one.

39. Joseph M. Murphy, "Santería," *Britannica*, last updated March 24, 2025, https://www.britannica.com/topic/Santeria.

40. Murphy, "Santería."

41. "*Church of the Lukumi-Babalu Aye v. Hialeah*, 508 U.S. 520 (1993)," United States Courts, accessed May 15, 2025, https://www.uscourts.

gov/educational-resources/educational-activities/exercise-religious-
practices-rule-law.

CHAPTER 10

1. Blue Letter Bible, s.v. "ἀπεῖπον," accessed May 15, 2025, https://www
.blueletterbible.org/lexicon/g550/kjv/tr/0-1/.
2. "Lewis B. Smedes Quotes," BrainyQuote, accessed July 11, 2025, https://
www.brainyquote.com/quotes/lewis_b_smedes_135524.

ABOUT THE AUTHOR

Vladimir Savchuk serves as the lead pastor of HungryGen Church, a vibrant multicultural congregation dedicated to soul-winning, healing, deliverance, and raising up young leaders. In addition to pastoring, Savchuk extends his ministry through the written word and digital media as an accomplished author, YouTuber, and traveling preacher. He also offers free e-courses through his online learning platform, VladSchool, making theology and Christian living accessible to a global audience.

Savchuk's journey began in Ukraine, where he was born into a devout Christian household. After moving to the United States at age thirteen, his calling manifested early when he took on the role of a youth pastor at just sixteen years of age. His dynamic style and deep understanding of Scripture quickly made him a sought-after speaker at various conferences and Christian gatherings.

Sharing life and ministry with his wonderful wife, Lana, Savchuk embodies a dynamic approach to leadership and the preaching of God's Word, enriching lives both in his immediate community and well beyond.